Acknowledgements

Scripture taken from the New King James Version®. Copyright © 1982 by Thomas Nelson. Used by permission. All rights reserved.

Cover illustration by Sophie Lunn

Thanks to all the people who have helped and supported me in writing these devotions.

Published July 2021

Journey Through the Psalms

I know many people who read, or even sing the psalms every day as a part of their quiet time, and that is a wonderful way to express your worship to God.

The psalms are like journeys with a beginning, a middle and an end. Sometimes they double back on themselves, twisting and turning, other times they go through rough ground. There are highs and lows, shouts of praises and shouts of desperation. Life is a journey which can, and does, go through similar things. These devotions take thirteen well known psalms and lead you through their journey.

Some may resonate more than others with you, but journey on and allow them to enrich your life no matter what part of the journey you are currently on.

A List of the Psalms and the Dates They Start

Psalm 1	July 16th
Psalm 8	November 29th
Psalm 22	March 3rd
Psalm 23	February 14th
Psalm 24	October 22nd
Psalm 34	January 1st
Psalm 37	May 1st
Psalm 51	September 14th
Psalm 100	November 17th
Psalm 103	August 1st
Psalm 117	February 29th
Psalm 121	February 1st
Psalm 150	December 19th

1st January
Psalm 34:1a
'I will bless the Lord at all times'
Mad Words or True Words

Psalm 34 is entitled, 'A psalm of David when he pretended madness before Abimelech, who drove him away, and he departed.' This first part certainly sounds like the words of a mad man, 'I will bless the Lord at all times'; 'at *all* times'. It is ridiculous to bless the Lord at all times; life is full of ups and downs, in the up times sure bless the Lord, but when things are tough, God ought to be blessing us!

But no, we must get into the habit of blessing the Lord, making the God of all happiness even more happy. It is easy to bless God when He has openly blessed us, but there is a deeper blessing, a richer happiness when we choose to bless God even when He appears to turn His back on us.

This psalm is so often reduced to one verse (8), but there is so much more to be found here; much to cause us to bless God every day. We shall look at verse 8 in due course, but that is not the starting point or even the key verse. As we consider each verse and phrase, my prayer is that you will bless the Lord more and more as you see what a great God He is.

Are these the words of a mad man, or the wise teachings of a man who knew these things to be true?

2nd January
Psalm 34:1b
'His praise shall continually be in my mouth'
An Antidote to Complaining

Do you find moaning and complaining about people comes very naturally to you? If so, you are not alone, I think most people find it all too easy to pick out mistakes in others and then spread the devil's fire by sharing them. The Lord doesn't want you to be like that, He wants your mouth to be full of good things, rather than poison. By putting His praises continually in your mouth, you give no room for negative words to form there.

Praising the Lord has the remarkable effect of lifting you out of the darkest places you may find yourself in. When you feel better about yourself you will feel better about others around you. This is no 'self-love' exercise, this is putting God first, not yourself. Don't praise yourself or belittle others in order to make yourself feel good, bless the Lord and praise His Holy Name.

When you are tempted to have negative thoughts about someone, don't start by trying to think positive thoughts towards them, but instead actively praise the Lord for something He has done for you. You will discover that you do not deserve God's goodness, and yet He pours it out on you nonetheless. There may be nothing good to say about that person, but grace is a gift God has bestowed on you, and you will find the more you meditate on that grace, the more it will pour out of you towards the people you deem unworthy.

3rd January
Psalm 34:2a
'My soul shall make its boast in the Lord'
What do you boast in?

David said, 'My soul shall make its boast in the Lord', and Paul said something similar in Galatians 6:14, 'But God forbid that I should boast except in the cross of our Lord Jesus Christ, by whom the world has been crucified to me, and I to the world.' So then, what or who do you boast in?

Boasting can be such a tiny thing, unconscious, unmeant; but we do it. We boast in our achievements, we boast in our children, we boast in our favourite football team or even in that my preferred superhero franchise is better than yours. All of these can be genuine and harmless, but all run the risk of turning sour. When you meet someone, who thinks differently to you or worse proves you wrong, you can become bitter against that person for destroying your boast. Boast in the Lord and leave His detractors to Him. No one can belittle the Lord, they may shake your faith to the core, but the Lord's goodness will remain untouched. Most people who talk negatively about God, have no ground for doing so, they do not know Him or what He is like; you do know Him and have met Him, let your boast be only in the Lord and stand in the knowledge that that boast is in a sure thing.

4th January

Psalm 34:2b

'The humble shall hear of it and be glad'

The Humble Shall Hear

Yesterday we looked at boasting in the Lord, and the fact that some may try to belittle the Lord. Well, the outcome of this is that the proud hearted will rejoice in the apparent bringing down of Jesus and His followers, but the humble of heart will be glad in your boasting in the Lord.

The humble are not swayed by strength of numbers but rather by the humbleness of others. Pride is the anathema of the humble, they reject the word of proud men, but are drawn to those whose boast is not in themselves but in the Lord.

We may wonder how we can reach this generation when so many, highly qualified, people tell us that the Bible is old fashioned and should be forgotten about in favour of their 'wise' words. If we directly attack these fools, we make ourselves out to be the proud, but if we put our trust, our boast, in the Lord, humbly yielding to Him, the humble will be drawn, quite naturally, to us. Leave the fight to the Lord, He knows what He's doing; as for you get down on your knees and pray and praise the Lord, the creator of all things.

5th January
Psalm 34:3
'Oh, magnify the Lord with me, and let us exalt His name together.'
How Big is Your God?
I promised a key verse in the psalm and this is it. 'Oh, magnify the Lord with me.'

When we think of magnifying something, we often think of making it bigger, or at least appear bigger, than it really is. Is that what David is saying? Is he saying we should try to make God bigger that He already is? Is that even possible? The more I read this verse the more I am convinced that what David is saying is that we should make our view of God bigger. God is already bigger than we can ever imagine, but our view of Him is often so small in comparison. David's challenge to us is to see God as He truly is, in all His marvellous immensity.

The question you may ask is, 'How should I do this?', and my answer to you is, read this Psalm, it is full of wonders that will enlarge your view of God – go on read it through now. Once you've done that, we can join David in the second part of the verse, 'And let us exalt His name together.' Fill your speech with the truth of how big and wonderful God is; tell Him in your praises, share it in your Bible Studies and House Groups, and tell the World your God is a great big God.

6th January
Psalm 34:4
'I sought the Lord, and He heard me, and delivered me from all my fears.'
Seek the Lord
This is a verse written by someone who has magnified the Lord. David knew God could deliver him, so He sought Him earnestly.

Do you expect God to deliver you from all your fears? Or do you think God is not interested in your worries? God is ready and willing to deliver you from *all* your fears. There are many things people are afraid of; some real, some imaginary. You may have a phobia; a phobia is defined as an 'irrational fear', irrational maybe, but no less real to the sufferer. I had an irrational fear of spiders, those little guys literally petrified me; if I saw one I could not move, my hands would become clammy, my breath irregular and my heart would race. A very real experience. But I sought the Lord, and He delivered me from the fear of spiders. Almost immediately after I had been prayed for, a spider fell from somewhere right in front of me and I didn't even flinch – God is good.

That is only a small fear really, but if God cares about Arachnophobia, I know He cares about your biggest fear. What is it that fills you with dread? I'm not going to give any examples but think about yourself, what fears do you have? Perhaps you can't put it into words that thing that frightens you, lurking at the back of your mind. God can deliver you from all your fears. Seek Him today and receive freedom.

7th January
Psalm 34:5
'They looked to Him and were radiant, and their faces were not ashamed.'
Look to the Lord

Who is the 'they' that David references here? It is the ones who have magnified the Lord and have sought Him in their fears. They stand radiant and unashamed.

Are there people in your church fellowship, who are radiant, shining out for God? I can certainly think of some in my church. You think, 'I could never be like them, they must be so holy and close to God. They don't have the problems I face.' You want to know the truth, they are just like you, only they are trusting in the God of Psalm 34 and proving Him every day, and you can do the same.

You want to be the 'radiant ones'? Get to know God better, I'll say it again, magnify the Lord more and more, trust Him with all your fears. Believe the words of this psalm, if God could do that for others, He can do it for you.

Do you feel ashamed? not ashamed of the Gospel but ashamed of some sin you have done? Adam and Eve's relationship with God was tainted by the shame of their sin and they hid from the presence of the Lord. Jesus' death on the Cross has made a way to restore your relationship with God and now you can look to Him without being ashamed.

Stand as one of the radiant unashamed children of God, others will look to you as inspiration and you can show them how to be radiant themselves.

8th January

Psalm 34:6

'This poor man cried out, and the Lord heard him, and saved him out of all his troubles.'

Cry Out to the Lord

David called himself a 'poor man', or a humble man, a nothing. You may see David as a giant killer or a great king, and yes, he was all those things but as he wrote this psalm he was a fugitive, hunted by king Saul. He had no status or position; why should anyone listen to him, especially God? And yet God did listen.

Do you feel like a poor man, a poor woman, a nothing, too insignificant for God to listen to your troubles? David saw himself as a nothing, but also knew God to be everything the Bible says He is. God was interested in David's heart's cry, not because he was David but because he was a child of God. You too are a child of God and that makes you significant in God's eyes.

Everything that troubles you, matters to God and you can cry out to Him in those troubles and He will save you out of them. I'm not saying your life will be trouble free, David's certainly wasn't, but God will be your constant deliverer, your shield in the day of trouble. You can then hide behind God who will not be overcome by troubles and He will not allow you to be overcome by them either.

What will you do: Continue in your own strength to get through your troubles or rely on God's strength to do it? Cry out to God today.

9th January
Psalm 34:7
'The Angel of the Lord encamps all around those who fear Him, and delivers them.'
Safe in the Camp

This might well be my favourite verse in this Psalm. The thought of the Angel of the Lord camping around me keeping me safe is amazing. Who is the Angel of the Lord? Usually this phrase refers to God Himself, the Second Person in the Trinity, Jesus Christ as He manifested Himself in the Old Testament. There is no reason to suspect there is anyone else in mind here. However, the Angel of the Lord is not seen as 'meek and mild' but rather the Leader of God's armies. Jesus encamps His warrior angels all around those that fear Him.

Do you feel hemmed in on all sides, with no way of escape; every which way you turn there is only dread, you are merely counting down to the inevitable? This is the good news for you: you don't need to stay in that place a moment longer, the Lord of Hosts is coming to rescue you! Call out to the Lord for help and He will deliver you and then place armed guards to protect you from the Enemy. Don't be afraid of the circumstances you are in but turn in reverent fear to the God of salvation and cry out to Him, 'Jesus! Save me!' No longer will the circling demons be able to reach you, you are free. Get down on your knees and worship the God who delivers and protects His people.

10th January
Psalm 34:8a
'Oh, taste and see that the Lord is good.'
Taste of the Lord's Goodness

This is the verse everyone thinks of when psalm 34 is mentioned; yes, even me. 'Oh, taste and see that the Lord is good.' It is not enough to hear about God's goodness, you must experience it for yourself, just as it is no good to hear that a cake is tasty without trying it for yourself. Go on try it for yourself (the Lord's goodness, not the cake!). We have already covered many wonderful things God can do for His people, and you may have praised the Lord for His goodness, but have you tasted of it yourself?

This verse is usually used as an evangelistic tool, and a great one it is too! But more, it is a challenge to God's people to experience Him to the full. Don't be content with the meagre portion you have so far received, there is so much more yet to gain from the Lord's abundant table. What are you waiting for? Are you afraid God's gifts will taste bitter? Are you afraid by accepting God's plate you will have to give up what you have so far enjoyed? Firstly, God's gifts are not bitter, He is good and all He gives He gives out of His goodness. Secondly, I don't care how wonderful your life has been so far, it is nothing compared to the bounty God has in store for you. Give it a go, what have you got to lose? What have you got to gain?

Taste of the Lord's Goodness.

11th January
Psalm 34:8b
'Blessed is the man who trusts in Him!'
How to be Blessed

So often at awards ceremonies the winner expounds how 'blessed' they are, they gush with such phrases as 'I'm so blessed.' Or, 'My life is just so full of blessings'. These people do have amazing lives especially 'A-List' celebrities; but I do wonder just how 'blessed' they really are. Does their jet set lifestyle really make them happy? How happy and blessed are you?

You may not live the celebrity lifestyle, or maybe you do; you may not have achieved all you set out to do, or perhaps you have; it doesn't make any difference to you having real blessings. Real blessing comes from God and you receive it by trusting in Him. In verse 1 David wrote, 'I will bless the Lord at all times', was this wise words? At the time I left the conclusion open but now I put it to you that blessing the Lord at all times, no matter what, is what trusting Him is all about. Real personal blessing isn't about what you can get out of it, but rather how God is glorified through it.

Choose to make your life a blessing to God and He, in turn, will fill your life with His eternal blessings. I have always found Him to be true to His word, but don't take my word for it. Taste and see, find out for yourself.

12th January
Psalm 34:9a
'Oh, fear the Lord, you His saints!'
But What Kind of Fear?

I was always taught that the fear we should have for God was a respectful, reverential honour. The Hebrew word Yare' certainly contains those sentiments. However, there is a broader meaning to that word which covers such thoughts as, 'dreadful', 'fearful', 'awe inspiring', 'terrifying'; we limit the full meaning of this verse if we only concentrate on one aspect of fearing God.

A fuller, more complete understanding of Godly fear is to come to Him in awe and reverence, knowing He is the Holy God of all creation and we are lowly sinners. There is a dread associated with entering God's presence and we do well to remember it. He is, however, a loving God whose arms are always open to receive repentant sinners like you and me.

The fear of the Lord is not to be a negative thing that drives you away from Him, but rather the lure that draws you closer to Him and provokes you to share His goodness and wrath with others. What do you fear more, the slight of your friends for sharing the Gospel with them, or the rebuke of the Lord if you don't?

13th January
Psalm 34:9b
'There is no want to those who fear Him.'
What do you Want?

What do you want? What is it that you most desire in life? Many people are afraid to fully commit to God because they think they may lose out on what is most important to them; their wants are more significant in their lives than God. Is that you? Be honest.

This is what David says, 'The Lord is my Shepherd; I shall not want.' Psalm 23:1, 'Delight yourself also in the Lord, and He shall give you the desires of your heart.' Psalm 37:4, 'There is no want to those who fear Him.' Psalm 34:9b. David understood that all His wants and desires were found in God. Putting God first in his life brought everything David could have ever needed and I'm not talking about wealth, wives, the kingship etc.; no, I mean those inner wants and desires that material things can't touch. The fact he had wealth, was secondary to all he received as one of the saints of God.

Without intending to offend anyone, saints, in the biblical sense, are anyone who fears the Lord, putting Him first in their lives; we call them Christians. If you are a Christian, you are a saint and God gives everything needed to His saints; not necessarily outwardly, but certainly inwardly.

What do you want? Outward ease, or inward peace?

14th January

Psalm 34:10

'The young lions lack and suffer hunger; But those who seek the Lord shall not lack any good thing.'

But do you Lack?

We are nearing the halfway stage of this psalm and have covered many good things God has for us: blessings, deliverance, gladness, radiance, being unashamed, the Angel of the Lord encamping around us, all our wants found in Him. We have been encouraged to 'taste and see that the Lord is good', but do you still lack some good thing God wants for you?

The psalmist says, 'those who seek the Lord shall not lack any good thing.' You have got on you knees every day, and poured your heart out to God, seeking Him earnestly for His answer and yet you still lack some of His goodness towards you. Let me assure you if you have sought God with all you heart, He will answer you and pour out His goodness on you. Could it be that God has answered you and you missed it because it wasn't the answer you wanted or expected? This psalm expounds some of the good things the Lord does for us and they cover many experiences we go through. Your situation may be tough, beyond anything I could imagine, but I know that God can and will do for you all that is written in this psalm He will not withhold any good thing from you, but, remember the definition of 'good things' is God's definition not yours or mine.

15th January
Psalm 34:11a
'Come, you children, listen to me'
Come and Listen as Little Children

It seems that in today's society no one wants to be a 'child', everyone wants to be the most important, the greatest they can be. When the disciples asked Jesus, "Who, then, is the greatest in the kingdom of heaven?" (Matthew 18:1) Jesus replied, "Truly I tell you, unless you change and become like little children, you will never enter the kingdom of heaven. Therefore, whoever takes the lowly position of this child is the greatest in the kingdom of heaven. And whoever welcomes one such child in my name welcomes Me." (Matthew 18:3-5). The Kingdom of God is very different from the Kingdom of men. In Man's kingdom, it is all about 'me' and what I can get out of it. In God's Kingdom it's all about Him, we are His little children.

Come as little children and listen to what God has to say; don't assume you know everything, or anything – it often surprises me how much I thought I knew, turned out to be false. I have had to come before God humbly and relearn many, many things and I'm still learning now.

Don't be wise in your own eyes but come to the Lord as children eager to learn from the Master; sit at His feet as Mary did and listen to Him.

16th January
Psalm 34:11b
'I will teach you the fear of the Lord.'
Why You Should Fear the Lord

In times past parents would say things like, 'If you do that again, I'll put the fear of God into you.' And the child would know not to do that thing again. Is this David's meaning here? Is this the words of a disapproving father? Not exactly, but David wanted the best for those who read these words.

Yesterday I used the phrase 'don't be wise in your own eyes'; that comes straight out of the Bible, Proverbs 3:7. I'm going to quote a bit more from that chapter now, 'Trust in the Lord with all your heart, and lean not on your own understanding; In all your ways acknowledge Him, And He shall direct your paths. Do not be wise in your own eyes; fear the Lord and depart from evil. It will be health to your flesh, and strength to your bones.' Proverbs 3:5-8. This, inevitably, follows on from the last devotion, do not to 'lean on your own understanding', or be 'wise in your own eyes' but rather, 'in all your ways acknowledge Him' and to 'fear the Lord and depart from evil.' Learn the fear of the Lord, the fear of offending Him above offending others. He loves you and only wants the best for you.

Living God's way and obeying Him, will bring 'health to your flesh, and strength to your bones.' Proverbs 3:8. This doesn't promise you will not have any serious illness, but living a godly life is preferable to living a sinful, destructive life that can cause ill health. What is sure is that if you live your life honouring God your soul will be well, and peace will inhabit your heart.

17th January
Psalm 34:12
'Who is the man who desires life, and loves many days, that he may see good?'
This is a call out to you!
Is there anyone out there who this verse does not speak to? There surely can't be many people who do not desire life, many days and above all to see good in their lives! So, this is a call out to all whom this verse relates to. For the minority who do not want what this verse speaks of, my prayer for you is that God would touch your life just where you are and bring you great goodness, peace and blessings. The rest of this devotion is dedicated to those who say, 'yes, yes, yes' to the sentiments of this verse.

If your hearts desire is to see good in your life, then over the next few devotions I will look at the answer to this riddle. What do you need to do to be blessed in life by Almighty God? Verses 13 and 14 of this are a good place to start and they will be our next stop on the way. Below are verses 12-14 to have a preview of what is to come:

12 Who is the man who desires life, and loves many days, that he may see good?

13 Keep your tongue from evil, and your lips from speaking deceit.

14 Depart from evil and do good; Seek peace and pursue it.

Start practicing these today even before I reach them.

18th January
Psalm 34:13a
'Keep your tongue from evil'
Be careful what you say

It is easy to open our mouths and say all kinds of things that may seem okay to us but are offensive to God; from the downright vile and vulgar to the unnecessary and silly. Jesus, when teaching on how to tell a righteous person from an evil person, said this in Matthew 12:36-37, "I say to you that for every idle word men may speak, they will give account of it in the day of judgment. For by your words you will be justified, and by your words you will be condemned." We are judged by our words.

It is important then, what we say and how we say it. Fill your mind with good things and good things will come out of your mouth. There is so much bitterness and strife in today's world; people only have bad things to say about each other, putting others down so that they can appear better. Everyone gets offended over tiny little things people say. We may think we shouldn't offend anyone, my reading of Jesus is that He never went out of His way to offend people, but also, He never went out of His way not to offend people, He simply spoke the Words of His Father. We too should be careful to speak God's words even if they hurt but never to deliberately offend or hurt someone out of religious superiority.

19th January
Psalm 34:13b
'And your lips from speaking deceit'
Don't be deceitful

The Ninth Commandment as found in Exodus 20:16, reads, 'You shall not bear false witness against your neighbour.' It is often shortened to, 'Do not lie', but really it is better rendered 'Don't be deceitful'. Deceitfulness goes beyond lying; being deceitful is telling half-truths and misinformation in order for your statements to appear true. Consider this illustration: You see a child with biscuit crumbs round his face and you ask him, 'Did you take that from the biscuit tin?', he answers with an emphatic, 'No!' Is the boy lying? If he took it from the biscuit tin, he is lying, but if he took it from the half-opened packet in the cupboard, he is technically not lying, but is being deceitful. You see the child didn't take the biscuit from the tin but did take it without asking. Don't be like that child, speak the truth at all times.

There are times to remain silent on an issue; Jesus refused to answer the mocking questions at His trial, but there are times you must speak and speak the truth. Children are naturally deceitful, they will tell you what they want you to know and will hold back incriminating evidence. But there is a time to grow up and put away childish things; to go against the flow of modernism which cries, 'Don't put the blame on me!' and stand up and speak the whole truth.

Remember verse 12? 'Who is the man who desires life, and loves many days, that he may see good?' If you want that then choose today to speak the truth, the whole and nothing but the truth.

20th January

Psalm 34:14a
'Depart from evil and do good'
Depart from the evil city and enter the good

We continue to find out how to receive the blessing of verse 12, 'Who is the man who desires life, and loves many days, that he may see good?' So far, we have seen it is important what comes out of our mouth. Keep your lips clean and your words true. Now we come to the big decision.

We must choose to depart from evil, no one will choose for us. Make that your priority today, 'I *will* depart from evil.' Once that choice is made, we find that Jesus is already waiting for us, not outside but right there leading us out of the wicked city. It must be our decision to leave but reckon on the fact we have no strength of our own to go; it is only Jesus who brings us out of evil.

It is also our choice to enter Good. Jesus will not force us to do good but once again we are powerless to do good without Him. Jesus has the Keys to the Good city, only He can open the doors and let us in. Trust Him and enter His city.

If your desire is to see good in your life (verse 12) enter Jesus' Good City and good will be all around you.

21st January
Psalm 34:14b
'Seek peace and pursue it'
Chase after Peace

How much do you want verse 12 to be true for you? Today's verse is very active, we are to seek peace and more than that, pursue it. Romans 12:18 reads, 'If it is possible, as much as depends on you, live peaceably with all men.' Not everyone wants to live at peace with you, some are argumentative for no reason; but that is not an excuse to fight against them. The Bible makes it clear it should be our aim to live at peace with everyone. Seek a peaceful resolution to difficult situations but if none are found and if the other person is not interested, you remain in peace.

If others are not interested in peace then leave that to God, we are not instructed to force others into peace only that 'if at all possible' we live at peace with them. How much do you want peace? Enough to pursue it wherever it may lead?

Open your heart and let God's peace in; His peace passes understanding and will guard your heart from the hurts of life (Philippians 4:7).

Remember these verses: 'Keep your tongue from evil, and your lips from speaking deceit. Depart from evil and do good; Seek peace and pursue it.' Psalm 34:13-14. Follow these guidelines and God will fill you with His life, He will give you eternal life and fill you will all good things. This is just the beginning of a wonderful adventure with God.

22nd January
Psalm 34:15a
'The eyes of the Lord are on the righteous'
The Lord God of Heaven Watches over you

Do you feel unnoticed, forgotten, overlooked and discarded? We can all feel like that from time to time, but today we see that God is attentive and His eyes are ever open, watching. As with all aspects of God's character this is not unconditional, the psalmist points out that the eyes of the Lord are on the righteous; in verse 16 we find out about the unrighteous.

Are you a righteous saint of God? If so, you are noticed, you are not forgotten or overlooked or discarded, the Lord God of Heaven watches over you. If not, choose to follow God today, there is no better time to get right with God than right now. He is waiting for you, His desire is to watch over you and keep you safe.

I will close today's devotion with the Old Testament Blessing from Numbers 6:24-26, 'The LORD bless you and keep you; the LORD make his face shine on you and be gracious to you; the LORD turn his face toward you and give you peace.'

Receive this blessing today.

23rd January
Psalm 34:15b
'And His Ears are Open to Their Cry'
The Lord Hears Your heart's Cry

Not only does the Lord watch over His righteous ones, He is attentive and listens to them. When we cry out to the Lord in a given situation we are not talking to thin air, Someone is listening; that Someone is Almighty God.

The Bible is full of accounts of God Hearing His peoples' cries, but there is one that springs to mind because it is a personal cry. In 1 Samuel 1:11 Hannah cries out to the Lord in hopeless desperation, 'O Lord of hosts, if You will indeed look on the affliction of Your maidservant and remember me, and not forget Your maidservant, but will give Your maidservant a male child, then I will give him to the Lord all the days of his life, and no razor shall come upon his head.' Eli the priest initially thought she was drunk, but when he realized she was praying blessed her and said, 'Go in peace, and the God of Israel grant your petition which you have asked of Him.' (vs 17). Hannah went away blessed, but did God hear? The wonderful answer is yes, the Lord did hear her heart's cry; Hannah conceived and gave birth to a son, and she called his name Samuel, which means God heard.

God heard Hannah's heart's cry and he will hear yours too. Open up your heart to Him and tell Him everything that you desire. He has His ears open ready to hear you, and He will move to answer in His time and in His way. Your hearts cry is important to Him.

24th January
Psalm 34:16
'The face of the Lord is against those who do evil, to cut off the remembrance of them from the earth.'
The Lord is against evil doers

Whereas before we saw God's face smiling on the righteous, now we see God as Judge turning His face against those who practice evil. Who are the people who do evil? They are anyone who sets themselves up in opposition to God; they are the unrighteous in God's eyes. These are not just the murderers, rapists, paedophiles and the like, they are everyone who is not a born again saint of God. This kind of truth is unpopular and always has been, but the fact it is unpopular, does not change the fact it is true.

The Lord will cut off all remembrance of the evil, unrepentant unrighteous from the earth leaving the world for Himself and His people. We make much of wicked people today, lauding them and putting them on pedestals, but we should be wise and follow God's example, looking to Him, to see who we should listen to and who we should shun.

Whose side are you on, the Lord's or the World's? Keep your eyes on the eternal; this world will pass away and take all it's citizen's with it. The Lord is making a new heaven and a new earth, one with no evil thing in it; a world populated by the righteous. The saints of God will live happily with Father God; the unrighteous will live terribly forever in Hell. Choose today to be on the Lord's side, that you may inherit eternal life.

25th January
Psalm 34:17
'The righteous cry out, and the Lord hears, and delivers them out of all their troubles.'
Haven't we had this before?

Haven't we heard this one already? Doesn't verse 6 say exactly the same thing? As a reminder here is verse 6, 'This poor man cried out, and the Lord heard him, and saved him out of all his troubles.' Is it the same? Without backtracking on what I said about that verse, it is David's personal testimony to how God heard him and delivered him even though he was only a poor nothing. Verse 17 takes it a step further and underlines the fact that the Lord has not changed. This time the verbs are in the present tense, giving the idea that this is a present continual state. We continue to cry out to Him and God continues to hear and deliver us. Our deliverance is not once and for all but every day, as we need Jesus, He is there to deliver us.

You may have heard others giving testimony to how the Lord has helped and delivered them, similar to David, but for you the Lord has seemed distant or uninterested in your situation. You have cried out to Him but have had no response even though you are a righteous child of God. You think, 'It's not fair!' or 'Why won't You help me Lord?' There are no easy answers to these questions, but I know the Lord does care; seek Him out and ask for His view of your situation. You may be surprised what He is doing behind the scenes. Nothing may appear to change outwardly, but God can change you, so that you can live for Him, regardless of your circumstances.

Cry out to God and He will hear and deliver you today.

26th January

Psalm 34:18a

'The Lord is near to those who have a broken heart.'

Nearer to a broken heart

In our culture we usually associate a broken heart with an ended romantic relationship, 'He broke my heart.' a girl might say when her boyfriend leaves her for someone else. Although this can be a true heart break and God does care, it is a narrow view of how hearts are broken. You can become heartbroken by any form of broken relationship, the loss of love or even the lack of love, betrayal or abuse. There may well be other avenues to a broken heart, but I will concentrate on these ideas. Someone has done something to crush you or has not shown you the love they should have. This leaves you broken, wounded, damaged and even looking for someone or something to fill the aching void in your heart.

This is why people run from one disastrous relationship to another or settle for second or third best. The Lord doesn't what anyone to be heartbroken, vulnerable or open to further heart break. He longs to draw near to you, His hearts desire is to fill your aching void with His tender love; love you can trust because He has promised to 'never leave you nor forsake you.' Deuteronomy 31:6. Don't put up with a broken heart, unlock the door to your heart and let the Lord in, He will sooth your soul and heal your broken heart, so that you can live as He intended and not allow the hurts of the past to define you. You will also be free to forgive those who have betrayed you.

27th January
Psalm 34:18b
'And saves such as have a contrite spirit.'
The amazing transaction

The Bible is all about salvation, getting right with God; this verse points to the direction of how you can be saved. It is the amazing transaction between God and man; the Lord gives salvation to the one who is contrite in spirit. But what is a 'contrite spirit'?

To be contrite is to be 'cut to the quick', absolutely regretful of past mistakes. Last time we saw that the Lord was near to the broken hearted, those who had been hurt by others; today we are looking at something different. Contrition is the immense sorrow for a thing that you have done yourself. There is an oppositeness to being contrite, or contrary, that implies you are going in a different direction. This is the underlying idea behind biblical repentance; not just saying sorry for doing wrong, but actively turning away from wrong doing.

When the Lord sees a soul is in true contrite repentance, He comes in and fills that soul with His Holy Spirit, as a seal and guarantee of salvation. It is God's Holy Spirit that gives the person the strength to walk as God intends, but the person must make that initial decision to turn around.

You may ask, 'When can I be saved, do I have to wait until Sunday?' The Bible answers this question, 'Behold, now is the acceptable time; behold, now is the day of salvation.' 2 Corinthians 6:2b.

Don't wait another day, make that amazing transaction with God, right now.

28th January

Psalm 34:19

'Many are the afflictions of the righteous, But the Lord delivers him out of them all.'

An honest world view

I love how honest this verse is. It says that the righteous will have afflictions in life; they will suffer as others suffer. There is no easy ticket here, life is tough; the question is who do you have in your corner?

Jesus told a parable about the wise and foolish builders, they both built houses and they both experienced a vicious storm. The difference was what they built on; the wise man built on the rock and the storm didn't affect him, but the foolish man built on the sand and the storm undermined his house and it fell flat. Jesus was saying if you build your life on My Words and Ways, then when the storms of life come along you will stand, because you have built your life on the Rock.

Jesus spoke another wonderfully honest Word when He said, 'These things I have spoken to you, that in Me you may have peace. In the world you will have tribulation; but be of good cheer, I have overcome the world.' John 16:33. Yes, afflictions, tribulations, the storms of life will come up against you, but Jesus has overcome all these things and is the Victor. Don't let these things win, trust the Lord to deliver you out of them. As each wave comes to batter your house, make sure it's built on strong foundations.

The Lord is honest with you; is it time to get honest with Him?

29th January
Psalm 34:20
'He guards all his bones; Not one of them is broken.'
He guards your bones

This is the verse John quoted in John 19:36. John recounts the Jews asking if the three crucified prisoners could have their legs broken so they would die before the Sabbath came. The soldiers broke the legs of the other two convicts, but Jesus was already dead, so they did not break His legs. John, who was there, noted that this is exactly what David prophesied would happen; Jesus' bones were not broken.

This prophesy was fulfilled to the letter in Jesus, but it is also fulfilled in His righteous saints. You may have broken a bone or bones (or perhaps you will at some point in the future); but what remains true however, is the essence of this verse; the Lord watches over you and guards you throughout your life.

Your bones are precious to the Lord and He guards or watches over them. Your bones are what keeps you all together and upright and God keeps His eye on those things that keep you together, both physically and spiritually. He cares. He watches over you and His desire is that you are not broken, remember verse 18? He is near to a broken heart and is close by to mend it for you.

Whether it is your actual bones or your spiritual 'bones', the Lord is actively watching and guarding them every day, so they will not be broken. He is on hand immediately if life breaks you in any way. Trust Him, He will never let you down. He guards your bones.

30th January
Psalm 34:21
'Evil shall slay the wicked, and those who hate the righteous shall be condemned.'
Man's judgement – God's judgement

There are two statements here; firstly the wicked will be slain by evil, secondly the Lord will condemn those who hate the righteous. We will look at each in turn.

'Evil shall slay the wicked': This is Man's judgement; he always resorts to killing in the end. From the very beginning, murder has been a convenient way of disposing of our enemies (Genesis 4). Injustice is sometimes dealt with by vigilante killings; we may even agree and say, 'He deserved what he got.' These killings, however are wrong. There are proper legitimate avenues for justice. It must be pointed out, that as Jesus Himself observed, '...all who take the sword will perish by the sword.' (Matthew 26:52). The wicked kill their own.

'And those who hate the righteous shall be condemned.': This, then, is God's judgement. This is a just statement by the King of all the righteous. He is saying, 'anyone who hates my people, are condemned.' Believe me there are many, many people who openly hate God's people. Jews and Christians, who seek to live a godly life, are some of the most hated people in our world. Christians are not able to speak the truth without being berated. I am not looking to start a 'hashtag' campaign, my hope is in the Lord. The King, He will judge. He will condemn all who hate and oppose His righteous ones.

Do not fear the world's condemnation, fear God's condemnation because it is eternal.

31st January
Psalm 34:22
'The Lord redeems the soul of His servants, and none of those who trust in Him shall be condemned.'
The righteous are not condemned
Last time we saw that in God's just judgement, He condemns those who hate the righteous; today we see that in that same just judgement, the Lord will not condemn those who trust in Him.

There is a lie that says that the Lord wants to condemn everyone, and bring sentence down upon them. The truth is that the Lord wants to redeem everyone, and release them from condemnation; the trouble is many people aren't bothered. If you are feeling condemned come to the Lord, He will free you from all condemnation. The world's judgement is temporary and often petty; God's judgement is eternal.

Christians are branded as 'judgemental', but it is the world that loves to judge others and 'pigeon hole' people to fit its views. If you do not agree with the world's view, it hates you. God's heart is that all men and women should walk together as equals under His rule. We are never free, we are either ruled by the world or by God. The Lord's desire is to redeem you; to buy you back from the slavery of the world and remove all condemnation from your back.

These words may offend some but remember that key verse? 'Oh, magnify the Lord with me, and let us exalt His name together.' (verse 3). That is the heart of this Psalm, and verse 22 is no different. Magnify God's great goodness and compare it to the emptiness the world has to offer.

Turn to Him, don't be condemned but be free.

1st February
Psalm 121:1
'I will lift up my eyes to the hills-- From whence comes my help?'
Where does my help come from? #1

This psalm was sung as the pilgrims walked up the mountain to Jerusalem and their eyes fell on the strong walls of that mighty city, and they saw the Temple in all its beauty. And so the question is: 'As I look at these things, is this where my help comes from?'

There are two things here: military might and religious observance. The walls represent the former and the Temple the latter. Where do we place our trust? Military might is important for protection, and it would be foolish to say we have no need of it, but this kind of protection can only go so far. An army may save your country, but it can never save your soul.

Then perhaps religious observance will bring us help? Religious observance is good, and will make you into a moral, upstanding person, but will it grant you eternal life? This brought to my mind the story of the rich young ruler: the young man asked Jesus, 'Good Teacher, what good thing shall I do that I may have eternal life?' He had already done many 'good things', but none were good enough to receive eternal life. Jesus told him to sell all he had and give the proceeds to the poor. He, no doubt, had given much to the poor throughout his life, but this and all his religious good works were not enough. Jesus concluded by saying, 'Follow Me.'

If your 'good works' only go so far as religious observance they are worthless to you. Look at all you do and ask, 'Is this where my help comes from?'

2nd February

Psalm 121:1b-2a
'From whence comes my help? My help comes from the Lord'
Where does my help come from? #2
If our help doesn't come from military might or religious observance, where does it come from?

The Israelites, after considering the mighty walls of Jerusalem and the beautiful Temple, concluded that their help did not come from these things but rather from the Lord. Those pilgrims walking up to Jerusalem for a designated festival, knew all this show was worthless without knowing the Lord who was behind it all. It was vitally important for the people of Israel to demonstrate their Jewishness by these festivals, it was what made them who they were, but without a relationship with God it was meaningless.

Where does my help come from? My help comes from the Lord. This I know to be true every day, all the time. Eternal life is not based on how many good deeds you have done, but on God's goodness to you. Good deeds are a practical way of saying 'Thank you' to God for meeting all your needs.

There are too many people who stop at religious observance and never get any further. They never see the need to seek God for help in their salvation. Don't be that person, call out to the Lord today and find the One who brings help.

This Psalm gives some of the ways God is our help and shield, going beyond physical protection and religious observance.

3rd February

Psalm 121:2b
'Who made heaven and earth.'
Your Creator cares for you

We live in a society where there are many 'lords' to follow, and many 'gods' to worship, and it was no different when this psalm was written. The psalmist wanted to make sure the reader knew the God he was speaking about, so he followed up the line 'My help comes from the Lord' with 'Who made heaven and earth.' This was the God of all creation as found in Genesis 1:1, 'In the beginning God created the heavens and the earth.' It is this God, and this God alone that can bring you help just where you need it.

Why does it matter whether or not God created the world in six literal days or used some other method such as evolution? It matters because a god who didn't make you can't understand your make up and so cannot help. Only the biblical Creator God who made you in His image can fully know what is best for you and bring you help at the right moment.

The Lord who made the heavens and the earth also made the delicate spring blossom, the iridescent feathers of a magpie and He also made you. Every aspect of your life is important to Him. You may feel He has abandoned you and left you to wallow in an impossible situation, if this is how you are feeling today, lift your eyes, not to the hills, but to the Lord your Maker and put your trust in Him even as Job did and you will find He has eyes on you and is protecting you on all sides. We will discover more about this protection later in the psalm but for now put your trust in God your help and Creator.

4th February

Psalm 121:3a
'He will not allow your foot to be moved'
Stand firm

There are many things in this life that trip us up. What is that one thing that always trips you? Others say it doesn't bother them but for you it is a snare. You know the thing. Well the Lord '...will not allow your foot to be moved', He will keep you from falling. Psalm 37:23-24 says, 'The steps of a good man are ordered by the Lord, and He delights in his way. Though he fall, he shall not be utterly cast down; For the Lord upholds him with His hand.' This is totally true and reliable. He will uphold you with His hand, however, you must choose to hold His hand and desire to stand.

Ephesians 6:11-18 says we should 'stand' four times and we do that by choosing to put on the full armour of God by obeying all He says. The armour consists of the belt of truth, the breastplate of righteousness, the shoes of the Gospel of peace, the shield of faith, the helmet of salvation and the sword of the Spirit. After we have done all this Paul says we should pray. But who does Paul say we should pray for? Ourselves lest we fall? No, Paul instructs us to pray for the saints, other believers, who may be struggling.

In a time of temptation don't be inward looking, look to others in need and pray for them. Leave yourself in God's care, He can keep your feet from stumbling. In that moment of near weakness don't fall into temptation but rather stand firm and pray for others.

5th February
Psalm 121:3b
'He who keeps you will not slumber.'
The Lord your help does not sleep

When my wife was in labour with our first child it took from about 8:30 in the evening to almost 6:00 the following morning, which is a very long time and due to certain circumstances I hadn't slept much the night before. This meant I dozed off several times during the long night when I should have been keeping watch with my wife. I am so glad that the Lord does not slumber or sleep, He is always watching over us.

For many the night is a fearful time when terrible things may, and do, happen. There are wicked people around who prey on the vulnerable and none of this escapes the attention of the Lord; He see it all. He will avenge, His Judgement will come. You may not be safe in this world but trust in the Lord because you will be safe in His Hands.

Whether or not your night terrors are real or imagined, know this that the Lord is with you and is watching over you. He cares for you so call out to Him day or night and the Lord will answer you. When the power of darkness surrounds you, remember that God's Power is greater and He is able to deliver you.

This is the truth to remember all day and all night, 'He who keeps you will not slumber.'

6th February
Psalm 121:4
'Behold, He who keeps Israel Shall neither slumber nor sleep.'
The God of Israel is the God of your nation and the Church

Yesterday we saw that the Lord is watchful over us day and night. This time we see that it is not just individuals the Lord watches over but whole nations and by definition His entire Church.

This psalm was written to the people of Israel and so that nation is naturally mentioned, and rightfully so because they are God's chosen people. However, I believe that this promise goes further, and God keeps your country too. No matter how awful things get, the Lord is ever watchful; His eye is on the lowest of the low and the highest of the high judging them to see if they match up to His Holy standards.

There is also, naturally, the idea of God keeping watch over His Church. Nothing that happens to the Church escapes God's notice. He sees the injustices brought against His people, the unjust violence inflicted on Christians; He knows the persecutions large and small. Others may not care but He does. It's true that the wicked seem to get away with treating the Church with contempt, but the Lord will Judge each one so leave that to Him. As for you, 'love your enemies, bless those who curse you, do good to those who hate you, and pray for those who spitefully use you and persecute you...' Matthew 5:44.

The Lord never sleeps, He is always ready to come to our aid anytime day or night. We are never alone. God watches over us, over our country, over His Church and over you.

7th February

Psalm 121:5a
'The Lord is your keeper'
The Lord is your keeper

The message of this psalm is clear, the Lord is your protector and He never sleeps so His protection is 24/7. This verse emphasizes the intimacy of that protection. The Lord is your keeper, or bodyguard; the one who takes the shot for you. The Lord stands between you and the wiles of the Enemy. He stops every attack that comes against you. Here's a thought, any attack that does strike you has stuck Him first! He went through it ahead of you and with you! If no one else knows the pain you're going through, God knows, and He is there to take and share that pain.

Proverbs 18:10 says, 'The name of the Lord is a strong tower; the righteous run to it and are safe.' If you are a Child of God, you are one of the righteous and therefore have access to the 'strong tower' of the Lord's Name. When you are in God's Tower you are totally surrounded by Him. His love will envelop you and the terrors will not be able to destroy your great hope in the Lord. Anyone who does anything against you, physically, mentally or spiritually in order to cause you harm is an enemy of God and He is zealous for you and your protection.

I can't promise an easy life or even an easy escape from trauma, but I can promise that the Lord will never leave you nor forsake you and He will keep you through your whole life. Put your trust in Him.

8th February
Psalm 121:5b
'The Lord is your shade at your right hand.'
Living under God's parasol

The psalm continues its theme of protection this time comparing God to a parasol. Whereas a parasol protects us from the harmful effects of the sun, the Lord shades us from the harmful effects of the world.

We are very aware of the dangers of staying out in the full glare of the sun without proper protection however, the danger from the sun is miniscule compared with the harm the world can inflict on us. The Lord is our shade, or parasol, but that does not prevent us from venturing outside God's cover. There are dangers in the world that are best avoided; many are obvious, some not so. These subtle dangers often take the form of everyday activities that promote health and wellbeing, such as yoga, martial arts, hypnotherapy, meditation techniques and the like. Many Christians do not see the harm in such things, but they are like going to the beach setting up your sun screen but then sitting in the full glare of the sun. That sun shield is of no use if you are not under its shade, and God's parasol is of no use if you move out from under it.

The sun may seem warm and inviting and totally harmless, but in reality, those warming rays can and do damage your body and the world's warm and inviting rays will damage your spirit in similar ways.

9th February
Psalm 121:6
'The sun shall not strike you by day, Nor the moon by night.'
Twenty-four hour protection
Okay, have you got it yet? God watches over you and protects you all day, every day.

These thoughts have already been covered, but this is a holy recap. The Lord will protect you from the temptations of the day. As the sun is injurious to our bodies so the world is injurious to our spirits, we must be on our guard and live beneath the protection of God's love. Likewise, the moon represents the night and its terrors. God is with you through the night and His protection continues. There are temptations of the night that can snare you, secret hidden things in the dark; the Lord's light will expose these traps and enable you to escape.

The world is a dangerous place to be; both day and night bring their own dangers, but the Lord is Master over them all. His protection is always available whether you are most vulnerable in the day or at night. Never rely on your own strength but rather live under the parasol of God all day, every day.

Twenty-Four hour protection – no sweat.

10th February
Psalm 121:7a
'The Lord shall preserve you from all evil'
The Lord's hedge of protection #1: Protection from evil

At the end of the psalm the word 'preserve' is used three times and we will look at each one in turn. The word translated 'preserve' is Shamar and literally means protected by a thorny bush. This means nothing can get to you without first getting through the thorns and it also means you can't get out without being scratched by those same thorns.

So, what does this hedge protect you from? The first thing is 'evil'; the idea the psalmist is making goes beyond wicked people to bad things that can happen. The worst of the worst experiences are blocked from coming too close by this thorn bush of protection. You may imagine the hedge to be beautiful and ornate, but actually the Lord's hedge of protection has huge thorns and ragged edges; nothing can get through it without ripping itself on those terrible spines.

They also protect you from the temptation of getting into danger. The thorns will hurt you as much as they hurt the evil things if you try to push through. But, why would you want to get out of God's protection? It's not a prison but a barricade against the Enemy.

There is safety within God's hedge of protection; safety from all kinds of evil that this world wants to destroy us with.

11th February
Psalm 121:7b
'He shall preserve your soul.'
The Lord's hedge of protection #2: Protection for the soul

Yesterday I boldly stated that, 'the worst of the worst experiences are blocked from coming too close by this thorn bush of protection.' The truth of the matter is bad things do happen to Christians; terrible things, even the worst of the worst things. This does not undermine the protection of God's hedge around us, but it does mean we need another layer of protection and this one *is* impenetrable.

God has placed a thorny hedge around your soul; that inner area of your life. If bad things happen to you, those things cannot get to your soul to destroy it. They may hurt your outward body, but your soul is safe in God's hands.

Remember if anything has got to you it has had to get through God's thorns first; this doesn't mean it is super powerful, it means it is wounded, torn by God's thorns. People may do and say all sorts of things to you, but the truth is your soul is Heaven bound, no one can get you there. You are God's child and He cares for you. Don't look to the outward appearance, look to the Lord He is where your help comes from.

12th February
Psalm 121:8a
'The Lord shall preserve your going out and your coming in'
The Lord's hedge of protection #3: Wherever you go, God is with you

The Lord protects us all day, every day. He stops us getting hurt by the wiles of the world, and ensures the eternal safety of our souls, but we live in the world and we have to go into it every day. The Lord has promised to protect us in our day to day life; hedging us in as we go to and fro. I remember walking from Buchanan Bus Station in Glasgow to Glasgow Central at night, about a mile walk. I had luggage and was tired after a day of traveling. I felt the eyes of everyone I passed, and I was totally vulnerable; in that dark and dangerous moment I knew that God was with me and His protection was in place.

I do not suggest putting yourself in danger as I did, but the Lord is gracious, and His protection extends to all areas of your life. Wherever you go, whatever you do, God is with you. He will see to it that anyone or anything that gets too close to you will be scratched by His thorns. Walk wisely, and know that God has your back, He will protect you at all times.

Don't move from under God's protection; stay safe and secure and close to the Lord. He is your protection and is ever working for your best, trust in Him and see what He will do for you. Jesus loves you and his hedge is always there.

Remember, wherever you go, God is with you.

13th February

Psalm 121:8b

'From this time forth, and even forevermore.'

Permanent protection

This psalm begins with a question, 'From whence comes my help?' and then goes on to answer it. We are wonderfully provided for by the Lord. He helps and protects us day and night. This last phrase gives us a wonderful promise; we are told when that protection starts and how long it lasts for.

I will break it down into the two parts, firstly 'From this time forth' this means the protection starts now; it is new every morning. We do not have to rely on yesterday's protection. God's protection always starts now. His parasol never gets holes, His thorn bush never grows old. Every moment of every day, God renews His protection on you. This means that it is perfectly suited for whatsoever situation you are going through right now.

So, to the second thought, 'and even forevermore.' When we buy electrical goods, they are generally guaranteed for a set period and then you're on your own. What is the guarantee period of God's protection? It is guaranteed forevermore. It is not dependent on you or on how long you live, it is dependent on God and He is eternal. God's hedge of protection does not disappear at death it continues with you for all eternity, although I imagine it to look more beautiful in Heaven!

Live under the protection of the Lord 'From this time forth, and even forevermore.'

14th February
Psalm 23:1a
'The Lord is My Shepherd'
The Good Shepherd

Psalm 23 may be the most well know psalm and perhaps the most loved. The psalm begins with this statement of faith, 'The Lord is *my* Shepherd'. It would be worth reading John 10:1-30 at this point as a reminder of what Jesus said about being the Good Shepherd. Jesus said in those verses that His sheep follow Him but flee from a stranger. He was also implying that those who are not His sheep do not follow Him. He went onto say the Good Shepherd lays down His life for His sheep, risking His life for them. Jesus literally gave His life for us on the Cross.

David, who was a shepherd, understood this mentality better than many of us; in 1 Samuel 17:34-36 David tells king Saul that he would risk his life to save one sheep that had been taken by a lion or a bear. One sheep was more precious to David that his own life. We are so precious to God that He risked everything to save us from the jaws of the prowling lion. David never had to go the full way and give his life for his father's sheep, but Jesus did.

Jesus is the Good Shepherd, but is He *your* Shepherd? It is very easy to read this psalm, but do you really mean it? Ask yourself today, 'is the Lord my Shepherd, do I listen to His voice and follow Him?' Be honest with yourself and the Lord, make Him your Shepherd today.

15th February
Psalm 23:1b
'I shall not want'
What do I want?

'The Lord is my Shepherd; I shall not want.' That is a very definite statement David sings to the Lord and we sing it along with him, but do we have wants and if so, what do we want? Is there something that you want the Lord to do for you today – a real need. Then bring it to the Shepherd, tell Him your need. David was a shepherd himself and so understood that sheep need things and as their shepherd it was his responsibility to provide for them. We shall be looking at green pastures and still waters in the next few days, but for today what do you need?

If the Lord is your Shepherd, He will ensure you have everything you need for the day; not necessarily what you want, but everything you need. It is His responsibility to give us 'our daily bread' but it is our responsibility to accept it, even if it was not what we wanted.

Trust the Good Shepherd to give you good things, come to Him expectantly with hands held open ready to receive of His bountiful supply. I don't believe David was implying that we should not have legitimate needs, but he was saying that we have a Shepherd who is not only able but willing to meet our every need.

Let this be our anthem for today, 'I shall not want, because I do not need to – The Lord, my shepherd will supply.'

16th February
Psalm 23:2a
'He makes me to lie down in green pastures'
Rest in the Lord

Today, we come to the 'green pastures' mentioned, in passing, last time. Since sheep graze on grass it must be assumed that David saw this as a place to fill one of our needs – to eat. We not only need to eat physical food, but we also need spiritual food. Look again, though, David says, the Shepherd 'makes me *to lie down* in green pastures.' This then is also another need being met, that of rest.

We, as sheep, struggle and kick and say, "No Lord, I am too busy to lie down at the moment. When I have finished all I have to do then I will rest!" But the Lord patiently makes us lie down to rest. Does the Lord have to force you to stop and rest in His presence?

We call Him Lord, but we do not do as He says. Often He's said, "Rest in My Love." But do we obey? Or are we embarrassed to appear to be not 'working'? Anything God asks us to do for Him is working for Him, even if it's resting! When the Lord comes to give us rest, yield to Him. The important work will still get done, but we will be able to do it with more energy and concentration.

Take the Shepherd's opportunity to rest today.

17th February
Psalm 23:2b
'He leads me beside the still waters'
Waters of rest

Yesterday we looked at a forced rest; the Lord who knows us *making* us lie down. Today we find a different kind of rest that the Shepherd leads us to. It is a still or quiet spot, a resting place. It gives me the picture of an oasis in the desert; an organised stop along the way. We may think about the Lord's Day this way; Sundays are there each week for us to stop and refresh ourselves in the Lord. There may be other organised stops the Shepherd has planned for us too; our daily Quiet Times with God, a holiday or retreat. Or, perhaps a stop the Lord has planned for us that we do not yet know about.

The Shepherd leads us to the waters of rest in order for us to drink. We need to constantly drink from the bottomless well of God's Life-giving Spirit in order to function and continue on in our Christian walk. These times of rest may be long, but they may only be brief, so we must take advantage of the waters of rest as the Lord gives them to us.

The Shepherd knows us better than we know ourselves, so when He leads us to the waters of rest, we must stop to drink, if only for a short time. Once we are refreshed the Shepherd will lead us on again down the paths He knows in order to bring us to the next resting place.

18th February
Psalm 23:3a
'He restores my soul'
Restoration

Ever wondered what the Lord restored your soul from and to? He restores your soul from its sinful nature to His nature. It made me think whether Jesus had this verse in mind when He told the parable of the Lost Sheep. In this parable Jesus asks the crowd, 'What man of you, having a hundred sheep, if he loses one of them, does not leave the ninety-nine in the wilderness, and go after the one which is lost until He finds it?' Luke 15:4. What a question! This is exactly what God does for His 'lost sheep', He not only seeks them, but He also brings them back into the fold. He doesn't leave us on the hillside alone He lays us on His shoulders and restores us to His flock.

Anyone who has been a lost sheep (and that is all of us) knows that wandering off alone is dangerous and often causes us harm. Therefore, our Good Shepherd not only brings us home but also heals our wounds and makes us whole again. This healing process may take time to complete, but be patient with God and He will restore your soul in His time. He knows what you can handle.

God's restoration plan began before you even knew you needed restoring. It begins with the Lord looking for you and finishes with the Lord making you whole as He desires you to be. This process will take your whole life, but the Lord is willing to put in the time, are you?

19th February
Psalm 23:3b
'He Leads Me in The Paths of Righteousness'
The righteous path

The Lord will lead His sheep along a path of righteousness, but it may not be an easy path. Do not be alarmed at the direction God leads you in as He has His own plan for you. His paths are the 'Paths of Righteousness'.

David called the Lord his Shepherd, and shepherds in the Middle East walk in front of their sheep, leading them. The sheep follow wherever the shepherd may lead. The Lord is not only in front of you, leading the way, He is also behind you protecting you and right by your side, walking friend with friend.

He walks before you, behind you and beside you for one purpose; to guide you along the Righteous Path. Where this path goes is different for each one of us, but the destination is the same for all! We therefore should not judge someone else based on our righteous journey but only by the light of the Bible. This will inevitably also ensure we are sticking to the path of righteousness; if our path does not reflect the Bible *we* are on the wrong path.

Follow the Good Shepherd and listen to His Words and you will walk in the Paths of Righteousness.

20th February
Psalm 23:3c
'For His Name's Sake.'
For His Name's sake

Yesterday we saw that the Good Shepherd lead's us down the paths of righteousness, today we find out why. We may think of all sorts of reasons the Lord leads us through certain things. We may think it is to teach us something, and we may well learn a valuable lesson. We might feel the Lord is mistreating us by taking us a hard way, or perhaps blessing us by leading us a pleasant way. There is only one reason why God leads us anywhere and that is, 'for His Name's sake'. It is for His Name He leads us through difficult places, and it is for His Name He guides us through fields of Beulah Land.

The issue is not where He leads us, but what our reaction is. Our life must always bring glory to God no matter what we are going through. If we gripe and complain, how is that honouring His Holy Name? What if we lounge in the bounties of God? Does that bring glory to His Name? In good times or bad, our face must be forever towards our Good Shepherd. It is not for our sake He leads us but for His Own Names sake. No matter what today brings, may your life bring glory to the Lord's Name.

21st February
Psalm 23:4a
'Yea, though I walk through the valley of the shadow of death, I will fear no evil; For You are with me'
He is with me through the valley

I have been breaking this psalm down into its phrases, but it would be wrong to break this section down any further. We all go through 'tough times', but sometimes we find ourselves in the deepest, darkest valley; a valley from which we see no escape. It may seem that death is the inevitable outcome. David said that even there he would fear no evil. It reminds me of Shadrach, Meshach and Abed-nego. When they were about to be thrown into the fiery furnace they affirmed, "O Nebuchadnezzar, we have no need to answer you in this matter. If that is the case, our God whom we serve can deliver us from the burning fiery furnace, and He will deliver us from your hand, O king. But if not, let it be known to you, O king, that we do not serve your gods, nor will we worship the gold image which you have set up." Daniel 3:16-18. What was their secret? Simple, they knew that the Lord was with them and would be with them even in the fiery furnace.

Do you fear that something bad is about to happen at any moment? You needn't if The Good Shepherd is walking with you; He will stay by your side throughout the darkest times in your life. The Lord can deliver you out of the valley of the shadow of death but even if He doesn't, He will remain by your side until the end.

22nd February
Psalm 23:4b
'Your rod and Your staff, they comfort me.'
Love in action

We like our Shepherd to provide for us, to lead us into safety, but we don't like the thought of discipline. God's discipline is for others, not us. We see people outside the Church disobeying God's Word, and we feel they deserve God's righteous punishment. We see other denominations, not worshiping the way we do and think God should sort them out. We don't often look at ourselves and see the need for God's correction.

The Rod and Staff speak of discipline: the rod was used to keep the sheep going in the right direction and the staff was used to bring back the stray animals that had got into trouble. We, like sheep, may find ourselves being disciplined by the Shepherd. His intentions are always for our good. It may not seem like it at the time but God's rod of correction will keep us from unnecessary harm and saves us from the need for God to use the staff to rescue us. When we stray from the path, the Lord will use circumstances to prod us and draw us back and if this is ineffective, He will use His staff to pull us back in line. It will be painful and upsetting but the final outcome will be good.

The Good Shepherd shows His love for us by necessary discipline. It is not cruelty but love in action. Knowing that our Shepherd loves us enough to show us where we are going wrong and is willing to do something about it, should be a great comfort to us.

23rd February
Psalm 23:5a
'You prepare a table before me in the presence of my enemies'
A table of blessing

You may call this 'typical Old Testament language'. In the New Testament, we are supposed to 'love our enemies'; but in fact, David is not really talking about loving or hating our enemies, but rather that God will bless us abundantly *despite* our enemies.

There is a feeling of the inevitability of enemies and David was all too familiar with them. So, David sings that although his enemies are trying to bring him down and cause him to be in want, God will prepare a table for him to enjoy and place it slap bang in the midst of them! The emphasis here is not on David's feelings for his enemies, but rather on God's overwhelming feelings for His friend David. God abundantly poured out His blessing on David even as everything was crumbling down around Him. When David was running from Saul, he was never in want; and later when through his own errors, he found himself running from his own son Absalom, the Lord continued to provide. That emphasis is the same for us, 'love your enemies, bless those who curse you, do good to those who hate you, and pray for those who spitefully use you and persecute you.' Matthew 5:44. Always rely on God's hand of provision even while these enemies are trying to starve you out, so to speak.

The Lord will prepare a table of blessing for you, eat of it and be satisfied.

24th February
Psalm 23:5b
'You anoint My Head with Oil; My cup runs over.'
A different kind of anointing

I looked up the Hebrew word for 'anoint', hoping for a good 'Messianic' connection; David is, after all, a forerunner of Jesus! But no, the word we translate as anoint, means to become prosperous, and when linked to the second part of the phrase you can see that God has made David very prosperous indeed; his cup runs over!

As we draw towards the end of this amazing psalm, it is good to consider the generosity of the Shepherd. This psalm is just packed with good things God desires to lavish on us His sheep: we will lack nothing, we will lay in green pastures, and be led to quiet waters, we will be refreshed and led on the right paths, and even when the going gets tough, the Shepherd is always there! When our enemies try to push us down, our Shepherd lifts us up and feeds us.

This is just a snapshot of God's lovingkindness towards us, the Bible is just full of promises direct from the Shepherd's heart to ours. Get close to the Shepherd and watch your cup fill, from full to overflowing!

If you thought this was as good as it gets just wait to see what comes next.

25th February
Psalm 23:6a
'Surely goodness and mercy shall follow me all the days of my life'
Goodness – more than goodness!

There is so much in this verse that I can't keep it to just one portion; I will, therefore, break it down into three parts, starting with 'goodness'.

Last time we saw that David was anointed with prosperity, all good things. This time we will look at those good things. What did David mean by 'goodness'? 'Goodness will follow me all the days of my life.'

The Hebrew word is towb and I suggest looking it up in a concordance, I can't possibly do the word justice.

Whole books could be written on this one word alone, but, okay, I will do my best. It means good things, almost any good thing you can imagine. Let me assure you *all* areas of life are bound up in this word; David said you would have goodness in every part of your life. A note of caution, this is not a prosperity Gospel saying everything and anything you desire God will give you; but rather that God will provide all your needs in each and every corner of your life.

The Lord wants to pour out His goodness on you with no limitations; all you have to do is accept what His goodness is for you. Yield to the Good Shepherd and enjoy His bountiful goodness.

26th February
Psalm 23:6a
'Surely goodness and mercy shall follow me all the days of my life'
Mercy – more than mercy!

We have looked at goodness, now we tackle mercy, or in some translations 'lovingkindness'. If you could fill whole books with the meaning of 'goodness' you could fill whole libraries with the meaning of 'mercy' and not even scratch the surface.

The word translated 'mercy' is hesed. It is in one sense the Old Testament version of agapē God's love, but really it is agapē squared! It is the love, grace, mercy, lovingkindness and overflowing generosity of God. The only way to understand what this amazing word means is to get to know the Shepherd; know Him, know His lovingkindness!

But, how do we get to know God? Surely, He is unknowable. Paul says in Colossians 1:15 that Jesus is the 'image of the invisible God'. Get to know Jesus and you automatically get to know God; He *is* God. Read the four Gospel accounts of Jesus' life and you will see lovingkindness and mercy on every page. Everything Jesus did or said was out of love, even the hard things.

We may argue over whether or not God's love is 'unconditional', but God's love is certainly eternal; it has no beginning and it has no end.

Not just mercy, but all of God's great love given to you.

27th February

Psalm 23:6a

'Surely goodness and mercy shall follow me all the days of my life'

ALL the days of my life

I will go out on a limb here and say that you, like me, don't feel as if all of God's goodness and all of His mercy are following you every day. Some days will be pretty grotty, dark and lonely. All your hopes and dreams dashed on the rocks and you cry out to God, "Where is your goodness? Where is your mercy? Are they not supposed to be following me *all* the days of my life?" At this point we'd better look back at verse 4, 'Yea, though I walk through the valley of the shadow of death, I will fear no evil; for You are with me.' Notice afresh those last five words, 'For You are with me.' Goodness and mercy are attributes of God's nature. If He is with us, they are with us! David knew God was with him through some terrible, as well as glorious, times; he lived in both a cave and in a palace!

God is with you all the days of your life, the good times and the bad, the highs and lows. He is your constant friend, and by this I mean our lives may change from day to day or even minute by minute, but God remains the same throughout. God's goodness and mercy *are* following you today because God is following you. Take comfort in the fact that the Good Shepherd is always looking after His sheep.

28th February
Psalm 23:6b
'And I will dwell in the house of the Lord Forever.'
Happily, ever after

We have been studying Psalm 23 and have seen how David builds his psalm up like a crescendo, culminating in saying, as we saw last time, 'goodness and mercy shall follow me all the days of my life'. Today we find out how David even looked beyond the grave to the time he would dwell with the Lord forever – in His house!

God's generosity does not end at death, in fact His generosity is only just beginning. If we have placed ourselves in God's sheepfold in this life, when we die the Good Shepherd will bring us into His house. No longer does He have to lead us to pastures and waters and lay up lavish meals for us; everything we need is eternally spread out before us. God will say to us, 'Make yourself at home, help yourself to anything your heart desires' and He will actually mean it! The whole of the Shepherd's house opened up to you and to me forever. For the first time we will truly be able to say, 'The Lord is my shepherd, I shall not want!'

Until that day we can bask in the overflowing generosity of our beloved Good Shepherd. His wonderful provision for us is a mere taster of what is in store for us when we meet Him face to face. Get to know the Good Shepherd, as described in this psalm, and He will abundantly bless you in this life and the next.

29th February

Psalm 117:1

'Praise the Lord, all you Gentiles! Laud Him, all you peoples!'

Not just for Jews

Psalm 117 is notable for being the shortest psalm, only two verses long. It is also notable because it is not aimed at the Jewish people, but rather the Gentiles, the non-jews, and specifically all peoples. Everyone is included here. Whoever you are, wherever you're from you can praise the Lord. There is not one person who can truly say, 'I cannot praise the Lord because... (insert a reason here).' People may choose not to praise, but they do not have any real reason not to.

The fact is, this is not an invitation to praise the Lord, but rather a command to do so. The Jewish people, to whom God had revealed Himself and given them the Covenant, have opened the doors so that all the peoples could praise God. There is the idea of a shout going up, calling everyone to praise God. Who am I and who are you to refuse the impartation to praise given to us by the Lord through His People?

Decide today to praise the Lord; you do not need to use many words, just look at this psalm! If you are not used to praising God start small, look out the window and tell the Lord of the beauty of creation, or else thank the Lord for His provision for you (perhaps, not so small after all). Short praises can be great praises. Go on, give it a go!

1st March
Psalm 117:2a
'For His merciful kindness is great toward us, And the truth of the Lord endures forever.'
Two praises to get you started
Although Psalm 117 is the shortest psalm it contains two wonderful praises to get you started on your praise journey.

The first is, 'His merciful kindness is great towards us.' This is a representation of God's perfect love for us. He is merciful and kind in all His dealings with us, even when we deserve nothing but punishment, He smiles on us. He has blessed us with unfathomable blessings, just look at His beautiful world He has given us to live in. He sends the rain on the righteous and the unrighteous (Matthew 5:45). We do not deserve His love, but He pours it out just the same. Praise the Lord for His merciful kindness that He gives so lavishly.

The second reason to give Him praise is that God's truth endures forever. What He said in Genesis 1 to Revelation 22 is still true today. Ideas change, new knowledge replaces old, but God's truth remains the same. This means we can trust Him totally. We know what God is like because He has shown it to us in the Bible and that truth is still true today. Jesus is the embodiment of God's truth. He said, "I am the way, the truth, and the life. No one comes to the Father except through Me." Come to Jesus today and praise Him for His eternal truth.

Use these two truths to praise the Lord throughout the day.

2nd March
Psalm 117:2b
'Praise the Lord!'
Hallelujah!

The writer of this psalm ends it not with three words but with one: Hallelujah. One word that says so much! Our Christian culture and especially our music is filled with hallelujahs. It is a term that can be used all too easily in Christian circles without really praising God. Have you ever used 'Hallelujah!' as an expression of exasperation? I know I have. Wouldn't it be wonderful to fill our day with real hallelujahs. Make a point of finding things to praise the Lord for today and then each hour say 'Hallelujah for ...' and then say all the things you've found so far. You could accumulate all the praises adding to the list each time, or you could bring just the new found praise, either way fill your day with hallelujahs. You may find you want to do this on a regular basis.

That is all for later. Right now just where you are begin to express your praise to God. Write something down, perhaps as a poem or a song. Draw or paint a picture for the Lord. The Lord has given you a gift, use it for Him. You may think you do not have an artistic gift, just try something. I would never have thought I could write and yet here I am having a go.

If nothing else stand up and shout 'Hallelujah!' I dare you...

3rd March
Psalm 22:1a
'My God, My God, why have You forsaken Me?'
A real hearts cry

Most psalms I have chosen are positive and although they paint a picture of hardships God, is always there to intervene. Psalm 22 does not start like that, there is a feeling of utter desperation, God is not listening, David is forsaken; surely all is lost. Where is God in David's situation? I wonder if your heart's cry is the same as the psalmist's, 'My God, My God, why have You forsaken Me?' If it is, you are in very good company.

Jesus quoted this psalm while He was dying on the Cross; at His lowest moment He cried out, 'My God, My God, why have You forsaken Me?' Although He knew His Father was always there, at that moment He felt totally alone. Jesus wasn't just quoting this psalm, He was living through it from verse 1 to 31 when all was done, and it was finished (Psalm 22:31).

Jesus knows the pain of this verse every bit as much as you do. He went through terrible pain and torture on the Cross, whilst for the first time in Eternity being separated from His Father. Does it feel like God has forsaken you? Well, let us walk this path together, along with Jesus, and see the deliverance God has for you and me.

4th March
Psalm 22:1b
'Why are You so far from helping Me'
When God's help is far off

Notice the title is 'When God's help is far off' and not 'When God's help seems far off'. There are times when God's help *is* far off, you cry out to Him in your distress but nothing changes, and the fog of confusion get thicker every day. What should you do in these dark, unrelenting seasons?

What is needed in these times is faith; just faith the size of a mustard seed, or half a mustard seed if that is all you have. But faith in what? You may well ask. Faith in God and His goodness. When God is far off be assured, He has not forgotten you, His help is ready for when the time is right. God's timing is perfect but that doesn't mean it's easy. It can be very tough waiting for God when it seems like He's abandoned you. Habakkuk 2:3 says, 'For the vision is yet for an appointed time; but at the end it will speak, and it will not lie. Though it tarries, wait for it; because it will surely come, it will not tarry.' Help is coming, so wait for it, yes, it is a long way off but every day it gets nearer.

Why is God so far off from helping you? Because when He comes, He will bring abundant blessing on you and will bless many others through your testimony.

5th March
Psalm 22:1c
'And from the words of My groaning?'
Unheeded prayer

One of my bugbears is the so-called 'unanswered prayer'. Real prayer is always answered; it just may not be the time and way you would want or choose. This follows on from last time, when we were considering God's absent help. It is as if David is saying, 'Where is your help for me Lord, are you even heeding my hearts cry?' Is this where you are today? Are you crying (literally) before God, pouring out your soul to Him, begging for an answer and all you get is nothing? Day after day of the same response will drive anyone to despair. Why does God do this? We may not know fully until we meet Him in Glory, it is a test of faith; how much do you really trust God? Do you trust Him enough to come through for you when it seems He is not even listening! Or is there doubt in your heart?

If it is important to you, you can be sure it's important to God. If your heart is breaking over the situation you are living through, then God's heart is also breaking for you; He loves you. This may not make it easier, but He has heard and when the time is right He will answer you and bring light into your darkness. Remember, the same David who wrote this also wrote, 'though I walk through the valley of the shadow of death I will fear no evil for you are with me.' Psalm 23:4. He has heeded your prayer and more importantly He is with you in your distress.

6th March

Psalm 22:2

'O My God, I cry in the daytime, but You do not hear; and in the night season, and am not silent.'

Honesty before God

There is an honesty in David's plea to God; he is telling the Lord exactly what he has been doing. He has been crying to the Lord, day and night and yet there has been no answer. David does not soften his complaint down because he is addressing Almighty God, he tells it straight because of who God is.

Don't be afraid to pour out your complaint before God, He has very broad shoulders! Tell Him how you feel and how often you have cried to Him without response. It's okay, He already knows. As your Heavenly Father He loves to hear you being honest with Him, even if it is a complaint directed at Him. He will silently listen as you put your case to Him, allowing you to let off all those pent-up emotions. When you are done, it is time for you to sit quietly at your Father's feet. He may have a word for you, even the answers you crave, I don't know, but what I do know is that He will put His loving arms around you and weep with you as only a Father can. He will bring peace into your heart where before there was only turmoil. Nothing may change outwardly, but in your heart a connection is formed between you and God and your situation will never be the same again.

7th March
Psalm 22:3a
'But You are Holy'
But God

We are walking through the verses of Psalm 22 and discovering things are not always easy in the life of faith. God doesn't always bring relief from our burdens immediately. There is sometimes a long, long wait where it can appear as if God is not even bothered about us. In today's reading there is a change of pace; it is as if David has paused and has thought about all he has said, and all he knows about God and he confesses that God is holy. He has not changed.

In all your struggles you are going through, when you list them, finish by saying, 'But God...' The Lord is the same, yesterday, today and forever (Hebrews 13:8) and the God who sent His Son to die for you, is the same God who appears silent and stony. Put your trust in Him, He loves you and only wants the best for you. It may be tough at the moment, tougher than I could ever imagine, but God is still holy, He is still on the throne and in control of all that happens in your life. Do you trust Him to bring you though the 'shadow of death' you are currently walking through? Well, do you? When Jesus was on the cross, His life was at it's lowest, and even His Father had turned His face away; in that lonely moment the reminder from this psalm that God is still holy and had not changed must have been such an encouragement to Him. Jesus trusted in the Father, and you can too.

8th March

Psalm 22:3b

'Enthroned in the praises of Israel.'

Enthroned in praise

Is God enthroned in your heart? If you are wondering if He is even there, make the decision to praise Him. Your praise is the throne room of God in your life. It is a choice whether to blame God for your situation and become bitter towards Him and thus pushing Him out of your throne room, or else praising Him for all the good works He has performed; lifting Him high on the throne.

Praise has the effect of taking our eyes off ourselves and placing them firmly on the Lord. Instead of self-pity you begin to feel great joy and gladness; thankfulness for all the great things He has done for you. It is at the point of your lowest ebb that you need to praise God the most; He is your King and sovereign over your heart and life. It is not about reminding God of who He is, but rather reminding yourself of who He is. That reminder will change the way you see God and the way you see the dark path you tread. What is more changeless, your current circumstances or God? Praise Him for He is the Rock of your salvation.

If you are struggling to think of anything to praise God about read on over the next few verses.

9th March
Psalm 22:4a
'Our fathers trusted in You'
When you can see no reason to praise

David must have been in a very dark place, for even the great psalmist could not think of much to praise God for in his circumstances; but he praised anyway. He looked back into the history of his people and recalled to mind times when Israel had trusted God. You may think Israel never trusted God, but there were times when they did and saw great victories, such as Joshua claiming the Land for the Lord. David had learnt that God had been with Israel in their darkest hours and even when they turned their backs on Him, He was still faithful. This knowledge reminded him that God was still faithful now, and He had not forsaken David in his hour of need.

I wonder, are you in that place of utter darkness, where you can see no good at all in your life? You are desperately trying to find something to thank God for and you are coming up empty. Take my advice and turn your eyes to past glories in your life, in your parents lives, think about your church and it's history - whether your church is hundreds of years old or just begun there will be wonderful things to praise God for. Open you mouth and say, '"so and so" trusted in you.' adding in the name of the person or persons concerned. If He came through for them, He will do the same for you.

10th March
Psalm 22:4b
'They trusted, and You delivered them.'
A good deal

We are all looking for a 'good deal', a bargain we can't turn down: 2 for 1's, half price, three months free, the list is endless. The only thing is many of these deals are anything but good; they are certainly good for the retailer but are they really good for you? God's deal is very good.

Yesterday, we saw that David's ancestors trusted God in their situations, today we see God's response: He delivered them. The deal is simple, you trust God and He will deliver you. He doesn't expect you to 'snap out of it' or 'get up and do something' - although you may find you will be able to do so later - He only expects you to trust Him in and with your current circumstances. Are you able to do that? Are you willing to do that? Don't try to trust Him; it's a choice to either trust Him or not to trust Him, there is no 'try'.

If you will take that step and trust Him, He will remove every obstacle in your way and lift you up out of your low state. He did it for others and He will do it for you. This is a deal worth making; you will not regret shaking God's Almighty Hand on this one and signing on the dotted line. You will not be signing you life away you will be signing God's life into you. Go on make the deal.

11th March
Psalm 22:5a
'They cried to You, and were delivered'
Underlining the point

As if to underline the point, David repeats the previous thought, from a different angle. This time the people 'cried to You, and were delivered'. Terrible things may have been happening; crises upon crises, pressure weighing down on Israel and they cried out to God and He delivered them. They may have been in the dark situation due to their own foolish actions (they often were), but God delivered them none-the-less.

You may feel that your current situation is your own fault, and as such it is your 'cross to bear', but God is waiting to deliver you. Cry out to Him in the midst of your distress and whoever's fault it might have been will make no difference. You will need to repent if you have sinned or forgive if someone has sinned against you, but in the end God is willing to deliver you.

How much do you want to be delivered? Enough to cry out? Or, are you comfortable in your suffering? Stand up, cry out to the Lord and be delivered.

12th March
Psalm 22:5b
'They trusted in You, and were not ashamed.'
You need not be ashamed

This is a beautiful statement. 'They were not ashamed.' Shame is a by-product of sin. When Adan and Eve sinned in the Garden by tasting the forbidden fruit, they experienced shame for the first time and they hid from God's presence. Ever since then, men and women have been afflicted with shame everyday of their lives. People may deny it or shout to cover it up, but it is still there. In fact, it may well be that those who shout the loudest are the most ashamed!

What are you ashamed about? Something you can't speak about and God must never find out. The truth is God already knows! He may not call you to account as He did to Adam and Eve but never assume He doesn't know; your shame is proof He does know. Do you want to be free from shame and guilt? Then trust in the Lord, He already knows what you have done, and loves you anyway, so what have you got to fear? Own up to your sins, confess them before the Lord, trust that He will not hold them against you but forgive you and fully release you from them.

To have that weight of shame lifted from your shoulders is such a relief. Once it is gone you will wonder why you carried it for so long. Things happen, we all make mistakes and sin, but Jesus has the answer. You do not need to be ashamed any longer. Trust in Jesus and be free.

13th March
Psalm 22:6a
'But I am a worm, and no man'
Back to reality?

Suddenly David's eye flips back to himself and in self-pity he compares himself to those heroes of old and sees himself as short of their mark. He calls himself a 'worm', a worthless person less than a man, not worthy of God's deliverance. 'Great King David a worm! Never, he was a great man of God!' You may think, but David knew his faults and failings as well as his triumphs. David lived a real, genuine life with ups and downs, and when he wrote this psalm he was on a down.

After considering people of the past and the way God delivered them you may think, like David did, that you do not deserve God's deliverance because you are not as good as they were. You're a sinner and they were holy and spiritual. You forget to pray sometimes and they were always on the 'hotline to God'. You have made too many mistakes and your situation is all your fault. Let me assure you that we are *all* sinners saved by grace alone, none of us deserve God's great deliverance but He gives it all the same.

Stop looking at yourself in self-pity and start looking to Jesus, the Great Deliverer. Read the Gospels and see the kind of people Jesus helped, Zacchaeus (Luke 19:1-10); The Samaritan Woman (John 4); The Woman caught in Adultery (John 8:1-11). None of these people deserved Jesus' attention but He gave it to them and saved them, and He will do the same for you.

14th March

Psalm 22:6b

'A reproach of men, and despised by the people.'

Despised and rejected

We have been concentrating mostly on David the author of this psalm, but now we will look at Jesus who knew this psalm in ways we never can. While He was on the Cross, these words could not have been more accurate. The crowd despised, hated and rejected Him. The King of kings, reproached by His own creation even as the prophet Isaiah had said (Isaiah 53:3). Where were His friends and family? Only John, His mother Mary and Mary Magdalene stood by; His own brothers and closest friends were nowhere to be seen.

This was a dark place for Jesus, and as these devotions go on, we shall get a glimpse of just how dark it was. However, do not be dismayed. If you are in a dark place, Jesus knows and understands just how deep it gets; you are not alone. Don't give up, press on and walk with me to the end of the psalm. This is no easy road we are walking but Jesus has gone before us and He is walking right now with us. Jesus said in John 14:1, '"Let not your heart be troubled; you believe in God, believe also in Me."'

Hold on to your faith, Jesus understands.

15th March
Psalm 22:7-8
'All those who see Me ridicule Me; they shoot out the lip, they shake the head, saying, "He trusted in the Lord, let Him rescue Him; let Him deliver Him, since He delights in Him!"'
Mocking hurts
Do you feel like people mock and ridicule you? That nothing you do is good enough for them, and they laugh at your poor efforts! It is a horrible place to be, and often feels like there is no way out. The Mocker blocks all your paths of escape and laughs in your face. He loves the look of hurt he see in you and watches as you become smaller and smaller in your own eyes. If that is where you are today, then this is a message of real genuine hope for you.

Jesus was mocked and ridiculed. Just look at the cruel words thrown at Him while He was on the Cross, 'Likewise the chief priests also, mocking with the scribes and elders, said, "He saved others; Himself He cannot save. If He is the King of Israel, let Him now come down from the cross, and we will believe Him. He trusted in God; let Him deliver Him now if He will have Him; for He said, 'I am the Son of God.' "' Matthew 27:41-43. The words David wrote are uncannily similar. Don't ever think these words had no effect on our Lord. He was in a vulnerable place and each of the hateful words hit their mark, but He went through it anyway for you and for me. Mockery is always painful to go through, but instead of getting bitter turn your eyes to Jesus and cling to Him. Jesus knows what you are going through. Let Jesus be your Rock and Shield when all others are throwing their darts of hate towards you.

16th March
Psalm 22:9a
'But You are He who took Me out of the womb'
There from the beginning

You may think all is lost, the inevitable end is coming. David no doubt thought so and Jesus knew He was dying. Even in that desperate moment they were able to look back and see that God had been with them from day one. We don't know much about David's birth and childhood, but we do know about Jesus'. When Jesus was born, He was laid in a manger because there was no room for Him in the inn. Giving birth is a dangerous experience for both mother and baby, but God delivered Jesus and ensured His safety from that very first day. Father God ensured Jesus was out of Bethlehem when Herod's soldiers came to kill Him. God's protection on Jesus didn't stop at infancy, He stood with Him His entire life keeping Him safe in all His earthly dealings. Even on the Cross, Father God was overseeing all that was going on; just look at this remarkable psalm that foreshadowed Jesus' crucifixion. The Lord ensured all the words David wrote were followed to the letter. God is in control.

You may feel lost and abandoned, looking over the precipice of your life, but know this, God the Father is watching over you. His hand of protection holding so many things back. It may not feel like it, but God is in control. He has a plan for you, a plan to rescue you. God was there when you were born, and He is still with you today. Hold on, God will deliver you.

17th March

Psalm 22:9b

'You made Me trust while on My mother's breasts.'

The safest of safe places

When a baby is breast feeding, the child is in the best and safest place possible with all it's needs met, having the mother's milk and also her loving protection. Is this the safest place? The Lord said through the prophet Isaiah, '"Can a woman forget her nursing child, and not have compassion on the son of her womb? Surely, they may forget, yet I will not forget you. See, I have inscribed you on the palms of My hands..."' Maybe a mother (even your mother) may forget her child, but God will not forget.

For a child, it's mothers' arms are a safe haven, but a safer place still is God's loving arms. Trust Him in your place of uncertainty, when all other safe places are gone from you. A baby naturally trusts it's mother to give all it needs and to protect from all ills. The child also trusts that if anything should happen the mother will save it from danger. God will do all this for you and more. Trust Him, He loves you more than any mother or father ever could. Wrap yourself in His arms and He will meet all your needs.

18th March
Psalm 22:10a
'I was cast upon You from birth.'
Cast upon God

'Here Lord, catch!' are the sentiments David wrote here. His mother casting him into the safe arms of God. Jesus' mother Mary would have done the same thing. These mothers knew they needed God's help in bringing up their children, so they handed them over to the Lord. Not just David and Jesus but all their children.

Today mothers, fathers, grandparents, aunties, uncles, family friends and others are praying for children they know and care for. There is someone who prayed for you from the first day of your life. You may never find out who, but someone cares enough to bring your name before God daily. They cast you upon the Lord.

Jesus, Himself, intercedes for you, praying right into your situation. (Romans 8:34, Hebrews 7:25) You can rest assured He always prays in God's Will for your life and always for your good.

In this time of trial, is it time to pray for a child you know to find the blessing of Christ? Cast them daily upon the Lord.

19th March
Psalm 22:10b
'From My mother's womb You have been My God.'
Before you could ever know Him, God knew you

Before you could ever know Him, God knew you. In fact, before you could know anything God knew all about you. All that you would do and all that you would say, and He still loved you. This situation you are facing is no surprise to Him because He knew from even before you were born.

These thoughts might make you angry, 'Why has He let this happen to me?' or even, 'Why was I born at all?' Don't be angry with God; be confident that the God who knew your beginning also knows the end. He has a plan; He is your God. He was watching over you when you were too young to know about Him. He was there when you shrugged your shoulders when you heard the Gospel. He was there when you fell on your knees and cried out to Him for Salvation; before you called He was there. Your God has not changed. As you survey your life and consider God's hand at work at crucial points, know this, that God is working in your life today. You may not be able to see it yet but one day you will look back and marvel at how you missed God's ever-present help in your life.

20th March
Psalm 22:11a
'Be not far from Me'
Be near me

This reminds me of the famous Christmas Carol 'Away in a Manger', the third verse says:

> Be near me Lord Jesus I ask you to stay
> Close by me for ever, and love me, I pray.
> Bless all the dear children in Your tender care,
> And fit us for heaven, to live with You there.

It is a childlike cry from the heart, 'Be near me Lord Jesus!'

We can get so old in our faith, especially when we are suffering in some way. We look for grown up answers to our need, when all the time we should be coming to Jesus like a little child. A song like this is always best sung by a youngster, or someone with a childlike heart. Put away your grown up, self-assured faith and replace it with the simple trust of a child.

As Jesus said, 'Assuredly, I say to you, unless you are converted and become as little children, you will by no means enter the kingdom of heaven. Therefore, whoever humbles himself as this little child is the greatest in the kingdom of heaven.' Matthew 18:3-4.

21st March
Psalm 22:11b
'For trouble is near'
Eyes on the problem

Do you find it hard to see Jesus because of the trouble that is before you? Your eyes are focused on the problem. The whole of verse 11 reads, 'Be not far from Me, for trouble is near; for there is none to help.' There is terror and loneliness that comes over. We shall consider loneliness tomorrow, today we will be tackling terror.

Fear binds you up and stops you from functioning as God intended. 'Trouble is near!', trouble is always near, but Jesus is nearer. 1 John 4:18, 'There is no fear in love; but perfect love casts out fear, because fear involves torment. But he who fears has not been made perfect in love.' Do not fear, but cast it out with His perfect love. If you are in Christ, God's love is in you, 1 John 4:17 'Love has been perfected among us in this: that we may have boldness in the day of judgment; because as He is, so are we in this world.'

Take your eyes off the trouble that is before you and place it on the object of Perfect Love, Jesus. One last look at 1 John, verse 19 this time, 'We love Him because He first loved us.' He loved you first and filled your heart with His love. His love is stronger than fear, it emboldened Christ on the Cross of Calvary and it will embolden you in your trial. Yes, trouble is near but do not fear, Jesus loves you.

22nd March
Psalm 22:11c
'For there is none to help.'
When you feel all alone

There are times in life when you feel you are all alone. That no one understands what you are going through and all your friends have abandoned you. There is no one to talk to, there is no one to help. That feeling of utter loneliness crushes your spirit. It can cause you to hit out at anyone who is still nearby, which in turn will finally make them desert you too. A vicious circle that will destroy your soul.

Loneliness is a real thing and a problem that is so often misunderstood even by those going through it. We are not meant to be alone; we are social. Seek God in your loneliness, He is there to help. In your seeking of Him, seek also Christian friends to come along side. Yes, you seek them out. Instead of pushing people away, go out of your way to meet up with people. Go to church, find one that is welcoming and friendly, but also offers the help you need. What are you looking for in a church? It should be a place where God is present and central to all that goes on. In a Church where the people put God first, you will never be alone.

Don't be an outsider, come in and see who you can come along side.

23rd March

Psalm 22:12

'Many bulls have surrounded Me; strong bulls of Bashan have encircled Me.'

Taunts and gibes

The image is best understood as a gang surrounding their victim and taunting them with gibes about their weakness, family, skin colour, or any other unkind words designed to do more than just hurt. There is no escape, they push and pull and laugh and taunt and slap and kick. There is never any let up. They are like strong bulls that do not allow you to get away. Jesus was nailed to a cross and yet that was never going to be enough for His enemies. The Chief Priests hurled insult after insult at Him. A psychological attack on His mind. They had won, (or so they thought) their adversary was dying and they had the opportunity to stick the knife in, so to speak. How cruel. Have you known such cruelty in your life? Maybe they are there now taunting you at every opportunity. Jesus knows and understands the hurtful words of those who hate you. Do not be cast down but look to Him and praise God through the torment. The enemy cannot win.

Replace their nefarious taunts with the truth of God. Memorise Scripture, read the psalms daily. Remember what Jesus has done for you; that Psalm 22 is Jesus' biography of suffering for you. He went through this and He understands.

24th March

Psalm 22:13

'They gape at Me with their mouths, like a raging and roaring lion.'

No let up

When the Enemy attacks it can be one thing after another. There is no let up. First jeering bulls and now threatening lions. They sense victory, your defeat is assured. Do you feel you are about to be defeated, or perhaps it's already happened? The lions are moving in to finish you off! Jesus felt the same. David felt the same. No hope, no future. No way! There is always hope, there is always a future because God is over all. He is your Salvation and Jesus is the Way! The Lord delivered Jesus and David, but not before they went through the trial of lions. This reminds me of Daniel when he was thrown into the lions' den. His enemies laughed and taunted, but God delivered him. The Lord shut the lions' mouths and Daniel walked out whole. Do as Daniel did, pray amongst the lions and God will shut their mouths for you too.

The Lord is able to deliver you out of the lion's mouth. Be honoured that He has entrusted you with the same trial Jesus passed through. You are not alone, Jesus is walking this way with you. Trust your friend Jesus, He is your constant companion and victory has been given to Him. The lions cannot harm you while Jesus guards your heart.

25th March
Psalm 22:14a
'I am poured out like water'
An offering - but is it a freewill offering?

Do you feel like your spirit has been poured out on the floor, spilt and lost forever? You're empty, drained, broken and waisted.

By no choice of your own, you have become like a drink offering poured out before the Lord. The drink offering was seemingly waisted, poured out onto the dusty floor of the Temple; but in reality it was an act of worship before the Lord. This lifted the act up into a whole new realm. When David was on the run from King Saul he was hiding in a cave with little to drink and he desired the waters of his home town of Bethlehem, so his friends broke into the town and brought him some back, but David would not drink it but instead poured it out before the Lord (2 Samuel 23:13-17).

Being 'poured out' can seem awful and pointless, but it can become an act of worship if you give the dregs of your life to Jesus. Instead of your life going down the drain it can be lifted up into the heavenlies as an offering to God. It may not be a freewill offering but make it an offering none-the-less. Bless the Lord even as you are being poured out.

26th March
Psalm 22:14b
'And all My bones are out of joint;'
Stretched but not broken

The agony of the Cross is beyond my imagining. Jesus' body stretched out, bones and joints aching under His own weight. Every breath was a fight against gravity, pushing with His feet to enable Himself to draw air into His burning lungs. His bones were stretched to the limits, not by the soldiers but by the torcher of the Cross. His bones were stretched but not broken. John tells us in his Gospel that none of our Lord's bones were broken, even after death. We read this in John 19:36 and this is a direct quote from Psalm 34:20 'He guards all his bones; not one of them is broken.' Prophesy fulfilled!

Psalm 34:19 reads, 'Many are the afflictions of the righteous, but the Lord delivers him out of them all.' Before we even get to the not having our bones broken verse, David tells us the Lord will deliver us from our afflictions There may be many afflictions we have to face pulling us one way and the other. They stretch us beyond measure, but the Lord will not allow us to be destroyed by them. He will deliver us and guard our bones that not even one is broken.

You may be in a painful situation emotionally, physically or even spiritually (perhaps a combination of all three), but remember the Lord is guarding you, preventing you from being broken. All of Jesus' bones were out of joint but none of them were broken.

27th March
Psalm 22:14c
'My heart is like wax; it has melted within Me.'
A melted heart

A melting heart is often seen as a nice thing. A kind gesture melts the hard-hearted person. It is also cutesy; an attractive person melts your heart whenever they are about. The term has rightly been defined as an emotional effect you cannot control. So, yes it can be lovely to have your heart melted but it can also be devastating. Something out of your control happens and your resolve disappears you, are crushed emotionally, unable to understand what is happening and why; your heart has melted away.

When your heart has melted in this way it is hard to know how you can carry on without any strength. Perhaps Habakkuk can point the way. He was a prophet and had to watch his nation fall apart as they turned further and further away from God. Even when all was lost he prayed, 'Though the fig tree may not blossom, nor fruit be on the vines; though the labour of the olive may fail, and the fields yield no food; though the flock may be cut off from the fold, and there be no herd in the stalls-- Yet I will rejoice in the Lord, I will joy in the God of my salvation. The Lord God is my strength; He will make my feet like deer's feet, and He will make me walk on my high hills.' Habakkuk 3:17-19. It is the joy of the Lord that will be your strength (Nehemiah 8:10). He will enable you to get through even this.

28th March
Psalm 22:15a
'My strength is dried up like a potsherd'
All dried up

To be dried up like a potsherd is to be without strength, without use, without life. A potsherd is an old broken piece of pottery no longer any good for the use it was made for. It was tossed aside and forgotten about. What's interesting about a potsherd is that it has been found. It may not have seen the light of day for centuries but now an archaeologist has dug it up and carefully placed all the bits together, cleaning the delicate pieces and finally placing them on show in a museum.

What else can broken pieces of pottery be used for? An artist may take those bits of seemingly useless dried up clay and put them together to make a beautiful mosaic; no longer old and pointless, but a wonder to behold.

God can and does both these things; He takes our broken lives and gently lifts them out of the miry clay, cleaning them with expert care. He then makes something beautiful out of them (Ecclesiastes 3:11).

Only God knows what He will make out of the broken, dried up pieces of your life, but you can be assured it will be beautiful and a joy to many.

29th March
Psalm 22:15b
'And My tongue clings to My jaws'
I thirst

When Christ was on the Cross, after everything else had been accomplished He cried out, 'I thirst' - John 19:28. Jesus' tongue was so dry it stuck to the roof of His mouth, but all they had to offer Him was sour wine. He craved a drop of pure water but received none. All the good works He'd done, and no-one gave Him anything. He looked beyond the physical needs of the moment to the glories of His Heavenly Father.

That is a dark place to be, thirsty but unable to quench that desire. Your greatest need is withheld and all you get is sour wine. Life is like that; like being kicked when you're down. More and more things go wrong and even the good things are tainted. What is the answer when your spiritual tongue clings to your mouth because it is so dry? Call out again for a drink, cry to the Lord to quench your thirst. He will not give sour wine, He gives the 'Water of Life' that will refresh your tired soul and make you live again. Don't settle for the World's sour wine look for God's precious water and drink deeply of that.

30th March
Psalm 22:15c
'You have brought Me to the dust of death.'
Nowhere left to go
In yesterday's devotional, we saw that when Jesus was on the Cross, He was thirsty but there was nothing given to Him except sour wine. In the next verse we read that He gave up His spirit and died. In todays reading we have, 'You have brought Me to the dust of death.' There is nowhere else left to go; death is the final curtain. Most people reading this will know of someone close to them who has died, and we all know what it is to lose them. But perhaps you feel that you, yourself, are lying in the dust of death. Desperation has overtaken you, your life has gone down about as far as it can go.

For Jesus, death was the end of His earthly ministry; He had completed all things and now His suffering would end. However, He didn't stay dead, because three days later He rose again in glorious victory; 'death, where is your sting?' 1 Corinthians 15:55.

The dust of death is the end of one thing and the beginning of something new. Just like this psalm, there may still be dark times ahead but new life is on it's way - Resurrection Day is in sight!

Nowhere left to go? The only way left when you are lying in the dust is up. Jesus taught in Luke 21:28 that when everything is falling apart and your heart is failing, to 'look up and lift up your heads, because your redemption draws near.'

May this be an encouragement for you today.

31st March
Psalm 22:16a
'For dogs have surrounded Me; the congregation of the wicked has enclosed Me.'
How the wicked treat the righteous #1
Over the next few devotions, we shall be looking at how the wicked treat the righteous. David calls them 'dogs' because that is how they act; they gang up like a pack and surround the one who desires to follow Jesus. It's tough to stand up for Christ in a world that is at enmity with Him. To stand in front of your friends and live in a way that honours God will make you a target. You will be ganged up on and often, even the ones you thought were on your side will join the taunters.

These taunts may come in many different ways; you may have experienced some kind of taunt while trying to live the Christian life. King David knew what it was like to be an outsider, with everybody against Him. When Jesus was on the Cross the wicked took their opportunity and mocked Him, spat at Him and watched Him die.

Of all these devotions from Psalm 22 this may be the closest to my heart. I know what it is like to be pushed out, overlooked, derided, made to feel second best (to be honest sometimes I'd have settled for second best!). I have often been lonely because of my stand. What is the answer? Jesus had the answer, we do what He did, Luke 23:34, 'Jesus said, "Father, forgive them, for they do not know what they do."' Jesus forgave His tormentors and we must do the same.

1st April
Psalm 22:16b
'They pierced My hands and My feet'
How the wicked treat the righteous #2

This is a clear prophesy of what happened to Jesus; His hands and feet were quite literally pierced as He was nailed to the cross. The Hebrew word used here is karah and means to bore a hole. This isn't a gentle piercing but violent and deliberate. We may never have our hands or feet pierced in this way, but people can bore into our souls with their barbs, seeking to destroy us. The physical pain Jesus experienced by having nails thrust into His flesh, was more than matched by the violence of hatred poured out against Him as He hung, dying on the cross.

Dogs smell weakness and vulnerability, they circle their prey and tire it out, then when they see their victim stagger and fall, they pounce. The smug satisfaction is clear on their faces as the Christian is degraded in some way.

The wounds in Jesus' hands never healed. When He rose from the dead, He kept the nail marks as evidence of what had happened; the proof that He was alive. Our wounds do not need to remain as God is able to heal the deepest borehole we may have. Use the experience to help others going through similar things. Stand by your brother or sister, speak out in their defence and never let them feel alone.

2nd April
Psalm 22:17
'I can count all My bones. they look and stare at Me.'
How the wicked treat the righteous #3

Do you feel exposed, as if everyone is watching you, just waiting for you to do something 'unchristian'? The eyes of the World are permanently on your back, what will you do in this situation? What will you say to that unkind person? Will you 'go the extra mile' or stop halfway. They may judge you for actions that they would excuse themselves of. They have no basis for their judgement, we however are called to judge the World, 1 Corinthians 6:2. Paul wrote that while discussing Christian judgement, particularly in the Church. Christians judge one another in righteousness and never in pride. We judge the World in exactly the same way. God's Word is our measure on how we are to judge.

The World may surround you, staring at you to see if you fall off your 'Christian perch', but they have no idea what Christian righteousness is, so how can they judge? You are saved by grace and clothed in Christ's Own Righteousness. You do not need to feel naked before the eyes of the World - they should be feeling naked before you, exposed by God's Spirit within you.

Christians do not go out of their way to judge, as the World seems to think we do, but we are called to judge and by walking in righteousness we show up their shallow standards and bring glory to God.

3rd April
Psalm 22:18
'They divide My garments among them, and for My clothing they cast lots.'
How the wicked treat the righteous #4

Jesus' enemies thought He no longer needed His clothes; He was about to die after all. They cruelly divided them amongst themselves so His family and friends could not have them. They saw only death for Jesus, He had lost. It didn't matter any more if He was innocent or guilty. Dignity was stripped away, and He was left naked, exposed and dying a terrible, painful death.

When our enemies get to the stage of removing our dignity, there is nothing left, we are at an end and they appear to have won. Our Christian witness has been destroyed; no one will be drawn to Church by us now. Any time we try to tell someone about the Gospel, we will be reminded of our failure and that will be that. What a relief that although we are called to be witnesses it is God who does the calling, He does the convicting, He has the final Victory.

The soldiers thought Jesus had no more need for clothes to cover His body, but in three days He was alive and clothed; dignity restored. God will clothe you again with dignity and you will see His victory through you. I encourage you to read on to the end of the psalm right now (19-31) and see what the Lord will do for the righteous. We will begin to look into that tomorrow.

4th April
Psalm 22:19a
'But You, O Lord, do not be far from Me'
Assurance amidst the turmoil

In Verse 11 we read something similar, 'Be not far from me', the simple heartfelt cry of a child. After that the verses got worse not better; where was the Lord in verses 12-18?

When everyone and everything is against you, remember the Lord is with you. He is not far away. It may seem like you are all alone, but know the Lord is near. This isn't a cry of desperation, but a prayer of the assured knowledge that God is close by. When the psalmist felt the most alone, when his enemies were all around and his friends had all fled, he knew that God was there, that the Lord had not deserted him after all. Did he expect God to abandon him? No, not at all. That is the heart of this psalm, it begins with, 'My God, My God, why have You forsaken Me?' and travels through many dark places, but the conclusion is that God has not forsaken him, the Lord has been his constant companion all through the valley of death (Psalm 23:4).

Where is God in your dark lonely walk? Right beside you, just where He always is. Just because you have lost sight of Him, doesn't mean He has lost sight of you. He has not left you abandoned amongst your enemies; He is your constant Help and Salvation. Today is not a day to cry out, but rather be enfolded in Father's Eternal loving arms.

5th April
Psalm 22:19b
'O My Strength, hasten to help Me!'
Know your limits

It is all too easy to believe that you have to do it all by yourself, that you must fight your battles because no-one else will. David knew this was an empty lie. The Lord God was his strength and he gave the place of champion to the One who could overcome all enemies.

Don't fight battles you don't need to, the Lord is more than able to defeat the fiercest foe. You do not have the strength to win the day, you must give way to the Lord. Someone may quote that we are 'more than conquerors', so we can fight any battle and vanquish any foe, but no, the verse is 'Yet in all these things we are more than conquerors through Him who loved us.' Romans 8:37. It is in Jesus we are conquerors not in our own strength. Let Jesus be the Victor He is. It is His nature to be Victorious and His desire to fight on our behalf to make us conquerors.

Today, let God be God in your life; yield your fight to Him and see what victories He brings about for you. He is more that able - He is your Strength.

6th April
Psalm 22:20
'Deliver Me from the sword, My precious life from the power of the dog.'
Deliverance

Last time David called out to the Lord his Strength to 'hasten to his help', this time he states what he needs help from. 'Deliver me from the sword'; he was in danger of death, his enemies were surrounding him with drawn swords.

In the midst of mortal danger cry out to God for deliverance. Our Enemy roams about like a roaring lion, seeking people to devour. We'll look more on this next time, but for now remember the Lord is more powerful than Satan and He can deliver you out of his grasp. Looking back over this psalm, this imagery has been used before, but now there is confidence in God. Nothing appears to have changed, however, everything is different when God is near. He will deliver you from the sword of the enemy even when you think you are backed into a corner with no escape.

Your life is precious to Jesus, He gave up His life for you. He hung on the cross and suffered more than David could imagine or write about, just so you could be saved. Being saved isn't merely a ticket to Heaven, when all your troubles will be erased, it is Heaven on Earth, where you can be free from the Enemy today. Let go of your bonds and walk free with your Deliverer.

7th April
Psalm 22:21a
'Save Me from the lion's mouth and from the horns of the wild oxen!'
Hosanna! Save me!

Following on from last time, the psalmist prays, 'Save me from the lion's mouth'. This is taking one step further than we saw before. Not just a coming attack but, too late, the lion has got me in his mouth. Peter warns us in 1 Peter 5:8, 'Be sober, be vigilant; because your adversary the devil walks about like a roaring lion, seeking whom he may devour.' Life has been unkind and you have taken your eye off the path you have not been able to be sober and vigilant because of the intensity of the attack, and so the lion pounced and has you in his merciless teeth. Even there, at the brink of the inevitable, God can save. The Devil may be a lion, but Jesus is *the* Lion and at His roar even Satan must bow.

Your situation may be grave, but Jesus is well able to save you. If there is nothing else that comes to mind in that dark hour just sing 'Hosanna' to the Lord. Hosanna means 'save me' and the Lord will move heaven and earth in order to reach and deliver you even from the jaws of an angry lion. He is able, He is your Strength, He is your Deliverer. So 'Sing Hosanna to the King of kings.'

8th April
Psalm 22:21b
'You have answered Me.'
The Lord's answer

This psalm has been a bit of a one-way street with David crying out to God for help in his dire situation, or Jesus baring His soul to His Father, but no response is made, God is silent. Until now. David writes, 'You have answered me.' What the answer was we do not know, but from this moment on the psalm is very different. The Lord has answered. I love the fact that David withholds God's actual words, because it means we can receive this into our situation, whatever that is. No doubt different to David and Jesus, but real none-the-less. The Lord has heard your cry and has answered.

What the Lord's answer is depends on what your situation is and what you've asked, but once He has answered that is it, no more debate. For David there is no more crying or calling out, God has answered. No matter what the outward appearance may be, it is settled.

The psalm changes from a psalm of desperation to a psalm of praise and it all hinges on this one short phrase, 'You have answered me.' The Lord has answered you too, I am sure He has, and if not listen for His voice because it will be there. Stop striving and start praising the God of Heaven, make His name known far and near. Stop living in verses 1-21 and choose to live in 22-31.

9th April
Psalm 22:22a
I will declare Your name to My brethren
Testimony begins at home

What has the Lord done for you? What is your testimony? Only you know, only you can answer this. Have you spoken of His great deliverance with your family? The Lord has been with you in the dark valley and has spoken a word of deliverance, isn't that worth sharing? You know your brothers, sisters, mother, father, uncles, aunts etc., and you know what they are going through right now. Will not your testimony be an encouragement to them? You have the answer to their need, the Lord, your Strength.

The Lord God who rescued David and raised Jesus from the dead, is able to deliver your family member from the darkest pit. You know it is true, because He did it for you! They may not want to know, but they need to know. Tell them all of what the Lord has done for you.

Testimony begins at home.

10th April
Psalm 22:22b
'In the midst of the assembly I will praise You.'
Share with the Church

Don't forget to share your deliverance with those who have been praying for you. A real church is a praying church and one that doesn't just pray for its own needs, but cares for the wounded sheep, bringing them before the Lord.

There is little that delights this kind of church more than the testimony of someone they have been praying for. Tell them that the Lord has answered, and deliverance is assured. Fill your words with praises.

Then go on praising the Lord each time you meet; you don't have to give updates all the time as your countenance will be testimony enough for all to see. Lift up your hands to the Lord and shout to Him words of thankful praise. You can start by praising Him for what He has done but soon you will find even that is left behind in a stream of unfettered praise to the great God of the Universe, who is your Father.

To stand up and declare the Lord has answered your prayers and the prayers of the church is a big thing, and quite daunting, but it is a statement of faith in the Lord your Strength. The Lord has done it.

11th April
Psalm 22:23a
'You who fear the Lord, praise Him!'
That means you!

It can appear that the only people who need to praise God are those He has delivered from some great difficulty, or those who have all they need. But the Bible says, 'You who fear the Lord, praise Him!' If you are a Christian you are by very definition one who fears the Lord. This verse is therefore for you. There is a sense here of sharing in David's deliverance, praising God for His goodness to a once stricken soul. More than that, there are countless blessings He pours out on us each day; remember to praise.

Praise isn't giving thanks for things, although thanksgiving does play a part; praise is telling God how great He is to you. What is your view of God? Tell Him all about it, kneel in the quietness of your room and pour out your espousals of love. Don't stop there, if your church has an opportunity for praise, use it. Speak out 'in the midst of the assembly' how awesome and wonderful God is. If you don't have the words to say, read a psalm or a poem, write something down before hand and read that. Never try and compete with others. Your praises are as precious to God as any the greatest orator could say.

You who are reading this, the Lord loves to hear your praises, speak them to Him now.

12th April

Psalm 22:23b

'All you descendants of Jacob, glorify Him, and fear Him, all you offspring of Israel!'

The children of promise

David turns and addresses his own people, the children of Israel. They were to glorify and fear the Lord. Israel, or Jacob as he was also known, was one of the Patriarchs. He was the grandson of Abraham and an inheritor of the promise. The Lord had promised Abraham that he would be the father of a mighty nation, a nation that would bless the whole world, but at the time he had no children. Isaac was the fulfilment of that promise. Through his son, Abraham would be the father of a nation, but Isaac was only one person. Isaac had two sons Esau and Jacob. The Lord chose Jacob and imparted the promise to him. Jacob also was only one man; a true nation was still a long way off. Jacob had 12 sons and they were the seeds of the nation of Israel. Those seeds were planted in the fertile ground of the land of Egypt and after 400 years the nation of Israel emerged. The descendants of Jacob, the offspring of Israel, were the children of the promise and they were to glorify God in the presence of the nations and fear Him by honouring the Covenant.

The fulness of God's promise to Abraham was fulfilled in Jesus, and through His blood we too are the children of Promise. That said, it is our responsibility to glorify God in all we do and say, especially when the World looks on, and to fear Him as we walk in this world of darkness.

13th April
Psalm 22:24a
'For He has not despised nor abhorred the affliction of the afflicted'
The Lord does not despise you

The Lord cares that you are afflicted. He is not disgusted with the hole you are in. Do you feel despised by God? That is a lie of the Devil. David passed through that lie and came out in the light of truth - God is a God of love. Take David at his word, for he knew affliction and he knew God delivered him. You may think, 'well that was great King David, God would treat Him kindly. But me? God isn't interested in me!' Well, David was a great King and is rightly remembered as being a friend of God, but he was a man like you and I. God cares for you as much as He did for David, you are His sheep every bit as much as David was. The Lord does not despise you or your affliction.

This is a wonderful reason to praise God. He loves you, He cares for you and He will do for you every bit as much as He did for the Saints of old. Psalm 34:19, 'Many are the afflictions of the righteous, But the Lord delivers him out of them all.'

14th April
Psalm 22:24b
'Nor has He hidden His face from Him; but when He cried to Him, He heard.'
He sees you, He hears you

It may feel like God is not interested in you; that He is preoccupied with other things. Why would the God of the whole universe be bothered about me? You may feel that a holy God wouldn't want to even look at you because of all the bad things you have done. The truth is that God is attentive to you and He hears you when you cry out. When you call out to Him, God turns His face towards you and smiles. His heart for you is only for your best.

Zephaniah knew about this side of God's love as he wrote in chapter 3:17 of his prophesy, 'The Lord your God in your midst, the Mighty One, will save; He will rejoice over you with gladness, He will quiet you with His love, He will rejoice over you with singing.' You see the Lord, the Mighty One is right in your midst and He will save; He will rejoice over you with gladness and singing, and then there this little phrase, 'He will quiet you with His love'. This is so much like a father comforting his child. It doesn't matter why the child is upset, the father hugs and speaks kindly to the child until it is quieted. The Lord does the same for you. He hears your painful hearts cry and looks upon you and smiles. Then He takes you up in His mighty arms and hugs you, protecting you from all ills; He will hold you there until you are ready to go on again.

He loves you, is ever watchful of you and He has heard you prayer.

15th April
Psalm 22:25a
'My praise shall be of You in the great assembly'
A future assured

Verse 25 is very definite. David is looking to a sure future. Our Lord Jesus saw the same sure future while hanging on the Cross of death. Throughout this psalm there has been the feeling of finality, that this was the end but now David writes, 'My praise shall be of You in the great assembly'. He was looking forward to a time when he once again would stand and give praise to God at the Sanctuary; he may not have been 100% delivered at this point - we know Jesus wasn't - but in faith he declared his assurance that he would be there.

Your future is assured. The path may be dark now, but Jesus has made a way of escape and one day soon you will be able to once more stand in the assembly and pour out your praises to God. Declare this certainty right now, speak it out, 'My praise shall be of You in the great assembly', say it and believe it. God is working and He is able. You don't need to tell anyone else; this is between you and God. You need to hear yourself say it in His presence. Keep declaring it until you know it to be so, and then wait for the glorious day when you stand there in the great assembly praising God.

16th April
Psalm 22:25b
'I will pay My vows before those who fear Him.'
I will

In yesterday's devotion we looked at the statement, 'My praise shall be of You in the great assembly', this time we will be considering the even more emphatic 'I will pay My vows before those who fear Him.'

'I will'. It is by an act of will that you will appear before those who fear Him. It is your will, but His Power. Say, 'I will', and take hold of His hand. This is not a half-hearted statement, and it is not a magic word, it is a statement of faith in the God of the Bible; the same God who delivered David from his enemies and raised Jesus up from the dead. He is able to make you stand, and He will walk by your side into the assembly of believers where you can pay your vows.

The vows that are to be made are vows of repentance and restitution, wiping the slate clean before God and His people. Then leave the past behind, start afresh, pick up past ministries, and perhaps new ones too.

Are you ready to say, 'I will' to the Lord? pray about it, seek Him and say those two words in faith, then go and do it. The Lord is with you.

17th April
Psalm 22:26a
'The poor shall eat and be satisfied'
He will meet all your needs

What do you need? By that I mean, what are you desperate for? The Lord will provide it for you. Notice it is not the persons doing. They are still 'poor', but God gives them food to eat and enough to be satisfied.

So, what is that thing you need, that thing that you have no power to do for yourself? Will you dare to let God provide it for you? Will you give your need to Him? Although the poor man is still poor, his poverty is gone. The same will be true for you; you will still have no power to provide for your deepest need, but that's okay, because God is there providing it for you.

If you can do it for yourself, there is no need for God to intervene, but in that area of weakness God can move in and miraculously provide for you. What a testimony of faith! You will be able to shout it to the world, that thing you could do nothing about has been turned around by the abundant grace and power of Almighty God. This is a miracle that is not easily hidden, just like the poor having enough to eat all of a sudden, so people will notice your need has been met.

Hallelujah, God will meet all your needs.

18th April
Psalm 22:26b
'Those who seek Him will praise the Lord.'
There is something you must do

Jeremiah 29:13 says, 'You will seek Me and find Me, when you search for Me with all your heart.' You have to do something, you must actively seek God out where He is. Pray, read the Bible, listen to sermons on a Sunday, or even during the week. Be active, desperate to be with Jesus. Why? Because of what the Lord's words were through Jeremiah in verse 11 of that chapter, 'I know the thoughts that I think towards you, says the Lord, thoughts of peace and not evil, to give you a future and a hope.'

You see God has good thoughts about you and a great plan of hope for your future, but you have to seek Him out, and do so with your whole heart. How desperate are you to get to Jesus? If you are half-hearted you will not get there, you will remain in the place you are right now. If you are fully committed to get to Jesus and are more desperate than the woman with an issue of blood in Luke 8, then you will find Him and He will open up His wonderful plans for you.

What will your response be to His plan? Will you say, 'Thank you' and walk away, or will you fall on your face in praise and worship? If you have truly sort Him with your whole heart, the latter option will be the most natural response imaginable.

19th April
Psalm 22:26c
'Let your heart live forever!'
Who want's to live forever?

'Who want's to live forever?', you may well ask, as you watch the News, or as a close family member falls terminally ill. Or perhaps, you're the one who is ill and longs to be free of this body. It may seem like you are living forever as you struggle in an ever-failing body.

Nobody want's to live forever here, in the world as it is, but God promises something better, life forever with Him. There will be no bad news, no suffering and no more tears. It will be joyous when we can see Jesus face to face. We don't have to wait to be in Heaven to experience Eternal Life. God's life will fill your heart right here, right now. Do you want that? If you said yes, these words are for you, 'let your heart live forever'. It is David's words of blessing on you, words that Jesus Himself spoke as He died for you on the Cross and words that are in my heart for all who are reading this. Don't go away without receiving God's special blessing in your heart today.

'Let you heart live forever!' and may that start today.

20th April

Psalm 22:27a

'All the ends of the world shall remember and turn to the Lord'

To the ends of the world

This is quite a statement! 'The ends of the earth shall remember and turn to the Lord.' But how will they remember and who will remind them. Last time we looked at being filled with God's life, that is His Spirit. Acts 1:8 bridges the gap between these two thoughts; Jesus said to His disciples and also to you, 'You shall receive power when the Holy Spirit has come upon you; and you shall be witnesses to Me in Jerusalem, and in all Judea and Samaria, and to the end of the earth.'

'You shall be My witnesses', that is you and me. Some people reading this will travel around the world to its furthest edge and witness there, but if that is not you, you can witness in your locality. This may worry you because you don't know where to go or what to say, but don't worry, the Holy Spirit will give you power to witness, so that your stuttering words will hit home and God's seed will grow in their hearts. Remember it is not your power, it is God's Power. Your testimony is step one for the Word to be taken to the ends of the earth. 'One small step for man; one giant leap for God.' Take a breath, open your mouth and leave the rest to the Lord. He has given you the power to be His witness wherever He sends you.

21st April
Psalm 22:27b
'And all the families of the nations shall worship before You.'
The families will worship

First let me explain what is meant by family here. It is not the 'nuclear family', mum, dad and children, or the extended family, uncles, aunts, cousins, grandparents, etc. It is the families of the nations; for example in Britain we have distinctive differences across the nation; we could start with the four countries England, Scotland, Northern Ireland and Wales - four distinct countries. We could cite the 'North/South divide', but look closer and you will see each town has its own flavour and even within towns there are districts, all different and yet a part of the whole. This is what is meant by families. Most, if not all, nations are like this.

There are churches in every town, district and area of Britain, representing the families of our nation. Across the world almost all people groups have representatives in the family of God. Even in the darkest parts of the world the Gospel lights the way; pray for your brothers and sisters who defy their culture to worship God. There are waring tribes that are united in the love of God. Worship being offered to the ends of the earth.

You are a part of that, you are in a people group, a family and you can worship before God and you can be the one that tells other families about Jesus.

22nd April
Psalm 22:28a
'For the kingdom is the Lord's'
The Kingdom of God is at hand

When David wrote this psalm, he was thinking about the kingdom of Israel. Israel was, and is God special, chosen people; the people of promise. Israel belongs to God. Through the Lord Jesus we have been 'grafted in' (Romans 11:17) to that kingdom. We are citizens of the Heavenly Kingdom; the Kingdom of God.

God's Kingdom is populated by those who love and fear Him. If you are a Christian, you are a part of God's Kingdom. Just as king David said, 'the kingdom is the Lord's', so I say 'The Kingdom of God is the Lord's'. You may think that is a moot point, but is it? do you obey the King of the Kingdom you claim to dwell in? Or, do you live your own way and do your own thing? Take stock of your life, do you live up to the mark of God's Kingdom? There are bountiful blessings in God's Kingdom, all ready for you to enjoy. These are not to be taken for granted but earned in the day to day living as a citizen of God's Kingdom. 'The wages of sin is death, but the gift of God is Eternal Life in Christ Jesus our Lord.' Romans 6:23. In God's Kingdom there is only life, make sure you are not gaining death instead.

23rd April
Psalm 22:28b
'And He rules over the nations.'
All the nations are His

You may not have thought of this before, but all the nations belong to God. This is because the earth is the Lord's, He made it, therefore He owns it. By the same logic, He owns the people (you and I included) because He made us. Whatever you do, whatever you say, wherever you go you are the Lord's. Will you please Him or please yourself - you can't do both. If you please yourself and rebel against God your Creator, He will throw you in His rubbish dump. But, if you obey your rightful master, He will honour you with glory and blessings and life forevermore. You are God's property so act like it!

Going back to the nations, God owns them too. Take a look at your nation, does it honour God in its law making, in it's dealing with other nations, in how it treats the poor? Please don't take a political view, but a godly view. Take off your political glasses, whether they have blue, red or any other colour tinted lenses, and look through God's perfect glasses (that's the Bible). No nation is perfect, but at the core are they godly? Pray for the government of your nation, and others, pleading for mercy and calling down God's blessing on them. Ask God to lead and direct them through the difficult decisions that need to be made. Remember your nation is God's nation and it should reflect His Holiness. If it doesn't God's judgement will come. Remember too that God is merciful, so pray on.

24th April
Psalm 22:29a
'All the prosperous of the earth shall eat and worship'
Is there room for the rich?

We often assume that God has no time for the rich, that there is no room for them in Heaven, or at least it is hard for them to even get in! We get this idea from the heartbreaking story of the 'rich young ruler' who loved money more than even eternal life. He went away sad, and Jesus remarked, "'How hard it is for those who have riches to enter the kingdom of God!' and again, 'Children, how hard it is for those who trust in riches to enter the kingdom of God! It is easier for a camel to go through the eye of a needle than for a rich man to enter the kingdom of God.'" Matthew 24:23-25. This is true, and in other places in the Gospel Jesus appears to favour the poor over the rich, but this does not mean there is no room for them.

The Bible is full of rich believers who put God before their riches. Job was one of the wealthiest men in the area, but continued to trust God even when all he had was stripped away. King David himself was rich and prosperous and yet he remained faithful to God all his life. There are New Testament examples too; Philemon, was a rich property owner who loved Jesus. Paul was probably well off when he became a Christian. The prosperous will eat and worship; the wealthy who know and understand where their wealth comes from will enter God's Kingdom.

There is room for the rich.

25th April
Psalm 22:29b
'All those who go down to the dust shall bow before Him'
Every knee shall bow

The Apostle Paul, quoting Isaiah, reminded the Christians in Rome that all people would bow before God's thrown of judgement. He wrote, 'As I live, says the Lord, every knee shall bow to Me, and every tongue shall confess to God.' Romans 14:11. This is the awesome, and dare I say, frightening truth. We shall all come before God and none of us will be standing. That's the negative out the way and now for the glorious positive.

Yes, we shall all be rightly judged by God, but those who have given their lives to Jesus will be found innocent and allowed into God's awesome presence. What will we be doing there you may ask? Well for a great deal of the time we will be bowing on our knees in holy reverence and praise. There are those who have gone before us and are right now bowing their knees before God. They may be dead to us, but they are alive in Christ Jesus.

You will bow the knee before God when you go down to the dust and die. My prayer is that it will not only be at the Judgement Seat, but forever, freely giving praise and worship before His Throne in glory.

Start now, get on your knees and pray in repentance for forgiveness of your sins.

26th April

Psalm 22:29c

'Even he who cannot keep himself alive.'

Even Jesus bowed to the Father

This third part of this verse is an ironic prophecy of Jesus. It is ironic because Jesus could have kept Himself alive, but chose not to. He bowed the knee to His Father God. Those famous words in the garden of Gethsemane, 'Not as I will, but as You will.' Matthew 26:39. Jesus surrendered His will to the Father. Jesus' will was not like ours. It was perfect and on par with God the Father's will, and yet He gave it up and chose to die for you and me. Jesus was and is 'The Life' He could have stayed alive indefinitely, but He put Himself in the place of the one who 'cannot keep himself alive.'

These events happened here on earth, Jesus humbled Himself and bowed before God. If Jesus, who is the Second Person in the Godhead, bowed before God, who are we to refuse to do it here and now. Put away your useless pride and give your life up to God. You cannot keep yourself alive, but God can and will guard your soul for all eternity. Surely that is worth giving your will up for! Don't miss this opportunity to become a follower of Jesus; follow Him onto your knees today.

27th April

Psalm 22:30a

'A posterity shall serve Him.'

The seed of the gospel

The King James Version puts this verse as, 'A seed will serve Him.' This 'seed' is Jesus, He is the One who was planted like a seed and produced a crop; that crop is His followers right down the ages. We are the caretakers of the seed. It is our responsibility to share it with others and keep passing the word on to future generations. In this way we serve the Lord.

We are not the seed, but the seed is in our hearts. Like a gardener we look for fertile soil to plant the seed in. Never shirk from your mission of spreading the seed of the Gospel. As in the Parable of the Sower there are different outcomes from your sowing, some will be more fruitful than others. It is our job to spread the Word and leave the outcome in God's hands. If they do not respond it is not you they are rejecting, but God. However, if they do respond and the seed takes root in their heart, take heed, it is not you they are accepting but Jesus.

Will you sow the Seed of the Gospel into somebody's life today? It is full of power and has the potential to change their lives forever.

28th April
Psalm 22:30b
'It will be recounted of the Lord to the next generation'
It's in safe hands

You may have heard that churches are closing at an ever-increasing rate, and that more and more people are turning to other things. So, what about future generations? Who will tell our children's children about Jesus? Here David prophesied a great truth that will last forever, 'It will be recounted of the Lord to the next generation'. Do not fear, the Gospel is in safe hands - the Lord's.

Look back into history and see how God has kept the Gospel message being passed down from one generation to the next. Even while heresies rose and fell, the truth kept on going. The so called, Dark Ages were a tough time to be a true believer, and yet the Gospel message was not extinguished. We do live in dark times, but fear not, God will see to it that the Gospel is recounted to the next generation. It will be done. This doesn't get us off the hook; if we are rightly concerned for future generations then we should be actively recounting God's goodness to them.

We can't see the future, we can't tell how bad or good it will be in the coming days, but I know who holds the future and He also holds the seeds of the Gospel safe and sound. Don't listen to what society says, listen to the Lord, He has it all worked out.

29th April
Psalm 22:31a
'They will come and declare His righteousness to a people who will be born'
The future assured

We have been walking this path with two people, David and Jesus. David wrote the psalm and Jesus lived and died with these words on His lips. David fore-saw a time when those who were not even born yet would hear the Good News about God. Jesus too, saw the great benefit His death and resurrection would bring. Hebrews 12:1 says, 'looking unto Jesus, the author and finisher of our faith, who for the joy that was set before Him endured the cross, despising the shame, and has sat down at the right hand of the throne of God.' He saw you and me being told of the wonders of Easter Sunday. The future is assured, the future is in safe hands.

We who have been entrusted with the Good News have a vital role to play - sharing it with others. There is an unbroken line from David, through Jesus and on to you. Will you break the chain or will you allow it to pass on from you to the next generation? Imagine this, there are people who are not yet born who will hear about the Good News of Jesus because you shared it with someone today!

This is as true now as it was when David first sang it. We are part of the 'They' who will declare His righteousness, and our declaration will pass the baton on to the next people to declare it and so on until Jesus returns. Never think your witness is unimportant; you are extremely important, and God will use you to bless a people who are yet to be born.

30th April
Psalm 22:31b
'That He has done this.'
It is finished!

Only John wrote the final words Jesus spoke on the Cross, this maybe because he was standing closest to Him. Jesus' last words were, 'It is finished!' (John 19:30) This was the end of His life, and it is the end of the psalm. 'It is finished!' is just another way of saying, 'He has done this.' Or to put it another way 'Job done.'

It has been a hard walk through this psalm, many a time we may have nearly given up, but here we are at the end. Yes, there is an end, and at that end we find the Lord is waiting for us. At the beginning He seemed so far away that we thought He could not hear us and if He could, He was not interested in our problems. But soon we saw that God was with us we were not forsaken. We have a purpose and future. This chapter of our lives, like this psalm will come to an end, and when it does Jesus will be there to say, 'It's finished, job done.'

I don't know where you are in your trek and you may not either, but I do know that the God who saved David and raised Jesus from the dead is there with you, walking every step of the way. Stop believing that God has forsaken you and look for the glorious finish line; it is there. God will never leave you nor forsake you (Deuteronomy 31:6). Take it by faith that as far as Jesus is concerned, 'It is finished.'

1st May

Psalm 37:1a

'Do not fret because of evildoers'

Don't worry

As we look out at our world, we see many people who do terrible, wicked things. It is all too easy to fret and worry about them, especially if they are not brought to justice. If you see an evildoer getting away with his wickedness, don't allow that to rob you of your God given peace. Whatever they might say, or the excuses they may make, they do not have God's peace in their hearts, they can't have as God only gives it to the righteous!

Worrying and fretting makes you the wrong kind of person because you become judgemental and angry, both with those around you and with God. We are called to judge and see if a person is living a life worthy of God, but when you see an 'evildoer', leave them with God, don't worry and lose your peace over them. Guard the peace in your heart as if it were a precious stone and it will keep you from stumbling. This psalm isn't about ignoring evil but rather taking hold of what God has given to you; cherish it, live in it and use it. Don't spend all your energies fretting over what other people are doing (or not doing), instead pray for them and show them the glories of a righteous life.

2nd May

Psalm 37:1b

'Nor be envious of the workers of iniquity.'

Don't be envious

You may not fret about evildoers, but do you envy those who gain positions and possessions by works of iniquity? There is an idea that the only way to make it in today's world is to step on others around you. There is no room for kindness or mercy; if you want to be rich you must be ruthless. And yes, it does appear that this is so. Those who make it big are often the worst kinds of people. You may think to yourself, 'If I am going to make it in the world, I must emulate what the successful people do.' This is the way to destruction. Listen to the words of David and do not be envious of the workers of iniquity. Don't copy them, don't be like them.

Be like David who was a humble shepherd boy, living out on the hillside, not important enough to be invited to the meal when Samuel came to visit. He was totally overlooked by everyone, except God. The Lord lifted him up from among the sheep and made him the king of Israel. Don't look at others and see what they have, look to God who has everything and loves to give liberally. He will make you the exact person He wants you to be and He will make you a success in His Kingdom. You may not have everything this world has to offer, but you will have everything the Kingdom of God can give.

3rd May
Psalm 37:2
'For they shall soon be cut down like the grass, and wither as the green herb.'
Why worry? Why be envious?

The psalm opens by instructing the righteous not to fret about evil doers or be envious of the workers of iniquity and verse 2 tells us why. Workers of evil will be cut down like the grass and thrown onto the compost heap of life. They may prosper, they may get opportunities you will only ever dream of, but in the end they are gone. Like cut grass and withered leaves they will be no more.

So why worry about them? Why be envious? The Lord's Kingdom and all His statutes will still be standing long after the most influential person has died. God's Kingdom is an everlasting Kingdom, it will never end. Remember the worst that the worst person can do is only temporary, but God's Word is eternal. There are workers of iniquity who thrive and make life hard, even impossible for Christians, but their destiny is sealed in a place far from God. You, however, have a glorious future to look forward to, life with Jesus in Paradise.

Don't boast and brag about their fate, pray for them that they too may come to Salvation. Pray that they would fret about you and be envious of what you have and that they would cry out to God for a crumb from your table.

4th May
Psalm 37:3a
'Trust in the Lord, and do good;'
Trust in the Lord

We will now take a break from considering evildoers and instead think about the righteous for a while. David advises us to 'trust in the Lord and do good'. Stop worrying what others are doing or what you need to do to have a successful life, instead trust God with it, leave your destiny in His hands. If you want to be successful in God's Kingdom start doing good. You may only be able to do a small thing, but that's fine, God knows your heart. Keep your do-gooding low key, the least people who know the better. It is not about how many good things people see you do it's the fact you are trusting God and doing something.

Doing good is the easy part, anyone can do it, even the most evil person imaginable. Trusting God may seem terribly hard. Can you trust God in your immediate circumstances? What is the first thing that comes to mind that you desire the most? Will you trust God with that? Trusting God is hard because we don't know if He will do the thing; what if He disappoints? God never disappoints. He doesn't always say yes, and we don't always get what we most desire, but He never disappoints. Trust the Lord and do good, He has your best at heart.

5th May

Psalm 37:3b

'Dwell in the land, and feed on His faithfulness.'

Feed on God's faithfulness

You can trust God because He is faithful. He will never leave you nor forsake you, He has promised. It is safe to dwell in His Land because He has provided everything you need. He doesn't promise riches, but He does promise His faithfulness and that brings a reassurance that money cannot buy. When life has brought you to the end and there is nothing left in the house, trust God He will be with you in that low, dark place. Choose to praise the Lord and feed on His never-ending faithfulness. I do not know what God will do in your situation specifically, but I do know He will be faithful to you and as you trust Him and do good His glory will shine through you.

Turn your face away from riches and fame and look to the Lord, the maker of heaven and earth. He is with you and as you dwell in His land He dwells there too. He will make His home with you and will rejoice with you and mourn with you. When even your closest friends have left, He will never leave. He will give you of His sustenance and you will live. Feed on His faithfulness today.

6th May
Psalm 37:4a
'Delight yourself also in the Lord,'
Go on, delight in the Lord

Have you noticed that society thinks Christians are miserable, joyless and would never be seen to be having fun? Is that the impression you give to those around you? We are to delight in the Lord. To delight is to be happy, joyful and yes, have fun and laughter. As Christians, who have a destiny with Jesus, we should above all peoples be joyful and openly show it. Do you show your delight in the Lord, or are you afraid of what other Christians might think?

Our delight must only be limited by God. 'Delight yourself in the Lord' we are told. That means we can't just do anything that seems fun, but the Lord has given us a sense of humour, so use it. He has given us fun and games, so play them. He has provided for all your happiness, so dig deep into the treasuries of joy the Lord has for you.

The World has its joys, but they last only for a moment then they need to be replenished. The Lord's joys are like a river that keeps on flowing. How deep do you dare to dive into the delights of the Lord?

7th May
Psalm 37:4b
'And He shall give you the desires of your heart.'
What is your desire?

Let me clear this up from the start, the psalmist is not saying that God will give you everything you want. He will give you your desires in line with His Will and according to the caveat of you trusting in the Lord, dwelling in the land and delighting in Him. In other words, if you put God 100% first in your life and leave your desires to Him, He will give them to you.

To delight in the Lord is to be happy in Him and in the place He has put you. Instead of asking, 'Why have you placed me here?', ask, 'What can I do for You here?' Your first desire should be to serve your Lord. What can you do for Him where you are right now? Decide to let your delight be in the Lord no matter what, and He will open the storehouses of Heaven for you. He is not mean or stingy, no, the Lord is generous, and He will pour out His blessing on you.

We normally come to this verse with a specific desire on our hearts that we long for God to give us, and that's fine to a point, but I challenge you to change your thinking so that your hearts delight and desire is the Lord and let the other things fall aside. Trust in the Lord for He is good, feed on all His faithfulness, delight in Him and He will give you desires that are in line with His perfect Will for you and He will fulfil them.

8th May
Psalm 37:5a
'Commit your way to the Lord,'
Digging deeper

Verse 4 said to 'delight yourself in the Lord and He shall give you the desires of your heart.' Most of us stop there; put your hand up if Psalm 37:4 is your favourite part of this psalm (or perhaps any psalm)- I've got my hand up. Verse 5, however, digs deeper into the vein and we shall look at this verse over the next few days. The first part is 'commit your way to the Lord,' that is a hard thing to do. We want to go our own way and do our own thing and follow our own dreams. What if God leads us in a completely different direction to the one we planned?

Christian, you have said you have given your life to Jesus, that includes all your hopes and dreams. Your earthly destiny is in God's hands now, you have no right to dictate the direction your life may go in anymore. Commit your way to the Lord, choose today to follow God's plan for you. It may not be the heady path you imagined, but it will be glorious. As you walk it you may think to yourself, 'well this isn't the glorious path I was promised!' Well, let me tell you, it will be glorious because the Lord Jesus will be walking that way with you. There is nothing more glorious than that!

9th May
Psalm 37:5b
'Trust also in Him,'
I'll say it again, trust Him

We have been here before in verse 3, 'Trust in the Lord'. Trusting in the Lord is linked to doing good, dwelling in the land, feeding on His faithfulness, delighting in the Lord and committing your way to Him. All your Christian life is a life of trust. How much do you trust Jesus? You may have read the Gospels hundreds of times, but have you listened to Jesus' words, and do you accept them? The entire Bible is Jesus' Word; He is the Word. Do you believe and accept all He says, even if it goes against all you hold dear?

What did Jesus say on this matter? He said, 'If you abide in Me, and My words abide in you, you will ask what you desire, and it shall be done for you.' John 15:7. Abide with Jesus, dwell with Him, trust Him in everything and He will be everything to you. Are you still afraid He might fail you? Perhaps your life hasn't turned out the way you planned, and you wonder where Jesus was and why He led you here? I'll ask you again, do you trust Him? Take a moment to gather yourself and all those whirling thoughts. Now choose to trust God in every part of your life and remember all His words: delight in the Lord and He will give you your desires, abide with Him and let His word abide in you and He will answer your prayer, and this verse, commit your way to Him, trust Him and He shall bring it to pass.

Well, do you trust Him?

10th May
Psalm 37:5c
'And He shall bring it to pass.'
God will do it

What is God's will for you? God will shower you with His blessings, He will make you a witness for Jesus in the places you go, He will take you down a hard path, lead through the narrow way and He will form Jesus in you. That is God's will for you. On top of that He may do other things for you but all to His glory and to bring glory to Jesus. If God says 'no' to your heart's desire it is not because He doesn't think you can handle the thing, it is because it will not bring glory to Jesus. Seek God and ask yourself what is your heart's desire? What do you want to do for Him? Allow the Holy Spirit to mould your hopes and dreams into a shape that glorifies Jesus, at that time He will bring it to pass.

Have you committed your way 100% to God and do you trust Him totally? If you answered truthfully, 'yes and yes' then God will do the thing that is in your heart but not necessarily in the way you expect. If you are not quite there yet, then leave your desire at the feet of Jesus, kneel before Him and put your trust in Him.

Make the choice today to commit your way to God; He only want's what is best for you, trust Him, He will do it.

11th May
Psalm 37:6a
'He shall bring forth your righteousness as the light,'
Desire fulfilled

What is the desire of the Christian? What do all believers want God to do for them? The psalmist has said that God will give you the desires of your heart, that He will bring it to pass, if only you will delight in Him and commit your way to His perfect leading in total trust. If we do our part, He promises to do His. So, back to the question, what is the desire of the Christian? Your desire should be for righteousness as the light and who is the Light? Jesus. Our desire must be to more and more clearly reflect the righteousness of Jesus to the world around us The Lord will not fail to give you your heart's desire if it is in line with this noble position.

This may make you disappointed, frustrated or even think, 'what's the point in the things dear to my heart.' Whether or not the Lord grants you other desires is between you and God, but He will not give you them unless you put Him first in your life and make His righteousness your number one desire. I can't promise that God will give you what you have always desired, or that it will fade away until it is easy to live without. I can promise that if your first desire is for God's righteousness to be shining through you, your Christian life will be immensely fruitful. More fruitful than you will ever know.

12th May
Psalm 37:6b
'And your justice as the noonday.'
The Judge's good verdict

The desire for righteousness is all well and good, but we know we are sinners and have broken God's Law and so deserve nothing but retribution. God is the Judge of the whole world. He gets to say what is right and wrong and to hand out punishments. Our desire for righteousness must include the need for restitution before God. The righteousness is His and His alone. We, however, must come in a state of repentance before God and humbly ask for forgiveness. If you have followed the path of this psalm you can expect a good verdict from the mouth of the Judge. He will declare you just before everyone. He will not mumble your verdict in the middle of the night, hoping no-one will hear. He will shout it at noon so that everyone will know you are free from the sins you have committed.

You cannot make yourself clean before God, there is nothing you can do. Only the Lord, the Judge can declare a good verdict in your favour. Commit your way to Him today, choose to delight in God's way and He will see to it that all those around you will know His favour rests on you. You will be spotless before God, robed in His righteousness and becoming more like Jesus - isn't that the number one desire of your heart?

13th May
Psalm 37:7a
'Rest in the Lord, and wait patiently for Him;'
Rest in the Lord

Unfulfilled desire can make us restless. How can we rest in the Lord when our hearts are breaking because of that one thing we need God to do for us, but He is silent on it. As mentioned previously, receiving God's blessing of righteousness will not necessarily lessen the natural desires you have, especially when you see other, less deserving people, get what you so desperately long for. The Lord says to you my brother, my sister, 'Rest in me.' Take a break from crying out in prayer and just rest a while at your Father's feet. As you recline, gazing up at the Lord, think again about trust - do you trust Him? Wait patiently for Him to act. It is not easy, I know, but the Lord has your best interests at heart. If it is important to you it will be important to Him.

God's peace and rest are like no other, they bubble up in the most unexpected ways allowing you to live the life He most wants for you. A life that is not pulled downwards by the seemingly unfair ways of human life. Sometimes life is unfair, and everything is against you. It is at these times you must trust God and rest in Him patiently. Allow God's Spirit to envelop you in His Love and then proclaim 'God is good' no matter what you are going through.

14th May

Psalm 37:7b

'Do not fret because of him who prospers in his way, because of the man who brings wicked schemes to pass.'

Don't fret about the wicked

Do you ever look at certain people and think why have they got all they want, when they are evil and speak ill of God. Why do they get what I so desire? You may even have asked God questions along those lines. The Lord is not worried or concerned about the prosperity of worldly people and the wicked schemes they bring to pass. He is concerned with you and your eternal happiness. Don't get me wrong, when wicked men do wicked things God, who sees everything, is very angry and justice will be done, but He doesn't fret about them. His victory is assured and God's future plans will not be thwarted by the actions of men and women. Because God is not worried, we needn't be either. We can rest in God's great assurance that the Kingdom of God will be standing a long time after they are forgotten. Kingdoms come and kingdoms go, but God's Kingdom will last forever. As a citizen of Heaven, you are a child of God and co-heir with Jesus. You may see the wicked flaunting the thing you desire the most, but one day it will be them longing to be where you are and have all the riches of Heaven while they are languishing in Hell.

This life is so fleeting, and God knows your heart's desire. Don't fret because of others, rest in the Lord and look to your sure future with Him.

15th May
Psalm 37:8
'Cease from anger, and forsake wrath; do not fret--it only causes harm.'

It only causes harm

It is so easy to get angry when we see evil people not only prosper but appear to laugh in the face of God in their wickedness. Don't get angry with them, don't fret it only causes harm. The question that arises here is, 'who does it cause harm to?'

The first thing that is harmed is you because you lose your peace and the anger will eat you up inside, especially if you know there is nothing you can do about it; so, don't fret. Then there are those around you, family and friends, who you blow off steam to. They may also become angry or at least they will fret, and they just exasperate the problem; so, don't fret. Following on from the last thought, you may find you take out your anger on the wrong people; you get so worked up inside that you snap at innocent bystanders who have done you no wrong; so, don't fret. Finally, you can cause harm by blocking the way for the wicked to repent. If they see you ranting they will harden their hearts against God, but if they see your loving concern their heart will be moved; so, don't fret.

As far as it's up to you, live at peace with all men (Romans 12:18); pray for them and show them a better way. Don't fret it only causes harm.

16th May
Psalm 37:9a
'For evildoers shall be cut off;'
So, don't fret

We humans do tend to worry about things and not all that worry is wrong as such. When we fret about evildoers seemingly getting away with it, we are showing concern for righteousness sake. The thing is we don't need to worry about them, God is in control. We can rest in God no matter what others do or how they prosper when we don't, because in the end they will be cut off. This is not being smug, this is about being in God's Kingdom. As we look at the deeds of the Enemy's Kingdom we need not fret, the victory is the Lord's. Leave their sins with Jesus. He can forgive the worst sinner who truly repents and no matter what they have done, there is hope. However, for the arrogant who says, 'I can do as I please, you can't tell me how to live!' They will be cut off. Cut off from what? They will be cut off from God's eternal blessing; the Lord will cast them out of His sight, and they will be carried away captive to eternal exile.

So, don't fret because of evildoers. Rest in the Lord and wait patiently for His abundant blessing to transform your life.

17th May
Psalm 37:9b
'But those who wait on the Lord, They shall inherit the earth.'
A generous inheritance

There really is no need to fret or get angry when we see evil men prosper. There is a place for righteous anger and speaking the truth in love, but don't let them steal your peace. The sobering truth is the wicked will be cut off from all things good. The incredible truth is, if you and I wait patiently on the Lord we will inherit the earth! The earth is the Lord's and He can give it to whom He chooses and He chooses to give it to His sons and daughters as an inheritance.

What do you think of that! This wonderful, beautiful planet that we have been entrusted with will one day have our names on the deeds, no longer tenants but owners. We, as a whole, have not looked after it very well and our leaders haven't always been the best, but there will be a day when you and I will be joint owners of the earth and we will rule it as God originally intended. God is not giving us this gift to do as we please with it, but rather to do as He wills.

The World may not think that you're important and you may be overlooked by those around you, but God has promised you a generous inheritance that will lift your status to the top, second only to God Himself. This is worth persevering for; hang on in there for a little longer you're going to inherit the earth!

18th May

Psalm 37:10

'For yet a little while and the wicked shall be no more; indeed, you will look carefully for his place, but it shall be no more. '

A little while

As we look out at our world it can seem like things are never going to get better. Wicked people are more increasingly wicked, those who sin arrogantly get more arrogant against God and His people, the Kingdom of Darkness increases it's hold on the earth. Don't let this steal your peace, for God says, 'in a little while they will be no more.' God's Kingdom will have the victory and all those who refuse God's offer will be cast out.

These are sobering thoughts; there will be a day when we look out over our world and there will be no wickedness only righteousness. Do you long for that day? Hallelujah. Do you long for the souls of the lost to find Jesus? Pray that the earth will be filled with the citizens of Heaven all praising God as one. There is not much time, Jesus says, in the penultimate verse in the Bible, '"Surely I am coming quickly."' and our response should be the same as John's, 'Amen. Even so, come, Lord Jesus!' Revelation 22:20. He is coming quickly, in a little while. Hold on a little longer and you will see God's Kingdom finally established here on earth and God's perfect rule adhered to by all. There will be great rejoicing on that day, and no more suffering, because there will be no more sin.

19th May
Psalm 37:11
'But the meek shall inherit the earth, and shall delight themselves in the abundance of peace.'
The meek shall inherit the earth
The opposite of the arrogance of the wicked is the meekness of the righteous. It is not the strong but the meek that will inherit the earth. Jesus Himself echoed this in the Beatitudes, Matthew 5:5, "Blessed are the meek, For they shall inherit the earth." He even added they are blessed.

Do you want to be meek? It is not a glorious place to be in the World's eyes, in fact the meek are pitied by those who live in big houses and appear to have all they need. Meekness isn't weakness, it is putting God first in your life and then everyone else and lastly yourself. It is the very opposite of what we are taught to be by the World. Nobody wants to be the least of the least, but we must choose that way; it is the way that Jesus, the Son of God, chose when He walked on the earth. You say you are following Jesus and want to be like Him, well act like it and become meek and humble before God. Stop worrying what the World will say, God says it is the meek that will inherit the earth not the arrogant. It is the meek that will delight in the abundance of peace not the arrogant.

Choose the life of the meek and receive God's unending blessing today.

20th May
Psalm 37:12
'The wicked plots against the just, and gnashes at him with his teeth.'
A warning, but don't worry

This verse is a warning to us: it is a statement of fact that the wicked oppose the righteous and plot against them. We must open our eyes and see things as they really are. Looking through the lens of God's Word we see the truth of this all around us. David wrote these words many years ago but they still ring true, the wicked plot against God's people. Don't be fooled into believing it is the other way around, no, the righteous plot to help the wicked and bring them to Salvation in Jesus.

Don't let this steal your peace; don't worry, God has it all in His control. Let them plot, let them gnash their teeth, don't fear them and certainly don't join them, no, pray for them to become citizens of God's Kingdom where they will inherit the earth and have a sure future. Don't try and pray for everyone as it will exhaust you, but rather pray for those you know need Jesus. You can't make someone a Christian, that is between them and God, but you can pray earnestly for them and leave them in God's righteous hands.

So yes, this verse is a warning, but don't worry we are on the Victors side.

21st May
Psalm 37:13
'The Lord laughs at him, for He sees that his day is coming.'
The Lord laughs

We get so worked up when we see those who oppose the Gospel prospering and spreading their lies, but God laughs because He sees the futility of their actions. The wicked parade around saying, 'look how great I am, I can do anything I choose, and no one can stop me!' The Lord looks down from heaven and laughs at his haughty words, knowing that He will come down and stop him when the time is right.

Don't fret and get angry when you see the arrogant displays of the wicked because their day is coming, a day of judgement. God laughs at their puny attempts to topple Him. We don't need to laugh, but we can smile because we are at peace in God's Kingdom. The siege wall of Hell may be built against the Holy Walls, but they can't even scratch the surface. Life may well be tough, and you may cry as you see society falling further away from God's perfect plans but rest assured God's Kingdom will prevail. Pray that more souls would stop striving and find rest in Jesus, there is still time for them, but the day is coming when time will run out and Jesus will return to Judge the earth.

22nd May
Psalm 37:14a
'The wicked have drawn the sword and have bent their bow,'
Ready for the fight

The wicked may be defeated already, but they are ready for the fight. They have drawn their swords, bent their bows and made their battle plans. They are ready to fight, what about you?

These are Jesus' words when He sent His disciples out, and they are still true today, '"Behold, I send you out as sheep in the midst of wolves. Therefore, be wise as serpents and harmless as doves."' Matthew 10:16. These and what Jesus said afterwards, are a warning to be prepared for the fight, not in an angry, aggressive way but wisely. The wicked have schemes to entrap the righteous and we must be aware, or we will fall into them. We also mustn't bow the knee to them as we are God's people and we bow the knee to Him alone. How then do we get ready for the fight? By reading the Bible to see what God says about all things, and so we have a rounded knowledge of righteousness; pray, talk to God, ask His advice and then carry it out.

Don't get overrun by the battle, but draw your sword (the Bible) and bend your bow (your righteousness) standing firm as a soldier of the Kingdom of God. As in every war there are battles won and lost, but, remember that God has the ultimate victory. Get ready for the fight because your enemy already is.

23rd May
Psalm 37:14b
'To cast down the poor and needy,'
Defend the poor and needy

The Kingdom of Darkness has no time for the poor, it will cast them down as if they were something unpleasant. This has always been the case, because the wicked love power and detest weakness. This is not to say all unsaved people hate the poor and do nothing for them. This is evidently not the case, however wicked men and women do exploit those who cannot defend themselves and many are so caught up with defending their sin that they have no time to think of the poor.

Don't be like them, defend the poor and needy (Proverbs 31:9), plead their cause, stand up for them. You may not have time or money to give to charities, but there are things you can do. Show love to them by getting along side and offering help in some practical way. If they reject you do not get offended as the World does, instead pray for that person and continue to offer help if not to them then to others.

The World loves to be big and brash and get all the attention; they love you to know they are helping people. You on the other hand should help in secret, if people find out let it not come from your mouth. Defend the poor and needy not for your status but for the Lord.

24th May
Psalm 37:14c
'To slay those who are of upright conduct.'
Live a different way

It is logical that those who love darkness would hate the light. The Kingdom of Darkness sets out to destroy anyone who acts uprightly. Righteousness is an act of aggression against the wicked and they retaliate in the only way they know how, by trying to destroy the Kingdom of God by their unrighteousness.

If righteousness is seen as 'aggression', should we cease being righteous? No, we are sons and daughters of righteousness, that is what we are, so how can we live any other way? While the Kingdom of Darkness seeks to destroy it's enemies, we seek to show them a better way. Jesus said in Luke 6:27-28, 'Love your enemies, do good to those who hate you, bless those who curse you, and pray for those who spitefully use you.' Never agree with practises that oppose the Lord's Word, but we must conduct ourselves in the way Jesus instructed; love them, bless them, pray for them and in every way be kind to all. These are the weapons of the Kingdom of God and with them we fight for righteousness. Stand firm, do not yield and you will see the Kingdom of God established on earth.

25th May
Psalm 37:15
'Their sword shall enter their own heart, and their bows shall be broken.'
The battle turned on it's head

In Verse 14 those opposed to God's Kingdom drew their swords and bent their bows ready for the fight, but now we read that their own weapons will be used against them. The Lord promises us victory and we do not even need to fight. This is not to say we sit idly by and do nothing, but we do not have to enter the fray, we let God fight for His Kingdom. The Lord will turn things on their heads.

The Lord is the God of order and He will restore order where chaos has seeped in. The words of hate our Enemy uses will be God's weapon against him. The Lord will turn our persecution into praise, our darkness into light, our mourning into joy. This may remind you of Isaiah 61:3, but actually this is the message of the entire Bible. The Lord will turn the battle on it's head and the very thing that is meant to cause us harm He will use for our blessing. This may not make it easier to go through, but the knowledge that God will turn things around can be a great promise to hold onto in the darkest of times.

The Kingdom of Darkness may appear to be winning the war on the souls of Mankind, but ultimately it will lose, and God's Kingdom will be established here on earth and Jesus will be King. Look up, your redemption draws near.

26th May

Psalm 37:16

'A little that a righteous man has is better than the riches of many wicked. '

Godliness with contentment is great gain.

We have seen from this psalm that it does appear that the wicked prosper while the righteous suffer, but David asserts that even the little a righteous man has outweighs the riches of many wicked people; so how can this be? David new that following the Lord gives wealth that money can never buy. When Paul wrote to Timothy he said, 'Now godliness with contentment is great gain.' 1 Timothy 6:6; there is much to gain from living the Christian life, but it may not be financial. The gains of godliness are eternal and found only in the hearts of those who are contented with all that God has given them.

Contentment means you are satisfied with what God has given you; it doesn't mean you have no hopes and dreams, or if you do you bury them. No, drive is a good thing, but it must never eclipse God's greater goodness and wisdom for your life. As you look back over your life so far, do not be disappointed at God not taking you down the path you so desperately desired, instead live contented where God has led you. Look for the paths of righteousness in your life and see the godly riches they have produced.

The Lord may grant you your hopes and dreams, and if so, praise the Lord, but now live with godly contentment which brings great gain.

27th May
Psalm 37:17a
'For the arms of the wicked shall be broken,'
Strength removed

It is true that at present the worldly people have all the power, resulting in decisions that shock, baffle and upset us. The strength of the wicked grows stronger, but do not fret, because the Lord will 'break the arms' of the wicked; in other words remove their strength.

People with power, money and influence believe they are in control, but no, God is in control. He is still on the Throne of Heaven and earth and His ultimate plan of redemption is still unfolding. We do not worship a powerless god, but the Lord God Almighty, who raises people up and brings them down. The Lord may be upset by the decisions the World makes but He is not baffled or shocked. He knows the hearts of men and women and knows who are for and who are against Him. The Lord will remove the strength of the wicked and make them truly powerless.

Pray for the decision makers, that they would make godly choices. Do you have friends or relatives that are wilfully rebellious against God? Pray for them; God can break the strength that is controlling them and set them free. Prayer is a power that will never be broken.

28th May
Psalm 37:17b
'But the Lord upholds the righteous.'
Strength given

You may feel you have no power against the forces of darkness; well, the truth is you don't. Your strength will fail you. If you are relying on your own tenacity to make a stand for biblical principles you will not be able to do it. You will be overrun by those who hate all you stand for as they will take their wicked venom out on you and make out you are the wicked, hateful one.

Almighty God stands against the tide of wickedness and never tires, His arm is always ready for the fight. In our weakness we can lean on Him and He holds us up, so we stand. He holds our hand and keeps us from falling (verse 24); He will never let us go. Not only does He uphold us by His mighty hand, He also bestows His strength on us. The Lord gives us strength! We keep His hand in ours by reading His word each day, by praying continually and by the power of the Holy Spirit dwelling in us. If you lack any of these things come to Father God. He will help you to read the Bible and understand it, He will enrich your prayer life and He will fill you with His Holy Spirit.

Don't fight the good fight alone; the Lord upholds the righteous and gives him His strength for the battle. Receive the strengthening of the Lord today; you will need it.

29th May
Psalm 37:18a
'The Lord knows the days of the upright,'
Your life is in His hands

You may feel like your life is in freefall or in total disarray, or maybe a combination of the two. Life can be confusing and sometimes a little unsettling, but the Lord knows all your days and because of this He remains in control.

Commit your way to Him, trust Him (v3) and He will lead and guide your life. The Lord knows what is up ahead for you and is preparing the way. It may be overwhelmingly tough at times, but remember God knows and God cares, and He will make a way even through the valley of death. It is a comfort that the Lord knows all your days and the road you are traveling. He is traveling with you every step of the way and also He has been ahead of you and left milestones and signs to reassure you He is there and to show you His way.

If your path is easy right now get into the habit of looking out for God's signposts. The Holy Spirit in you will light them up like neon signs and that way when you travel a harder path you will naturally look out for them. Those already on the hard path, start today to look out for God and His guidance all around you. As you strain your eyes through the gloom you will begin to see God's signpost pointing the way you should go.

Rejoice, the Lord knows all your days.

30th May
Psalm 37:18b
'And their inheritance shall be forever.'
An eternal inheritance

'"Do not lay up for yourselves treasures on earth, where moth and rust destroy and where thieves break in and steal; but lay up for yourselves treasures in heaven, where neither moth nor rust destroys and where thieves do not break in and steal. For where your treasure is, there your heart will be also."' Matthew 6:19-21.

Some people have an earthly inheritance, and of itself there is nothing wrong with that; but the more you have the more you have to protect it - there is always someone with their eyes on your money! Heavenly treasure is safe, it is eternally yours, no-one can take it away from you. Our inheritance is forever, but you don't have to wait until you die to enjoy it; start storing it up today. Look around you at all the things God has done for you, things that no-one can take away from you; rejoice in the bountiful provision of God. He has given you an inheritance, treasure in Heaven, that no amount of money can equal. Don't be envious of the wealthy, but actively seek to 'imitate those who through faith and patience inherit the promises.' Hebrews 6:12b.

Why worry what people have in this fleeting life, you have an eternal inheritance.

31st May
Psalm 37:19a
'They shall not be ashamed in the evil time,'
Be not ashamed

Shame is the consequence of sin. Adam and Eve were ashamed when they listened to the lies of the Serpent and ate of the forbidden fruit. Shame has followed Mankind through the ages ever since. The righteous will not be ashamed because we are set free from the bonds of sin.

We live in an evil time when sin is praised and righteousness mocked, we may well ask, 'where is the shame?' People may cover it up but deep down we all posses the knowledge of good and evil and that knowledge condemns sin and praises righteousness. Shame is still the product of the knowledge of good and evil. In this evil day, live righteously, even if no one else does and you are hounded for it. There is no need to be ashamed if you have made Jesus your Lord and King.

Shouting, 'I can do as I please!' as loudly as you can, will not take the feeling of guilt and shame from your heart, only Jesus can do that. Remember, 'Commit your way to the Lord, trust also in Him, and He shall bring it to pass.' Psalm 37:5.

1st June
Psalm 37:19b
'And in the days of famine they shall be satisfied.'
The bounty of God's provision

In this evil day we live in there is a spiritual famine. People are starving through lack of truth, justice and godly behaviour. It doesn't matter how much food there is on your plate it will never fill the aching void in your heart. This is why so many have turned to 'alternative therapies' most of which have spiritual origins; just not the Spirit. This is like going through the bins of a restaurant that has enough food for everyone and it is all given away free and eating an old banana skin. Why would anyone do that!

The famine in our land is only there because people refuse to humble themselves and go into the 'restaurant' and sample the delights within. We are fortunate that even at this dark time we are satisfied by the bounty of God's provision. We have spiritual food aplenty and enough to share with those around us. Eat your fill so that you are strong and prepared, then go out into the 'highways and byways' and share the bounty of God with those who need it. Some may still refuse, but those desperate enough will accept what you offer and then come into the restaurant for themselves.

NB: Don't allow the spiritual famine to come into your church.

2nd June
Psalm 37:20
'But the wicked shall perish; and the enemies of the Lord, like the splendour of the meadows, shall vanish. Into smoke they shall vanish away.'
The end of the wicked

David acknowledges the splendour the World bestows on its subjects; they are like the splendour of the meadows, truly beautiful. When you walk though a meadow in summertime and all the flowers and grasses are in bloom it is quite breathtaking; but walk through that same park in winter and it is stark and bare, that is what David says will happen to the enemies of God. At present they seem so attractive and beautiful, full of vibrancy and colour, but the day is coming when those same people will be no more, they will have vanished away like smoke dissipating in the air. Your inheritance is forever it will never fade away.

So, why fret when you see the wicked prosper? Why get angry when they parade around as if there is no God? It is but for a time and then they will perish, vanishing forever from before your eyes. It is the Lord's work to bring the end to the wicked, it is our job to pray and witness to them. Don't usurp God by trying to make them vanish; we should judge righteously but God is the King who pronounces judgments. Pray for opportunities to share your faith with someone before it is too late for them.

3rd June
Psalm 37:21a
'The wicked borrows and does not repay,'
Take and not give

There is the thought here that the World takes and takes and takes and never gives back. This may not be true for individuals, but it is the heart of the Kingdom of Darkness. Out of the heart of darkness comes fraud, confidence tricksters, theft in all its forms and all other ways you are parted from your money without getting anything back. The World loves to take but does not want to make good on its debts.

This is not how we should be. We, as Children of light should operate in the light, giving what we owe and never taking for our own greed. We are called to show those around us a better way of living; not necessarily better than them, but better than the World's standards. This shouldn't be too hard because the World's standards are pretty low! However, we live in the world, we are tainted by it, and even tempted by it. Be wary that you do not follow them into the trap of taking and not giving, be honest and open in all your affairs so that those around you will not have anything to condemn you with. The World will judge you for your actions but they are hypocrites and will point you out even though they are doing the same thing. Deal honestly and give no room to the devil.

4th June
Psalm 37:21b
'But the righteous shows mercy and gives.'
Give and not take

We serve a generous God, a God who does not hold back any good thing from His children, so shouldn't we act in the same way? If we see someone in need we help them, it is second nature to us. We may not be able to solve their problems, for instance we may not have the money they need, but we can give of our time, show mercy and help them in other ways. We don't have to do what we can't, but we should do what we can.

Being merciful and generous can open us up to abuse, so we must be wise in our giving, but still give. The wicked borrows and does not repay, we should lend without expecting anything back in return. It's not about giving and giving and giving without any thought for yourself or your family, we must take care of ourselves or else we will have nothing to give away. If you see a need you can help in, seek God over it and then be bold and give. Always be generous with the bounty God has given you, share the Good News with those in the spiritual famine. If the Lord has blessed you with money, then give to local causes but give anonymously so no glory comes back to you.

There will always be people in need and you will not be able to help them all, but you will be able to help some or even one. Be generous where you can, it is, after all, what the Lord has done for you.

5th June
Psalm 37:22
'For those blessed by Him shall inherit the earth, but those cursed by Him shall be cut off.'
A summary

This is the message of the psalm; the righteous will inherit the earth while the wicked will be cut off. It may not seem that way now, but this is the eternal promise, a promise that one day will be fulfilled on the earth even as it is already established in Heaven. When we see the unrighteous prosper and be lauded by all we don't need to fear. They may say that this is the end for the Church, the days of Christianity are over, but that is not true. God's people will not only survive they will be lifted up to the highest place.

Let's consider the blessings and curses of God. What does it mean to be 'blessed' or 'cursed' of God? The word blessed, means to be honoured or saluted in this case by God, like the way God presented Job to Satan with great pride (Job 1:8); He does the same for you. You are blessed because God says you are. The word curse is the exact opposite, it means in God's opinion the person is a nothing, less than worthless. Those who have lifted themselves up in pomp and praise, are seen by God as the lowest of the low. Whose opinion will you listen to, the World's or God's?

6th June
Psalm 37:23a
'The steps of a good man are ordered by the Lord,'
Steps ordered by God

If, like me, you tend to start and stop with verse 4, then these next two verses may well be the only other parts of this psalm you know.

Life is a journey that is made up of many steps; we walk through life often not knowing where the next step may take us. Good things happen, or perhaps bad; joys and griefs; highs and lows. There doesn't seem to be any order, it's just a chaotic, random maze. Look again, if you are righteous before God, you are a good man, or a good woman and God has ordered your steps. He knows your destination and He knows the route you will take. Yes, there will be the good, bad, joys, griefs, highs and lows etc., but God has directed you down those paths for a reason, and by traveling the path God has ordained for you, you will be able to help and encourage others who walk a similar path.

God has not ordered the steps you should take and then gone off to order someone else's, no, He travels with you every step of the way. He knows the way, He is always ready to catch you or hold your hand if the unexpected should arise; nothing comes as a surprise to Him. Walk with Jesus everyday and He will guide your steps.

7th June
Psalm 37:23b
'And He delights in his way.'
The Lord is delighted with you

Did you know that when you walk God's chosen path for you it is a delight to His heart? He is not delighted by your hardships or pain; He is delighted that you are traveling with Him along the path of life. He loves your company and His constant desire is to be with you. Is your constant desire to be with Him?

The Prophet Zephaniah put it this way, 'The Lord your God in your midst, The Mighty One, will save; He will rejoice over you with gladness, He will quiet you with His love, He will rejoice over you with singing.' Zephaniah 3:17. The Lord is not far away from you, He is near, right in your midst and He will rejoice over you with gladness. He will quiet your heart and He will rejoice over you with singing. In the place you are right now, you may not be able to rejoice and sing, but that's okay, let God rejoice over you with singing as He delights in you. As for you, rest quietly in His love. The road is long, but your traveling companion is Almighty God and He delights that you have chosen to walk in His way.

8th June
Psalm 37:24a
'Though he fall, he shall not be utterly cast down;'
All have sinned, all sin

Let's get this straight from the offset, all have sinned and all sin; that means you and me. What then is the difference between the righteous and the wicked? It is not the ratio of good things to bad, although that should be a natural difference. Being 'good' will not get you into Heaven. We are righteous only because God declares us so when we put our faith in Jesus. As we walk this life on earth we will stumble and fall, but God will never cast us down.

The first part 'Though he fall' is us, we fall, we sin, we mess up and become less than God intended us to be. We may look around and find plenty of Christians who mess up more than we do, but it is not a competition, we have all sinned and fallen short of the glory of God, Romans 3:23, that is the bad news. The second part is, 'he shall not be utterly cast down' This is God, He will not cast you out no matter what you have done, this is the good news. God understands we are human and liable to fall but He also knows our heart and if it is righteous because He has declared it so, He will not cast you down. Get up, brush yourself down and return to the path of righteousness and resume your holy walk with God.

9th June
Psalm 37:24b
'For the Lord upholds him with His hand.'
Holding Fathers hand

When I took my children out for a walk as infants, I would hold their hands tightly, this protected them from dangers, particularly busy roads. As we walked, they would occasionally trip over their feet and stumble; because I was holding their hand, I stopped them from falling and gently lifted them back onto their feet. This is a great illustration of what Father God does for us. As we walk through the journey of life Father holds our hand tightly guiding us away from dangers and preventing us from falling headlong when we stumble.

Do you feel you are too mature a Christian to hold Fathers hand? Do you think you are ready for independence? If you do, beware, there are dangers all around and many pitfalls to stumble into. I love holding Fathers hand, I feel so safe and secure in His grip; it's not that I am immature, but rather well aware of my limitations. When I have wandered, even a short distance away, it is not long before I get hurt. I know where I am safe.

Stay close to Father God and keep a firm grip of His strong hand.

10th June
Psalm 37:25a
'I have been young, and now am old;'
The wisdom of years/the vigour of youth

David could look back over his life and see many things. This knowledge is only learnt by living. Wisdom comes with age; even Solomon only really learnt wisdom when he was old, just read Ecclesiastes and see that after many years of going his own way he realized God's way was so much better.

Churches are best served by both young and old; the young have the drive and energy needed to push the church on to new and exciting things. The old however have the wisdom to see what will and will not work - they have no doubt tried it before. Young people listen to the older generation because they have the words of wisdom to pass on to you, wisdom that will help and guide you in your ministry. Older people listen to the young, their youthful enthusiasm will lift your hearts as you see the next generations coming to Jesus.

Don't cut out the young because they are inexperienced, the future of the Gospel is given to them, and don't discount the old because they have had their day, their wisdom cannot be garnered any other way - listen to them. A balanced church is a wise and vigorous church with all generations pulling together - this is Godly wisdom.

11th June
Psalm 37:25b
'Yet I have not seen the righteous forsaken, nor his descendants begging bread.'
We are not forsaken

David could look back over his life and proclaim with certainty that the righteous are not forsaken by God. God will never leave you nor forsake you, no matter what. David lived a long life and he knew God was faithful to His servants even when they (he) didn't deserve it. I have not yet lived as long as David did but God has never let me down and I have never known Him to forsake anyone. Yes, there have been tough times, for some 'tough' doesn't really sum it up, but God has always been with them and I have never seen Him fail. You may forsake Him, but He will not forsake you.

Okay, it is very evident that some believers beg for bread; there are countries today that persecute Christians mercilessly cutting them off from even the most basic human needs. They hunger and thirst for a morsel of sustenance. However badly they are treated, God's blessing continue unabated; some may be offended by this, but it is true. God's blessings are not physical they are Spiritual and poured out from on high. They may lose everything, even their lives but God remains faithful and He will not forsake them. As you pray or give to help our persecuted Family, remember they are not forsaken, God holds a place in Heaven for them.

The righteous are not forsaken.

12th June

Psalm 37:26

'He is ever merciful, and lends; and his descendants are blessed.'

Blessings in, blessings out

This verse sounds like 'cause and effect'; if we are merciful and bless others, God will bless us and our descendants. This is not what this verse is saying. It is not blessings in, blessings out as if the Christian life is some kind of machine. No, there are blessings in and blessings out as a natural consequence of living a righteous life. Blessings are as natural as breathing. We can't help but bless others, to do good and be generous because that is how the Spirit moves within us. It has no bearing on the blessings God pours out on us! We don't bless others because God has blessed us, neither does God bless us so that we can bless others; we just pour out blessings on others and God just pours out blessings on us because it is the natural response.

Don't wait for God to bless you before you go out and bless someone, go and do it. You may be waiting for God to give you £1000 so you can share it with others, God may never give you that. Look instead to what you do have and give out of that, it may be time, experience, talent, gifting, often these things have a more lasting impact than money. The Holy Spirit in you longs to be generous, He also knows what you do and do not have, listen to Him and give. It is the same Holy Spirit that drives God to pour out blessings on you. He gives out of His abundant store, you give out of what you have. Blessings are as natural as breathing; blessings in... blessings out...

13th June
Psalm 37:27a
'Depart from evil, and do good;'
Easier said than done

Often the path of evil is more inviting than the path of righteousness. It may be easier said than done to walk the righteous path, but are you willing to take the first step? That's what departing is; it is opening the door and stepping through from evil to good. It is a journey to be made not an instant change. It may seem like a lonely path with your friends and family advising against such an adventure. This has always been the case; read Pilgrims Progress and you will see Christian deciding to leave the City of Destruction and everyone trying to stop him. However, it is only by making that first step and departing evil that you can ever begin to do good that really lasts.

Doing good is not impossible while dwelling in the camp of evil, but it is not the kind of goodness God is looking for; He is not interested in what you *do*, He is interested in what you *are*. The further you journey away from evil, the easier it will be to not only do good but to *be* good. Good people do good things and say good things and live a good life; evil people do evil things, say evil things and live an evil life. If you have taken the decision to depart from evil and follow Jesus you are on the way to good.

14th June
Psalm 37:27b
'And dwell forevermore.'
Rest in God's camp

The whole verse says, 'Depart from evil, and do good; and dwell forevermore.' So, where do we dwell forever? On the road outside the camp of evil, never reaching a destination? No, once we depart from evil, we gain the right to dwell forevermore with God. From God's point of view, we are dwelling with Him already but from our point of view we have not got there yet. We can't see from God's vantage point so we see things from a day to day, on-going perspective.

As we live our lives as Christians, we must strive to be more like Jesus. The Holy Spirit within us compels and helps us to get there. Less evil and more good. We must never rest on our laurels, but journey on each day. The pull of our old ways may be strong, but we must consciously choose to do what is right. It is a hard way and can be tiring, but, at the end there is rest as we dwell with Jesus forevermore. As you journey on, through the rough and the smooth, think of this, God already sees you at the end; you are already perfect to Him. We don't have to try to live up to God's expectations like the carrot and stick. We choose to live righteously, and God guides us to be the way He already know we will be. There is rest in God's camp, and we are dwelling there forevermore!

15th June
Psalm 37:28a
'For the Lord loves justice,'
The Lord loves justice

You may have thought that the Lord tolerates justice, but in reality, it holds Him back. It is justice that means God cannot declare us all righteous without the blood of His Precious Son, Jesus. It is justice that sends people to a lost eternity when God's will is that none should perish (2 Peter 3:9). These things are sad, and God would love all people to come to Him, but justice must be done; if you refuse God's offer and remain in the camp of evil you will go to Hell. Never let it be said that God hates justice or that God's justice is wrong. God's justice is perfect and right and good, and God loves it. He loves it because it is good and just to open the doorway of Heaven to any that leave the camp of evil and choose the path of good; verse 27 would be impossible without God's justice.

This psalm is a psalm of God's perfect justice. We all long for justice to be done but no earthly justice system is perfect. God's justice is perfect, He does not make mistakes. We can fully rely on God's Word, if God has declared you righteous then you are righteous and God is not going to change the rules tomorrow, or the next day or ever.

God loves justice as described in the pages of Scripture. God’s justice is a two-edged sword, bend the knee to Him to ensure you are on the right side of God's Law.

16th June
Psalm 37:28b
'And does not forsake His saints;'
He will not forsake you

The Lord loves Justice and therefore He is compelled to never forsake His saints. To be honest, it is as much out of His love for us that He will not forsake us.

We sometimes get the impression that the 'saints' are some kind of mystical upper class of Christian that God has singled out because they have done something significant or are especially holy. This is not what the Bible calls 'saints'; saints are God's holy ones, that is they are the people God has proclaimed righteous. Every Christian is a saint and God will not forsake them.

A better question is what are Christians according to the Bible? Using the words of this psalm, they have departed evil and are doing good, they trust in the Lord and delight themselves in Him. Christians have committed their way to the Lord and trust Him all along the way. They do not do this alone but they are filled with God's Holy Spirit who keeps their hearts from fretting.

If you are a Christian, you are a saint of God and He will not forsake you. Hold on, the Lord is with you.

17th June
Psalm 37:28c
'They are preserved forever,'
Preserved but not jammed

Fresh fruit and vegetables perish very quickly if uneaten, this is why they are preserved. They are made into jams and pickles which makes them last longer. God doesn't want us to perish (2 Peter 3:9) so He preserves us. This is where the analogy breaks down, God doesn't turn us into spiritual jam, although you may feel like He does. He preserves us by guarding our lives.

The Lord God Almighty is guarding the door of your life, keeping you safe from the attacks of the enemy. Bad things happen, but trust God to preserve you in them. If nothing negative impacted your life you wouldn't need to trust God, you would think you could go it alone. Our thinking is limited to this life, but God sees the eternal and He is preserving your life to that time scale.

The theme of this verse is that because the Lord loves justice He will never forsake you, but will guard your life, preserving you for all eternity. The truth is not only the theme of this verse, it is also the theme of the psalm and indeed the whole Bible. No matter what you are going through today be assured that God is with you preserving you that you will not perish. He will not leave you in a jam.

18th June
Psalm 37:28d
'But the descendants of the wicked shall be cut off.'
The wrong side of God's justice
Verse 28 is all about God's justice and so far we have looked at what can be expected if you are on the right side of the Law; but what happens in you find yourself on the wrong side of God's Justice?

There are two types of people who hate the justice system, the first are those who have been failed by it in some way, the second are those who set themselves up against the laws of the land. God's Justice is perfect and does not fail anyone, although some may feel it has let them down, but in truth is it has not. However, those who are not of the Kingdom of God have set themselves up as being opposed to God's Law and Justice, so they rant and rave about how terrible and intolerant God's Justice is. God's Justice is right and they are wrong.

The Justice that falls on the unrighteous is that they will be cut off from God's Eternal blessings; they will be forsaken by God and will perish for all eternity. It is not about how good you are, but whether you are righteous or wicked in the heart. If you have not been pronounced righteous by God you are one of the descendants of the wicked. Choose today to change camps and come humbly before God and yield to His perfect justice and be saved.

19th June
Psalm 37:29
'The righteous shall inherit the land, and dwell in it forever.'
An eternal inheritance

If you haven't grasped it yet, the righteous will inherit the land and will dwell in it forever. You have an eternal inheritance! Other people may have more than you do now, but don't be envious of them, their things will pass away but your treasure in Heaven will last forever.

The People of Israel were looking for an eternal kingdom where they would rule for all eternity. The Promised Land was supposed to be that land, but they could not live up to the demands of dwelling in God's Kingdom, so they were exiled. The land of Israel is God's land and He chose to give it to His ancient people as an inheritance. He has a land He wants to give to you too; an Eternal Land, a land from which you will never be cast out. Only the righteous will inherit this land. The only thing you can do to become righteous is to yield fully to God's perfect plan for your life. His plan may not bring you fame and fortune, you may be overlooked for that promotion, or not be given the recognition you deserve. Don't fret about it and don't get angry you as have a far better destiny than anything this world can give. You have an eternal inheritance.

20th June
Psalm 37:30a
'The mouth of the righteous speaks wisdom,'
Speak wisdom

Our future is secure, we have an eternal inheritance. We now, however, live in the world. It is essential we watch what we say because you can be sure your friends will be! Be wise in all you say and remember who you are representing. You may feel it is okay to say anything you like as long as it is not a-grade swearing. That may be the case, but what impression does that give those who hear you? Be wise in your speech. Seek God's wisdom in everything that comes out of your mouth, especially when discussing diversive subjects such as politics or football.

My advise is to learn from the Master, Jesus. When He spoke, He never went out of His way to offend anyone, but then He never went out of His way not to offend anyone either. He spoke the truth in love. We, as Christians, are bound to offend people. The Gospel is foolishness to those who are lost because it is the polar opposite of the World's message. You are going to offend, that is just the way it is, but don't go out of your way to offend; it is better to say nothing than to be cruel.

It should be natural for us to speak wisdom, unfortunately it is not that easy, and it takes practice to know what to say. Ask the Lord to fill you mouth with wise words today.

21st June
Psalm 37:30b
'And his tongue talks of justice.'
Speak of God's justice

There is a wisdom to God's Justice that the World hates. The World wants to do it's own thing and go it's own way, and in doing so has got itself tided up in knots; there is no justice because there is no wisdom. The simplicity of God's justice contrasts to the complexity of the World's justice. Saying everyone can be and do as they choose doesn't work; for one person to get what they want someone else must lose out - where is the justice in that! God's justice is so simple: come to Him, humble yourself before His Almighty Throne, repent of your many sins and God will give you the gift of Eternal Life, refuse and you will get eternal death. This is simple and straight forward and is the same for everyone, men and women, young and old, rich and poor, and covers all races.

When the subject of justice comes up in conversation, be quick to speak up for God's justice. It may not be liked but they will have heard the Good News. Spend time familiarizing yourself with God's perfect Justice that you will always be ready to give an answer. Add the talk of God's Justice to your wise words, that everyone will see your colours nailed to the mast.

22nd June
Psalm 37:31a
'The law of his God is in his heart;'
Is God's law in your heart?

The idea of God's Law is not a concept we like to think about, we are, after all, not under the Law but under Grace (Romans 6:14). Look again at that passage in Romans 6 and you will see it is all about living a righteous life and avoiding sin. It is true that we are no longer under the Law but under Grace, but that does not mean we can do as we please, 'Shall we continue in sin that grace may abound? Certainly not!' Romans 6:1b-2a. So, how do we avoid sinning? First, we need a concept of what sin is: sin is rebellion towards God, it is braking God's holy, perfect Law. To avoid the pitfalls of sin we must know and understand God's Law.

We are not under the Law, we are totally free from it. However the Law still stands and God still judges according to it. The Holy Spirit in you works according to the Law of God and He will guide you away from sin and towards righteousness. This doesn't absolve us from learning God's Law for ourselves as we should read God's Word and drink in His statutes. Let His Law dwell in your heart and direct your decisions.

You shouldn't avoid sin out of obligation, but out of love for your Saviour. Unless His Law is in your heart you will fall into sin.

23rd June
Psalm 37:31b
'None of his steps shall slide.'
Sure footed

The Walk of Faith is long with many hazards and pitfalls in the way, surely it is inevitable that we will stumble or slip at some point! Or is it...

The more we allow the Holy Spirit to reign in our hearts the less our feet will slide. It was God who inspired David to write this psalm. Everything that David sang was straight from the Fathers own heart and when He said, 'None of his steps shall slide.' He meant it. Do you believe that the Holy Spirit can do this for you? It may be impossible for you, but it is not impossible for God (See Matthew 19:26). The Lord can do it for you by causing you to be sure footed. Remember, as you walk the Lord is holding your hand so that if you do trip you do not fall headlong (Psalm 37:23-24). This is stage one, following Jesus so that we may become mature Christians able to walk without stumbling.

Take a step of faith and believe that 'none of *your* steps shall slide' Trust in God's infallible Word and know that He will not leave you or forsake you. He is holding your hand and everything will be alright. Listen to the guidance of the Holy Spirit and He will lead you down the safe paths avoiding the hazards and pitfalls that may arise. Good or bad may come your way but your feet will remain firm and you will be able to stand strong in the Lord. Trust in the Lord, with Him you are sure footed.

24th June
Psalm 37:32
'The wicked watches the righteous, and seeks to slay him.'
Watching and waiting

The Lord watches over us and holds our hand so, should we fall, He is on hand to pick us right back up and as we mature we fall less and less. The wicked also watch us, waiting for us to fall, but they will not pick us up, they will kick us while we are down seeking to slay our witness.

Have you noticed the World is largely uninterested in what Christians do or say, except when they either say something that offends their sensibilities or when they do something 'unchristian'? How many times have we seen the wicked seek to openly destroy a Christians life for daring to live according to the Word of God; this is usually reported in the News as a right and just response to Christian beliefs. However, when a professing Christian makes a mistake, a mistake anyone might make, they are immediately pounced on and paraded as a hypocrite.

You may have come across this behaviour in you own life. People will largely leave you to follow your faith as long as you never witness to them and should you ever do as they do, they will never let you (or anyone else) forget it. Don't be discouraged by this behaviour as they are only doing according to their nature. You are not of their Kingdom because your King is not like that. He is loving and caring and will uphold you with His hand. Show the World a better way, they will be watching.

25th June
Psalm 37:33a
'The Lord will not leave him in his hand,'
The Lord will save

We have seen that the wicked watches the righteous and seeks to slay him; what is God's response to this? Will the Lord stand idly by while His Holy Ones are attacked? No, He will not leave us in the hands of the wicked. The Lord will save and deliver you out of the power of your Enemy. The wicked may feel they have the upper hand and your defeat is inevitable, but God's Power is greater, and the Victory is in Him. The Wicked one may take everything from you, but He cannot steal your salvation that is assured in Jesus. Job is a great example of this. Satan took his family, livelihood and even his health, but Job was able to confidently state that, 'I know my Redeemer lives' Job 19:25. This is not sentimentality. Job was in a deep, dark place, a place that he could see no escape from, and yet he trusted God his Redeemer. God was always in control of Job's life, from beginning to end and He is in control of yours too. He will not let the wiles of the wicked take control of you, the Lord will save.

Do you trust Him, even when the World has entrapped you?

26th June
Psalm 37:33b
'Nor condemn him when he is judged.'
You are not condemned

The Enemy lies in wait for you to stumble and pounces when you do. The Lord comes down and delivers you out of his hands and what does the Enemy do then? He drags you off to God's Courtroom and announces to the Judge all your transgressions, knowing God has to punish sin; not only has he got you, but he has also got one over on God. The Lord must judge, it is the right thing to do. What will God do? He will tap his gavel to attract attention and pronounce righteous judgement. As the smirk on Satan's face is wiped off, you are proclaimed not guilty; you are not condemned. Satan squirms off and you are left before the Throne of God. The tension is unbearable, then Father God opens His arms and draws you into His loving embrace.

Not just pardoned and set free but made a child of God. The schemes of the Wicked one backfired on him and you are now closer to God than ever. You may make a mistake, and it may be a big one, but if you are righteous and repentant there is always forgiveness from God the Judge, and He will restore you. Don't let the Enemy's accusations wear you down. God has pronounced you righteous so live in that righteousness. You are not condemned.

27th June
Psalm 37:34a
'Wait on the Lord,'
Wait

This has been a tiring journey, full of ups and downs, but now it is time to stop. 'Wait on the Lord' the psalmist says and wait we must. There are times in our lives that are like lulls, nothing much happens. At such times as these we must not try to make anything happen, even if God has made promises. Take the opportunity to rest and breathe, wait for the Lord to begin to move again.

What are you waiting for the Lord to do? Bring it to mind right now and ask is there anything you could do to make it happen? If there is, don't do it, wait patiently for Him. There are things you can be doing, but God's promises are His business and we do well to leave them to Him. As a caveat to this we also shouldn't do anything to counter His promise; leave the whole subject well alone. God is working it all out, all you need to do is wait on Him.

Do you find it hard to wait? Well put your hand to other work for Jesus, but do take the opportunity to rest. You don't have to forget what God has promised. He hasn't forgotten, but don't worry or get anxious, God has got it all planned out. Wait on the Lord.

28th June
Psalm 37:34b
'And keep His way,'
Keep His way

Life is a journey and we are all walking along a way, or a path that leads us to our ultimate destination. There is another 'way' we must be aware of, it is the way we live our lives: our habits, our manner, the kind of person we are at heart. We all put on a persona to show those around us the kind of person we want them to see us as, and depending on the company, that persona may take different guises. There is however, a persona that does not change no matter who we are with. That persona is the deep one, the one that is truly who we are, the one from whom the other persona originate. I say it does not change, but it can and does change over time depending on how you live your life and what you do.

The more you do something the more it effects your inner persona and makes you the person you are. Walk in God's ways and that will mould your life to be more like Jesus. Choose to read the Bible each day and it will become a part of your life, as natural as breathing. Also, pray into every situation until it becomes the first thing you do. Today choose to make godly habits and form an inner persona that will shine out Jesus to all the people you meet.

29th June
Psalm 37:34c
'And He shall exalt you to inherit the land;'
God's work

There are things we must do: 'Wait on the Lord and keep His Way', but there are things that only God can do, and we must leave these things to Him. We have already touched on this, but like the psalmist it is wise to say it again. Wait for the Lord to fulfil His promises; if God has said it, He will do it. In this verse we come across a universal promise for all believers: He will exalt you. To be exalted is to be lifted up to the highest place, the place of honour, and as you have been lifted high no one will miss what God has done.

Don't try to exalt yourself; if you do it will end in humiliation. Don't exalt others by putting them on a pedestal they can never live up to. Leave the exalting to the Lord, He is an expert in exaltation and will never put you or anyone else in a place that is wrong for them. Never think God has raised up other people to a place that you could never attain. In God's perspective He exalts all His children the same; we all inherit the same portion of the Land with no Christian more exalted than another.

The single characteristic of a soul exalted by themselves or others is pride. The single characteristic of a soul exalted by God is humility. Wait for the Lord and He will exalt you.

30th June
Psalm 37:34d
'When the wicked are cut off, you shall see it.'
You shall see it

When you wait patiently for God and walk in His Ways, you will find you are at odds with the World. The World's ways are diametrically opposed to God's Ways; the difference will single you out as different. The wicked prosper in all they do, attracting plaudits from everyone around, while the Church struggles to make an impact. The only mention the media often gives the Church is to mock or ridicule it. This will not always be the case as there will be a day when God exalts His people to the highest place and at the same moment, He will cut off the wicked and bring them down to the depths. This may seem impossible now, but it will happen. God has promised and when it does you will see it.

This promise has been passed down the generations and largely the wicked still reign, so what does this mean? Will we really see the wicked cut off or is this just a pipe dream? This is a sure promise. We may see a partial fulfilment of this prophesy in our lifetimes, but when the end comes the Lord will have victory over His enemies. You will see wickedness cut off and all its participants. Your tears will be wiped away by Jesus and you will live forever with Him. This is a thing to rejoice over, not that your enemies are defeated, but that you have been vindicated.

1st July
Psalm 37:35
'I have seen the wicked in great power, and spreading himself like a native green tree.'
Trees of wickedness

Isaiah 61:3 speaks of 'Trees of righteousness, the planting of the Lord'; these trees are good and produce a good crop. The trees David mentions in this verse are very different. The Wicked have accumulated great power, and they have used it to establish themselves. It is as if a tree plants itself and causes itself to grow by its own power. No tree has ever planted itself, someone or something has always chosen the place where the roots will grow. Even wild trees that grow without the aid of Man are not planted by themselves, the seed does not choose where it will grow! The wicked believe they have planted themselves, but this is not the case.

The question then is who has planted you? Were you planted by 'accident', or by the designs of others, or has God planted you and established your roots? The wicked make themselves look like a tree of righteousness and virtue, but really, they are the planting of Satan. Christians are the planting of the Lord and He has placed you where you are for a reason and He will establish you forever. We shall see what the outcome of the wicked is over the next few days.

2nd July
Psalm 37:36a
'Yet he passed away'
Just what it sounds like

The Wicked spread themselves out like a lavish tree, dominating the horizon; when you look at the view it is them that catches your eye. That tree may look healthy but, in reality, it is sick to the core. That person who shouts to make his presence felt, and says, in effect, 'Look at me, I can do as I please, and there is nothing anyone can do about it!' That person will go the way of all men; that is to say he will die. All his rantings and ravings, all his parading around like a peacock cannot prevent the inevitable. Death comes to all; the trees of wickedness will be cut down.

Yes, the righteous die too, but our hope is eternal; we have life with Jesus to look forward to. There is, however, a finality in the way the psalmist describes the wicked person's passing; there is no Eternal life only Eternal Death. This should firstly give you joy and hope, in that those who oppose the Church will be cut off, while the Church will remain forever. Secondly it should give you the desire to see people saved, so that they too can avoid a lost eternity. Pray today for someone who needs Jesus, but at the moment is actively opposed to Him.

3rd July
Psalm 37:36b
'and behold, he was no more;'
Who do you trust?

As we look at the News we may think, 'How does that person get away with it? People love him and put him on a pedestal, but what he does is wrong. How come he gets to live when good people die?' Why does God allow that man, that woman to live? Even the Christian viewpoint that says, 'If God killed all the ungodly, who could stand?' doesn't quite solve it. As you bring that person to mind, the person who defies God in their every action, also bring to mind others who have done that: The Pharaoh in Moses' Day who enslaved Israel and would not let them go, or what about Pol Pot and genocide of millions in Cambodia, or Hitler and the Holocaust. It would have been terrifying to live in those days and yet where are those people now? They have all been brought down to dust along with their campaign of evil.

There may arise again someone as bad, or worse, than these, but do not fear, God is still sovereign; He reigns over all and even the most powerful person on earth will one day be no more. Who do you trust? Who do you put your hope in? Let the only answer to this be Jesus.

4th July

Psalm 37:36c

'Indeed I sought him, but he could not be found.'

Gone for good

There is the idea here that David looked intently for this wicked person when he heard that he was gone, to see if was true, but he could not find him. This person is gone for good. The wicked has gone but will good take his place?

When a corrupt, wicked person is removed from your circle of influence, they leave a gap that must be filled. It is like a vacuum that nature is desperate to fill. This is your opportunity to fill that gap with a godly, righteous person. Don't leave this to chance, go out and find godly people to surround you. As David sought the wicked man to see if he was really gone, you seek the godly man. There are godly men and women to be found, they are in churches up and down the land, quietly influencing those around them.

If you do not seek out the righteous when the wicked has gone, more wicked people will seek you out and you will be in a worse place than you were before. It is extremely important you fill those gaps as soon as possible so the Lord can begin to heal and guide you in the ways of righteousness.

Let the wicked be gone for good.

5th July
Psalm 37:37a
'Mark the blameless man,'
Watch the blameless

David encourages us to 'Mark the blameless man'; this means to watch him, keep a close eye on him. This can be tricky because the blameless do not seek to draw attention to themselves; they are often unassuming, quiet, unnoticed, but God will point them out to you and say, 'Watch this one.' Watch them, observe their mannerisms and how they conduct themselves, they are the ones to emulate. They may not be big, loud and glitzy. No-one may go to stadiums to see them, but they are the people to be like, because they are the people God will richly bless.

After observing them, copy them, do as they do and be as they are. Ask the Lord to make you one of the blameless. Being blameless will not make you famous or wealthy as the World views it, but you will be rich in God's eyes, and that is the best reward of all. There is no earthly reason to be blameless, but God has prepared a heavenly reward for them, a gift no one can take away; that is something worth grasping for.

Watch the blameless, so you can become blameless too.

6th July
Psalm 37:37b
'and observe the upright;'
Watch the righteous

As well as watching the Blameless, we too must watch the righteous. There are those in our churches and circle of friends that are righteous in a way that others are not. These are not 'holier than thou' or some kind of super Christian, they are normal, down to earth men and women who have dedicated their whole lives to God. The psalmist directs us to observe or watch them. How do the righteous conduct themselves? You emulate them. Ask the Lord to help you to be more righteous; you can bet those we see as righteous are praying everyday to God and asking for forgiveness for sins so that they may be righteous before Him. They know they are not righteous in their own strength but only in the Lord; this keeps them holy, this keeps them humble, this keeps them righteous.

Don't let observing the righteous bring you down; I know sometimes I think, 'I could never be like them!' If you think like that you are doubting God's ability to make you the person He wants you to be. Instead of turning inward and seeing how far you are from righteousness, look to God, the source of all righteousness and together as fellow workers, journey on to your desired end. It will be a lifelong adventure, but a road well worth traveling. Come on, get on your knees and begin that journey today.

7th July
Psalm 37:37c
'For the future of that man is peace.'
A future of peace

We have been urged to observe the blameless and righteous, with the idea of copying them. Today we find out the benefit of living in a blameless, righteous way.

There is so much talk of 'peace' today by people who seem to not know what it is. Peace is not the cessation of war; peace is a state of the heart. No politician, no matter how moral or how well-meaning they may be can give true peace to this world; only God can grant that. Look again at the blameless and the righteous, do they have peace? They conduct themselves in a way that shows that no matter what they go through their trust is in the Lord. Life is tough, but God is with you through it all, and you ought to live in the truth of this. There is a peace you can know now; a peace that comes from the assurance that God is by your side and is leading you to His beautiful home, where you will dwell forever. It is in that sure future, that true peace is. When you finally enter fully into God's presence and He says to you, 'Well done, good and faithful servant; you have been faithful over a few things, I will make you ruler over many things. Enter into the joy of your lord.' (Matthew 25:23) you will find you are surrounded by peace, inside and out; it will be the end of your inner struggles.

8th July

Psalm 37:38a

'But the transgressors shall be destroyed together;'

Ignore for your sake, witness for theirs

Verse 37 calls us to watch and take note of those that are blameless and righteous and verse 38 calls us to ignore the transgressor, as if they are irrelevant. Why do we ignore them? Because, no matter what they do and how loudly they proclaim they can do as they like, God with destroy them all. So, don't be anxious about those who openly oppose God.

The word 'transgressor' means rebel or sinner and covers everyone who is not in the Kingdom of God. The word 'destroyed' really means eradicated or exterminated and is exactly that, God will exterminate the plague of transgressors as we might a wasp's nest. That last word, 'together', means just that, every transgressor will be destroyed from the greatest to the least, with no exceptions.

Now stop and consider this. We all know people who are not saved by the Blood of the Lamb, the Amazing Grace of God, they are all grouped together under the banner of transgressors. So, yes, we should ignore the rise of wickedness and not become anxious by it, but we should witness to our friends and family and so rescue them from God's judgement. Who will you witness to today?

9th July
Psalm 37:38b
'The future of the wicked shall be cut off.'
A future cut off from peace

At the end of verse 37 we looked at the future of the blameless, righteous person and saw that it was Peace. All the cares and struggles of the world removed forever, an eternity dwelling with God. This verse mirrors that by contrasting the future of the wicked, transgressor. Their future is one that is devoid of peace. David says, they will be 'cut off', but cut off from what? They will be eternally cut off from God and His peaceful dwelling place. Jesus speaks of a 'great gulf' between the place of Peace and the place of Torment that cannot be crossed (Luke 16:26).

It doesn't matter how peaceful and easy the lives of the wicked are now, their future is one of eternal unrest. Often that unrest starts now. Deep in all our hearts we know what is right and what is wrong and living contrary to God will leave anybody agitated and anxious; the very thing God says we need not experience.

Our eternal destiny is secured at death, we either dwell in Peace or we are cut off from it forever. Live the blameless, righteous life and be a witness to all those around you, whether inside or outside the Church, let them see the way you trust God in everything. The Lord will whisper to them that your future is peace and theirs is not. Will they listen?

10th July
Psalm 37:39a
'But the salvation of the righteous is from the Lord;'
Salvation is from the Lord

As we draw to the end of this psalm there is one thing that you should take away from it: God is good and righteous, and He gives His servants good and righteous things. The number one, top of the list of good and righteous things God gives us is Salvation. Any salvation that is not from the Lord should be shunned.

Salvation is not merely being saved from the bondage and consequences of sin, no, salvation is a state of being right before God. The righteous are only righteous because God has saved them. There is nothing we can do for ourselves to become righteous, but God, who is gracious gives salvation liberally to all who call on His name in truth. Don't be fooled into believing there is no hope for those described as 'wicked' in this psalm, while they are still alive there is always hope that they will choose to turn from their wicked ways and come back to God.

It may sound like a contradiction that on the one hand there is nothing we can do to be saved and on the other we must choose to follow God. It is not a contradiction, but a wonderful transaction, one tiny move towards God results in a huge move by Him towards us. Salvation is from the Lord.

11th July
Psalm 37:39b
'He is their strength in the time of trouble.'
Strength is from the Lord

Philippians 4:13 says, 'I can do all things through Christ who strengthens me.' and in the context of the previous 2 verses Paul is saying, no matter what he goes through, from the very darkest days to the heights of the highest mountain it is God who strengthens him to get through it and to stay true to Him. Paul knew troubles in a way we may never have to live through: he was stoned, shipwrecked, imprisoned all in the cause of the Gospel, but this doesn't mean your troubles are not real.

What are you going through at the moment? Do you feel weak and jaded? The Lord is your strength right where you are and He has an abundance of strength He will pour into you. God may not deliver you from your troubles, but He will give you the strength to pass through them. The strength of the Lord does not turn you into a mussel-bound superhero able to defeat any foe. No, the strength of the Lord is like a stronghold where God is the walls to the fortress and no enemy can breakthrough. The Lord has built a wall of protection between His righteous ones and the wiles of the World; yes, you may go through some devastating things that no one should have to go through, but the Lord's strength will be with you and protect you even in those times. Call out to Him, He is your strength and salvation in all situations.

12th July
Psalm 37:40a
'And the Lord shall help them and deliver them;'
Help and deliverance

Let's jump right in and declare that the Lord will help and deliver you. I can't possibly know what you are going through right now as you read this, and I wouldn't presume to tell you everything will turn to sunshine and roses, but I will say with confidence the Lord will help and deliver you.

The help of the Lord is not like the help of even the most caring friend; if I were to help you that help would be a fleeting thing, but God's help is eternal. He has power to help in ways no-one else can, and He wants to help. Cry out to him for help in your distress and He will be swift to act; what that help will look like I cannot tell, but it will be the very help you need at that moment. This brings us to the second part, deliverance.

Are you in a situation where you need delivering from the grip of the enemy? Are you trapped in the stronghold of the wicked, unable to free yourself? Well, there is no place God can't reach, there is no prison God can not open. Call on Him for deliverance, do not rely on worldly remedies, the Lord has the keys to the stronghold you are in. If you truly wish to be free, call on Him in humble repentance and He will deliver you and set you free.

The Lord *will* help and deliver you.

13th July
Psalm 37:40b
'He shall deliver them from the wicked,'
Delivered from the wicked

This is a long psalm and David repeats the themes several times. Do you think He's trying to tell you something? The wicked, no matter how strong he might be, will be defeated by God; He will deliver you. It is a David and Goliath situation, where you are David standing before Goliath with nothing but faith in God; it wasn't the sling and stone that gave David the victory but God alone.

Do you feel like that today, standing unprotected before the might of the enemy? David had no armour; he had no sword or shield, only a shepherd's sling and 5 stones. Goliath had all the weapons of the day only supersized. Israel were cowering, the Philistines were waiting to attack. This was a hopeless situation, there was no earthly way David could win. Fortunately, David didn't rely on an earthly way, he relied on the Lord. David didn't wait for Goliath to strike he, in the power of God, struck first and it only took one shot to fell the giant. God delivered David and Israel in a miraculous way and He will do the same for you.

Take off the ill-fitting worldly armour you have been protecting yourself with and put on the armour of God. This may seem like foolishness, just think what David wore when standing against Goliath. I'll leave you with this thought from 1 Corinthians 1:25, 'the foolishness of God is wiser than men, and the weakness of God is stronger than men.'

14th July
Psalm 37:40c
'And save them,'
Salvation

Although in a real sense this is a future event, it is true to say that we are saved now. Jesus came to save sinners like us; and He didn't die on the cross just for some far-off future glory, He did it so we could have abundant life right now, today. Salvation means you can enter into all the glorious truths of this psalm right now. God's Good News is that we can be victorious in our lives no matter what we are going through. We may not have everything we could want, wealth, health, fame, renown, intelligence, but we have everything we need and more. Jesus will make us victorious in the hole we live in. The darkest place can seem as light as day if Jesus is there. The one promise worth claiming for yourself is that Jesus will never leave you nor forsake you, Hebrews 13:5.

You may think you don't deserve to be saved, well God has never saved anyone who deserved it; everyone that has been saved has been saved by the grace and mercy of God. Turn away from looking inwards at how bad or good you are and start looking up to God the perfect righteous One who sent His Son to die in your place. Fall on your knees, open your heart and call out to God for Salvation, and He who sees your heart will begin to do a wonder work in you.

15th July
Psalm 37:40d
'Because they trust in Him.'
Trust in Him

Those who, like me, stop at verse 4 may get discouraged because although you delight yourself in the Lord you have not been given your desires yet. However now we have reached the end of the psalm we can look back and see, it is not about short-term blessings but long-term gains. Yes, life may be unfair for us and perhaps the ungodly get more than we do, but in the end the righteous will inherit an eternal reward. It really is worth the wait.

While we wait, we trust in the Lord to deliver us out of bondage, to keep our feet from stumbling and yes, that He would give us the desires of our hearts. Do you trust Him to fulfill all these promises in this psalm, even if it looks as if the opposite is the only truth? It is easy to say yes, but not so easy to live it. Ask the Lord to fill you afresh with His precious Holy Spirit to enable you to live in the trust of the Lord. The Holy Spirit naturally trusts God and all He says, but then He would; the Holy Spirit *is* God. When the Holy Spirit fills your life, His nature becomes your nature and you too will naturally trust God.

David trusted God time and time again and each and every time God delivered Him, even after He had sinned. God will deliver you too if you will trust in Him.

16th July
Psalm 1:1a
'Blessed is the man'
Blessed basics #1

Everything has a beginning and that includes the Psalms. Psalm 1 is the first poem in the book, and it gets right back to basics. The opening line is 'Blessed is the man'. Let's make this clear here, the psalmist meant everyone; the term 'man' means mankind, humanity, you and me regardless of gender. So, who of us does not want to be blessed? If you want God's blessing in your life this psalm will give you the basics to receive His favour.

This blessing is not reserved for certain people who are more godly than you; it for reserved for you. As we go through this psalm listen to what God is saying. Are you living up to the basics of Christianity? If not, you won't be able to have God's blessing. For some, you will have heard all this before; it is the basics after all! But, it is always wise to refresh our minds with these first things from time to time, taking stock and asking the poignant question, 'Are you still living like this?'

Take this time to get back to the Blessed Basics and be the one who has God's great blessing on their life.

17th July
Psalm 1:1b
Blessed is the man: 'Who walks not in the counsel of the ungodly'
Blessed basics #2

The first basic question to ask yourself is, 'Who do I take advice from for my life?' Who do you listen to; who is your first point of call in a dilemma? Think about it for a moment, who is it? Is it your spouse, your parents, your pastor, your colleagues at work? Or perhaps it's the bar tender, the traditional source of wisdom? Who do you go to? The point the psalmist is making is it matters a lot who you take counsel from. Be very careful whose advice you listen to; is it godly?

If you walk in the counsel of the ungodly you will be walking away from God's blessing in your life. There is much ungodly counsel out there, so be wise where you go for help. Weigh up all advice you are given, no matter where it comes from, even well-meaning Christians can give bad advice. Not all counsel is ungodly some is merely neutral and may be helpful, but the best counsel comes straight from God's Word the Bible. Go speak to your pastor, or elder or failing that your friend who will speak the truth to you no matter what. Listen to them, pray it over and walk in counsel of the godly.

18th July
Psalm 1:1c
Blessed is the man: 'Nor stands in the path of sinners'
Blessed basics #3

If you desire God's blessing don't stand in the path of sinners. Does this mean we shouldn't stand in their way? Should we ignore their actions allowing their sin to increase? No, that is not what is meant here. When the psalmist says, we should not stand in the path of sinners he means we shouldn't stand with them doing as they do. This can be a stumbling block for some who wish not to look judgemental so go along and join in with sinners. It is not even about judging sinners, it's about standing separate from them; that is the meaning of holiness.

If you want God's blessing, there are things you can no longer do and places you can no longer go; there may even be TV programmes or films you can no longer watch. Be aware of the little things that offend your Big God; do not overlook them. If you are standing in the path of sinners, dwelling in their land, you have alienated yourself from Gods Kingdom; your Salvation is assured in the Grace of God, but His blessings will be far from you.

Make your choice of where you stand, remain with the sinners and see if they give you any blessings or dwell with Holy God and receive countless blessings.

19th July
Psalm 1:1d
Blessed is the man: 'Nor sits in the seat of the scornful'
Blessed basics #4

If to stand in the path of sinners is to dwell with them, then to sit in the seat of the scornful is to be one with them. To sit in a seat is to be comfortable; are you comfortable in the company of the scornful? Are you okay with people who mock Jesus and His followers? If so, beware that you do not sit too long in their company or you will become like them. There are those who will happily speak about any frivolous topic you care to name, and they seem to know all about it but often it has no bearing on them, but bring up Jesus, or mention a Christian and they turn, not necessarily nasty, but they mock and deride; they are scornful. Don't sit with them, choose to take your rest in godly company. Stop making excuses for yourself, stand up and walk away. These people will mock you once they see you stand up for Jesus, but God will abundantly bless you.

Don't be the one who sits with the scornful, sniggering behind others backs, laughing at them, mocking Christ, or if you do you will be numbered with them. Be numbered with the holy ones, whose words are upright, edifying, godly and pure. You may feel that you miss out on the fun, but no, there is no fun in the scornful, only hatred. God is the Father of happiness and He will bless you with fun and laughter all the days of your life.

20th July
Psalm 1:2a
Blessed is the man: 'But his delight is in the law of the Lord'
Blessed basics #5

We have seen what not to do in order to be blessed, but there are things to do and attitudes to have that will enable God's blessing to flow through you. The Christian life is not about not doing anything and stoically resisting all temptations that come your way. There are practical activities to be involved in. The number one activity is to delight in the law of the Lord.

It is an active choice to delight in God's Law; we are naturally repulsed by it. To be honest, most people hate being told what to do by anyone, because we are selfish, and all want our own way. Just a casual look at today's society that promotes that way of thinking will show you what a mess it brings. To choose to not only follow God's Law but to delight in it is tough and takes the Holy Spirit moving in you to accomplish it. If you take up the challenge to delight in the law of the Lord, God will pour out His abundant blessing on you, so that your life is more joyful than you could ever imagine. Things that you may have to give up, the Lord will replace with better things; things that bring blessing to you and to all those around you, and also bring all glory to God.

21st July

Psalm 1:2b

Blessed is the man: 'And in His law he meditates day and night.'

Blessed basics #6

Many people think that meditation is a passive exercise in order to remove unwanted thoughts and give clear thinking, but that is not what is implied here. When we meditate on God Word it is active, not just our minds are taxed but our whole being. The word means to study, to ponder, to speak, to mourn and even to roar. Meditation on the Bible is not silent or passive, it is loud and active. Your whole life will be changed by meditating, and not only yours, but also the lives of everyone around you.

In the previous devotion, we looked at delighting in the law of the Lord. Today we are thinking about what the outworking of that is. If our desire is to delight in God's Law, we need to know what it is, right!? The way we learn what God's Law is, is by studying and meditating on it; reading the Bible daily, thinking about what God is saying to us and acting on it. As mentioned above, there may be mourning involved as we see our sinful nature as opposed to God's Holiness. We may even roar, whether in laughter or pain as we meditate. Speaking is always first to God, praying honestly before Him; then speaking out to Christian friends, family, others around. Share with them what God has shared with you.

God will bless the person who meditates in this way. Don't get side-tracked into meditation from a secular, pagan or false religious origin; God's way is always the safest and best.

22nd July

Psalm 1:3a

Blessed is the man: 'He shall be like a tree planted by the rivers of water'

Blessed basics #7

We have been considering what we need to do to be in the position to receive God's gracious blessing in our lives. The person who does those things will be blessed and their blessing will be evident to all. Today's verse says 'He shall be like a tree'; a tree is a symbol of life, and also of being immovable. There is a permanence to trees that we can all understand. It is not easy to move a tree, because where they begin to grow is usually where they stay. So too, is the one who is living in God's blessing. The Lord makes him immovable, so nothing can shake his faith. He will stand in the strongest gale and all the time will be proclaiming God's goodness. This tree was planted in the best possible place - right next to a river. It is not in dry ground, trying to find water, or in stagnant pools trying to find fresh springs; no, it is planted on a riverbank where pure, fresh, clear water abounds daily. God's blessing is like a never-ending river bringing joy after joy into the Christians life. Every moment of every day those blessings are available, so reach out your spiritual roots and drink them in.

If you are feeling dry it is because you have stepped outside of God's blessing; read the previous devotions again, bow the knee and ask God to show you where you have strayed. Turn back to God's paths and return to the watering hole of God's blessing. Be an immovable tree planted by the rivers of God's blessing.

23rd July
Psalm 1:3b
Blessed is the man: 'That brings forth its fruit in its season'
Blessed basics #8

Trees may be immovable as we have seen, but they are not passive. Trees produce fruit.

The fruit of a tree of God's blessing, brings forth fruit of its kind, in this sense fruit of God's blessing. An apple tree produces apples, an orange tree produces oranges and a blessing tree produces blessings. As God pours out His abundant blessings on you, don't keep them for yourself, pass them on; bless others as they are in need. The more God blesses you the more you should bless those around you. It doesn't matter if they have a specific need or not, just pass on to them God's blessing. We are to be trees of blessing, producing a bounty of blessed fruit, so that anybody can reach out and sample God's goodness. We should be living examples of Psalm 34:8, 'Oh, taste and see that the Lord is good; blessed is the man who trusts in Him!'

Are you living in such a way that your life oozes God's blessing to all those around, tempting them to try of His glorious goodness for themselves? You will if you are living a God blessed life.

Share the fruit of God's blessing with someone today.

24th July
Psalm 1:3c
Blessed is the man: 'Whose leaf also shall not wither'
Blessed basics #9

I wonder what the word 'leaf' brings to your mind in this context. Leaves are where the plant receives and stores its power; so, to have good leaves is to have open hands to receive God's blessings. I think there is more to it than that, I believe the psalmist is pointing to the life and health of the tree. Leaves are a good indicator of the health of a plant, if they are withered or brown the plant is not well. I have a rose bush in my garden and I have tried several times to take a cutting from it but each time the leaves turned brown and there was no life in it, and then one cutting took, the leaves remained green and it even survived the winter! How healthy are your spiritual leaves?

The leaf is an outward expression of what the tree is like inside. We don't need to be a tree surgeon; we see the leaf and know whether the tree has life or health. The same is true for our spiritual lives. Others around can see your leaves, so to speak, and they will know how much spiritual life and health you have. If you are following these blessed basics you are on the right path for a healthy spiritual life that God will bless, and others will not fail to notice.

May your leaves be ever-green and never wither, that your life will be a witness to the blessings of God hidden in your heart.

25th July
Psalm 1:3d
Blessed is the man: 'And whatever he does shall prosper.'
Blessed basics #10

There is an element of poetic licence here; it is very clear that not all Christians prosper in all they do, just take a look at your own experience, and ask if you have prospered in whatever you have done?

Let's look at this again, in the context of the psalm and 'Blessed Basics'. This psalm is about not going the World's way but putting God first in everything you do or say; that is the basis of a strong Christian life. God will honour and bless you if you choose to put Him first. So, if whatever you do is done to honour and bring glory to God then you can expect that to have God's blessing poured out on it and it will prosper. This is not a carte blanche prospering, but rather prospering in doing what God asks and mediating on His laws.

Can we expect God to prosper us in whatever we do? We can, if we are following His lead and doing as He commands. God wants to bless you with a prosperous life, but first you have to put the basics in place, so the channel of blessing can be open.

26th July
Psalm 1:4a
'The ungodly are not so'
Blessed basics #11

The psalmist changes tack now and looks at the antithesis of those whom God blesses. They are the 'ungodly', those who walk in the counsel of other ungodly people, who stand in the paths of sinners and sit, lounging, in the seat of the scornful. You won't find these people delighting in God's Law, no, they will replace God's directives with anything that seems good to them at the time. They are like weak trees planted in desert places, where there is no water. Because they are famished, they produce no fruit of blessing and their leaves reveal the deadness of their hearts - if they have any leaves! They may appear to prosper but in God's eyes they fail every moment of the day.

We were once all ungodly, but God, '...has delivered us from the power of darkness and conveyed us into the kingdom of the Son of His love.' Colossians 1:13. That is, of course, if you are on the path of righteousness. We have seen the blessing God pours out on those who walk uprightly, we shall now consider the opposite; what is it really like to live without Heavenly blessings?

27th July

Psalm 1:4b

The ungodly are not so: 'But are like the chaff which the wind drives away.'

Blessed basics #12

Whereas the righteous were described as a living, thriving tree, the ungodly are described as 'chaff'. Chaff is dry and useless; it is the leftovers when what is wanted is gone. Chaff blows away in the wind; it has no substance and even a gentle breeze will carry it away.

However great they may appear all ungodly people are like this in God's eyes; they are here but for a moment, and then they are gone and then the Lord will forget them. They are dried out husks because God has not rained down His blessings on them. Don't look on the outward appearance look at the spiritual evidence. If you have spiritual life in you, you will begin to see that the ungodly are nothing at all, there is nothing to see. There are many good people in our world, people we should thank God for because of their generosity, or kindness, or being a helpful hand in time of need, however, unless they are following the Blessed Basics, they are at heart ungodly.

Remember, we were once all ungodly chaff, so, pray for the good people and your family and friends to be replanted by the rivers of God's blessing.

28th July
Psalm 1:5a
The ungodly are not so: 'Therefore the ungodly shall not stand in the judgment'
Blessed basics #13

We all shall one day stand before Almighty God in the Judgement. In Matthew 25:31-46, Jesus speaks about the sheep and goats: they may look similar from the outside, but they are different. The same is true for the righteous and the ungodly, but God knows who are His and who are not. Jesus said the things the righteous will do and the ungodly will not do, 'I was hungry and you gave Me food; I was thirsty and you gave Me drink; I was a stranger and you took Me in; I was naked and you clothed Me; I was sick and you visited Me; I was in prison and you came to Me.' These are the things the righteous will do and be rewarded for. The ungodly may do similar things, but it's not about what you do or even who you do it to, it is Who you do it for. The Christian's number one focus is always Jesus. The ungodly, may do good works for all sorts of people but never Jesus.

When they come before God, they will be faced with the truth that even the good they did was worthless, because they didn't follow Jesus. They will not stand; terror, guilt and shame will cripple them.

Even the smallest thing you do, if done for Jesus sake and His glory will be counted to you as righteousness, not because of you but because of Him.

29th July
Psalm 1:5b
The ungodly are not so: 'Nor sinners in the congregation of the righteous.'
Blessed basics #14

The ungodly can appear so proud, so strong; able to win any argument with Christians, laughing at our sad, outdated morals. So, it may come as a surprise that they cannot stand in the congregation of the righteous - we are victorious.

Remember verse one where the psalmist warns the righteous not to stand in the path of sinners? Well this is saying a similar thing: the ungodly can't stand with us, because they are from a different kingdom, the truth will always come out. Everything a Christian stands for is abhorrent to the ungodly, they have no place with us. Sinners justify their sins, whereas Christians are justified by God because they have turned away from their sins.

A sinner cannot stand in the congregation of the righteous, unless he denies himself, picks up his cross and follows Jesus (Matthew 16:24, *my paraphrase*). Pray for the one who is a sinner, who has drawn near to your church, he may look uncomfortable, or even angry, but God can change his heart - after all he did it for you!

30th July
Psalm 1:6a
Blessed is the man: 'For the Lord knows the way of the righteous'
Blessed basics #15

We can all be bewildered sometimes, not knowing where we are going or what we are doing. It can be like walking in a thick fog, but remember this, the Lord knows the way you are going. He is totally in control of your ultimate destination. The way may be hard, but the goal will be glorious.

God knows exactly where you are in your life and He is watching over you every step of the way. You may not be able to see the next step ahead, but God can. Do you trust Him enough to place your foot on the unseen ground in front of you? You may wander from the pathway, going your own way but God sees the bigger picture, and He will ensure you come back to the paths of righteousness. This is not an excuse to go your own way and do your own thing, but a blessed reassurance that God knows the way to the Heavenly City and He will guide you there step by step, day by day, up hill and down valley until you reach your Heavenly Destination and you can rest with God forever.

What a wonderful blessing! The fact God is walking by your side is such a Blessed Basic we can often forget. May you be reminded today that He is with you.

Keep going, God knows.

31st July
Psalm 1:6b
The ungodly are not so: 'But the way of the ungodly shall perish.'
Blessed basics #16

This brings to mind the well-known verse, John 3:16, 'For God so loved the world that He gave His only begotten Son, that whoever believes in Him should not perish but have everlasting life.' Those who believe in Jesus will not perish, however those who do not believe in Him will. The ungodly are walking the way of death; like proverbial lemmings rushing off a cliff together.

What does the word 'perish' bring to your mind? Are any of them good? Probably not. There is only one thing you can do when something has perished and that is throw it away, it's useless. This is what will happen to the ungodly, everything they do is worthless, good for nothing but the scrap heap. Let us not rejoice in the destruction of the ungodly, whoever they are, and dare I say, whatever they have done. The ultimate end of the ungodly is everlasting destruction in Hell. If they die today that is where they will be, but the Good News is that God's free gift is available to the vilest offender who truly believes, and if they turn to Jesus they too will have everlasting life.

As we bring these Blessed Basics to a close, remember the basic truth Psalm 1:6 tells us: there are two destinations we can end up in, Heaven or Hell, choose today where you want to go.

1st August
Psalm 103:1a
'Bless the Lord, O my soul;'
Talking to yourself #1

Talking to yourself is usually thought of as a sign of madness, but actually it can be an extremely wise thing to do. David begins this psalm by talking to himself and saying, 'Bless the Lord, O my soul'. We don't know what David was going through when he wrote this, but he needed a pep talk to remind himself of the importance of blessing the Lord.

Life is full of ups and downs; sometimes these can be short, at other times they can last years. When I say this, I am referring to 'ups' and 'downs', both can be short or long periods of our life, but no matter where you are today, tell your soul to bless the Lord. This psalm is a great way to remind yourself of what the Lord has done for you, and what He is doing for you and what He will do for you. In the good times it can be easy to forget where your blessings originate, so tell yourself to praise the Lord for His goodness. On the other hand, when in the dark times, instead of wallowing in self-pity, make a decision to praise the Lord. Do as David did and say, 'bless the Lord, O my soul.'

No matter what the season of the soul you are currently living through, tell yourself today to 'bless the Lord', remember that He is good.

2nd August

Psalm 103:1b

'And all that is within me, bless His holy name!'

Talking to yourself #2

Open up your heart to God, bless Him with everything you have inside. Just how deep is your well of praise? Dig deep inside, rooting out all the hard, ungodly areas and bring up the blessings of God. Speak to Him from the depths of your heart all that He means to you.

Bring every area of your life into God's holy presence and bless Him with all that is there. This is a statement that you will not hold anything back from God. Just take a moment to think about that. Can you do it? Will you do it? Choose today to take that step to bless God's holy name with *all* that is within you. Don't hold anything back from Him. It may be a terrifying thought for you to be that open with someone, but God is gentle, He is good, and He will turn your life around if you let Him. Open up your heart to God and fill His courts with your praises, and in return He will fill your heart with His blessed Spirit who will make the deep places of your heart His home.

Speak to yourself today and say, 'I choose to open my heart fully to God, to let Him in to the deepest parts of my life.'

3rd August
Psalm 103:2a
'Bless the Lord, O my soul,'
Talking to yourself #3

Verse 2 opens in the same way as verse 1, with David telling himself to 'bless the Lord'. This is a poetic way to emphasise David's need to bless the Lord in the situation he was in. It is almost as if he didn't convince himself the first time and so he talks to himself again.

Your soul may need some convincing today in order to bless the Lord with all that is within you. Take control and tell yourself to bless Him. Your senses and feelings may be telling you that God has forgotten you, but He has not; His loving eyes are still on you and He is good. Our feelings change from day to day, in fact from moment to moment, but the Lord does not change. Talk to yourself and remind yourself of all the things God has done for you. It may be hard at first, but be encouraged because David also found it tough. In this psalm, as we shall see, David begins slowly and tells himself of generalizations and never quite gets round to attributing God's goodness to his own life but speaks in terms of 'we' and 'us'. There is the feeling, however, that he is speaking from his own experience of God.

Think for a moment or two of all the things God has done generally, and then bring to mind what He has done for you personally, then tell yourself to bless the Lord for these things.

4th August
Psalm 103:2b
'And forget not all His benefits:'
Talking to yourself #4

In this psalm David is urging himself to bless the Lord, and today we see that he tells himself to remember God benefits. Actually, he doesn't say to remember them, he says not to forget them! He didn't need to actively remember all the good things God had done for him, they were always with him. He knew, however, how easy it is to let these truths slip into the background and be forgotten. As the psalm progresses David lists some of God's benefits to us, but before we look at them, choose to keep God's benefits in the forefront of your mind.

The benefits of following God are the things He has done for you personally; His dealings with you. Look back over your life with Him and see what He has done, don't forget them. When we are going through difficult times it can seem like God is far off. At these times we can forget God's goodness to us. Job went through terrible things, losing everything and although he questioned God as to why he should suffer in that way he never forgot God's benefits to him as a righteous man.

In both good times and bad, tell yourself each day to, 'forget not all His benefits.' Keep them constantly before you. As we go through David's list of benefits, ask yourself are they true for you.

5th August
Psalm 103:3a
'Who forgives all your iniquities,'
Bless the Lord because He forgives

In the first 2 verses of the psalm, David has been telling himself to 'bless the Lord', and now he comes to the first reason to bless the Lord. Over the next few days, we will travel with David to remind ourselves of God's benefits. While this is by no means a comprehensive list it is a wonderful starting point to blessing the Lord.

Top of David's list is God's forgiveness. He forgives all your iniquities. You may not know exactly what iniquity means, I looked it up and it is very bad. Iniquities are the worst things you have done, the depraved things, wickedness. The most terrible, secret thing you have done the Lord will forgive you for. The thing that everyone looks at you in distain about, the Lord God of the universe will forgive you. He is the God who forgives all your iniquities, there is nothing you have done that His forgiveness cannot cover. Stop holding onto your iniquities, let them go and hold onto the One who forgives.

If God is willing to forgive you, surely you can forgive yourself! David knew God's forgiveness. After the terrible things he did concerning Bathsheba, he humbly came before the Lord in repentance and God forgave him and I know the Lord will do the same for you.

Bless the Lord because He forgives.

6th August
Psalm 103:3b
'Who heals all your diseases,'
Bless the Lord because He heals

The Lord is the God who heals. He can heal *all* your diseases, not just your physical ones but mental illness too. He heals body, mind and soul; He makes you whole. You may be sceptical because He hasn't healed you, or you have seen too many 'healing meetings', but I know He heals because I have seen it with my own eyes, and known it in my own body. God heals.

Everything God does is to bring glory to His Name. He will not heal for money or to make someone famous. He doesn't even heal because you have enough faith, but He heals because He is a loving God who longs to see us well. Faith is important, but God sees faith differently to us, His measure of 'enough faith' is vastly different to ours (Matthew 17:20).

Are you in need of healing today? God can do it. Ask your pastor for prayer and see what God will do. Remember, God heals to bring glory to His name, but sometimes not healing brings more glory to Him as you rise above your difficulty and are used by Him to encourage others.

Whether well or sick, bless the Lord today because He heals all your diseases.

7th August

Psalm 103:4a

'Who redeems your life from destruction,'

Bless the Lord because He redeems

God is the God who redeems. But what does redeem mean? To redeem something is to take a useless thing and make it useful again, (this brings to mind upcycling), or to buy it back so that it is yours once more, or to make good on a promise or pledge. When God redeems, He does all this and more.

We are all heading for destruction, that is our destiny. The Lord longs for each of us to have a new destiny, a destiny of Life with Him. He takes our old, worthless life and transforms it into something new, something totally different. His aim is to repurpose your life, to upcycle you into the image of His Beloved Son. He can only do this if you belong to Him. While you are the World's possession God cannot make you new, but once He has brought you back into His Kingdom, the sky's the limit of what He can do. God promised from the very beginning to send a redeemer to bring the lost people back to Him. The Lord made good on His promise by sending Jesus into the world. Jesus died on the cross to pay your unpayable debt and bring you back to Him. He will then fill you with His Holy Spirit and transform you into a new creation.

Bless the Lord today because He totally redeems. Praise Him for what He has done for you or pray to Him that He might redeem you today.

8th August
Psalm 103:4b
'Who crowns you with lovingkindness and tender mercies,'
Bless the Lord because He crowns you

Being crowned is like being made a king or queen, a prince or princess; it is a sign of authority bestowed on the person. That authority becomes the possession of the barer of the crown. God has crowned you with His lovingkindness and tender mercies; He has bestowed these priceless gifts upon you. This is not a one-time blessing but a continuous daily blessing - notice David wrote 'crowns' not 'crowned'.

The word translated crown can also be translated surround, and that gives a fuller understanding of His lovingkindness and tender mercies. These attributes of God are an outpouring of His love as they are protective words, encompassing words; but not protective like a wall, as if you are in a prison. No, they are like a womb where a mother loves and protects her unborn child. When God crowns you, He brings you in to His house, the safest place in the universe. God's house isn't a prison of restrictions, it's a safe place to grow, develop and to feed on God's Word.

Only those who have been crowned by God can enter into His protection; they are the redeemed, those who have come to God in humble repentance and have been lifted up to the highest place.

Bless the Lord because He crowns you with lovingkindness and tender mercies.

9th August
Psalm 103:5a
'Who satisfies your mouth with good things,'
Bless the Lord because He satisfies you

Are you satisfied with your life? Or, is your soul starving, desperate for something to eat. I'm not talking about bodily hunger, but spiritual hunger. The hunger that comes from an empty soul. You may have everything this world can offer but be empty inside. You have food on the table, a roof over your head, a good job and yet you are not satisfied.

The world we live in gives many good things, blessings to make our life happy, but it can never fully satisfy. Only the blessings of God can reach to the centre of your being so that you are totally satisfied. There is nothing more than God. The only thing you need more of is Him. Open your spiritual mouth and feed on the Lord. Read His word, pray, bless the Lord, go to church on Sunday, feed daily on the good things from God and He will satisfy you.

There are so many people who appear to have everything, but really have nothing and are empty inside. Bless the Lord who satisfies you and show them the feast that they are missing. Monetary wealth is good, but it never satisfies. God's wealth is better and does satisfy.

Put a smile on your face and be an advert for God's spiritual food that has filled your heart.

10th August
Psalm 103:5b
'So that your youth is renewed like the eagle's.
Bless the Lord because He renews

To say the Lord will renew your life to as it was when you were young, may fill some people with morbid dread. There are those who do not want their youth back; it's gone, in the past. To those people I will tell you that when God renews your youth, He literally renews your past. The past is still the past, but God has redeemed it, He has sanctified it, so that the memory of your youth is no longer hurtful. Only God can reach those areas and renew them. Instead of your youth being a stumbling block, it now has wings to make you fly. Don't let the past hold you down, allow God to renew it.

God's renewing isn't constrained to the past, He wants to renew your life today. A wise friend of mine often comments that 'age is just a number', and she is right. It doesn't matter how old you are in years; some people are old even when they are young and some always have that touch of youth even when they are too frail to walk. God wants all people to be youthful no matter their age, that means you too!

Spend a few minutes meditating on verses 1-5, and then bless the Lord that He does all those things to renew your youth like the eagles. He does it for you.

11th August
Psalm 103:6a
'The Lord executes righteousness... for all who are oppressed.'
Righteousness for the oppressed

The full verse is 'The Lord executes righteousness and justice for all who are oppressed.' We will consider God's justice tomorrow but, for today we will look at how God executes His righteousness for the oppressed.

Firstly, the Lord cares for all those who are oppressed, no matter what. He hates to see men and women pushed down, persecuted and made out to be less than human. However, God is righteous in all He does. He is holy and cannot condone sin. The Lord will reveal His favour to the oppressed and show them the high status of being God's people. The oppressed will gather under His wing and God will contend against the oppressor. In order for those oppressed to receive God's righteousness they must choose to turn from their sinful ways, and when they do, they find freedom in Him. Oppression cannot rock the heart of one who is in Christ, they are no longer pushed down, but pushed up to the highest place.

Pray for the parts of society you see as oppressed. Pray that they would turn to God and receive His righteousness as a shield.

12th August
Psalm 103:6b
'The Lord executes... justice for all who are oppressed.'
Justice for the oppressed

God is not only a God of righteousness, He is also a God of justice. His eyes roam around the world searching out oppression. There are people who are oppressed, pushed down and despised and whether or not you feel they deserve to be in that state is not relevant. God will bring His justice from on High and condemn the oppressor. This does not mean God condones the lifestyle of the oppressed, but it is not for us to allow those people to live in a lowly state.

As I write this Christians around the world are increasingly being oppressed, even to the point of death. Although it has not got to that stage yet at home, those who hold a traditional Christian viewpoint are being oppressed more and more. If God will bring justice for the unbelieving oppressed (and He will), how much more will He bring justice for His own people? The Lord will judge our increasingly secular society, which tolerates anything except Christianity. He will bring justice to His oppressed people, not just here but right across the world.

Keep standing for righteousness, even when that will cause you to be oppressed. The Judge of all the earth will bring justice for you. The kingdoms of men will fall, the Kingdom of God will last forever.

13th August
Psalm 103:7a
'He made known His ways to Moses,'
He revealed Himself

The Lord is unknowable, unfathomable, no-one can work Him out on their own, but He chooses to reveal Himself to us. Moses was nobody special, he was just another child born to the Israelite slaves in Egypt. Not by choice or intelligence he found himself living in the palace being brought up as a prince. He tried to use his princely position and authority to set Israel free, but it all went horribly wrong and the prince was reduced to a shepherd. After 40 years of tending his father-in-law's sheep the Lord appeared to him in the burning bush. We may have a lofty view of Moses, but he was nothing and yet God made known His ways to him. God chose Moses to lead His people out of slavery in Egypt. Moses was God's mouthpiece, but all the wondrous miracles were God's doing. Moses was greatly used of God but only because he had no power of his own.

What is your view of yourself? It may be high, but many people have a very low opinion of themselves. Turn your eyes away from yourself and fix them on Jesus. He has chosen you and is making His ways known to you. He has lifted you up from your lowly state and is making you a prince or princess of the Kingdom, just as He did for Moses.

Bless the Lord for revealing His hidden attributes to you.

14th August
Psalm 103:7b
'His acts to the children of Israel.'
His acts

Not only did God reveal His ways to Moses He also showed His mighty acts to Israel. They were captive slaves in Egypt, who had no power, no strength; there was no way out. They were in an impossible situation; impossible for them, but not for God. The Lord made known to the children of Israel first-hand what He could do. Not only did He bring the people out of Egypt, but He also brought the Ten Plagues to show just how powerful He was. Every step of the way from Egypt to the Promised Land God acted on Israel's behalf, even when they didn't deserve it.

When Peter was arrested in Acts 12, there was no hope of release or escape, so he contented his heart to meet His Lord once more. However, the Lord acted on his behalf, answering the prayers of the saints, and Peter walked out of the prison free to continue the Lord's work.

Do you need the Lord to do the impossible for you? He is able to do just what you need Him to do. Where you have no power, God is all powerful; where you have no strength, God is almighty; where you have no way out, Jesus is the Way. Call on the Name of the Lord in your impossibility and see what only God can do. Remember, although it may be impossible for you it is not impossible for God, He is able.

Bless the Lord for His mighty acts.

15th August
Psalm 103:8a
'The Lord is merciful and gracious,'
Grace and mercy

David knew the primary benefit God gives is His grace and mercy. Grace is God giving us what we don't deserve, and mercy is God not giving us what we do deserve. David then goes on to unpack these wonderful truths for us in the following verses of this psalm. We will linger a for a little while with David in God's grace and mercy.

The reason why God shows us His grace and mercy, even though we do not deserve it, is because that is who He is. As David says, 'The Lord is merciful and gracious.' God cannot help being merciful; He is merciful by nature and His desire is to show mercy to all mankind and to a limited extent He does. We, as sinful people, should all die before God, with no good things at all, but God shows mercy by providing for the unrighteous as well as the righteous. Grace is different, grace goes further, and God can only give grace to His righteous people. He has poured out His Spirit on us and opened up the way to live with Him eternally. This is grace, we do not deserve these things, but God gives them generously.

Bless the Lord today for His abundant grace and mercy.

16th August
Psalm 103:8b
'Slow to anger,'
Slow to anger

I'll get this out the way right now. By saying the Lord is slow to anger implies He will eventually get angry with us. David explores this in verse 9 of the psalm and we will do the same; for now, we will continue with God's great grace and mercy.

God sees what we do as individuals, communities, nations and across the world and He is stirred in His heart. How far have we fallen from God's perfect Way? How many not only reject Him but speak disrespectfully against the King of kings? God has every right to destroy us all and yet He hasn't. God waited about fifteen hundred years before He brought the Flood and wiped out everything except Noah, his family and the animals on the Ark. He has held back His righteous anger ever since and has even sent His Son to make a way back to Him avoiding His ultimate wrath altogether.

God is slow to anger; this does not mean that nations will get away with their atrocities, neither will you get away with your sinning. Rejoice that God is not angry with you and repent on bended knee before your merciful God.

Bless the Lord today because He is slow to anger.

17th August
Psalm 103:8c
'and abounding in mercy.'
An abundance of mercy
The Lord has mercy to spare!

God is not about to run out of mercy. His patience may run out with us and His anger, one day may overflow, but He will always be merciful. When you sin, don't hide yourself in fear but rather get up and come to the Lord who will forgive. Our God has plenty of mercy to go around; He has enough for you. Don't say, 'I have gone too far this time, He will never accept me back.' This is not true; God's mercy will not run out. He is waiting for you to return to Him in repentance and when you do, He is ready to draw from His storehouse of mercy towards you.

There is no end to God's mercy. He will give it to any who will call on Him in truth (Psalm 145:18). Go on try Him, He is a merciful God, He will not reject you. Don't judge God on what we humans are like. We are often anything but merciful. We do and say things that are unkind and unforgiving, but God is not like that at all, He loves you and pours out His mercy on you. You may have strayed far from God, but you can never wander outside His abounding mercy. Kneel before Him today and receive this wondrous gift of mercy.

Bless the Lord for He abounds in mercy.

18th August
Psalm 103:9a
'He will not always strive with us,'
A warning

Over the past few days we have been thinking about God's abundant grace and mercy that He lavishly pours out on us. The danger of this is that we can begin to take these gifts for granted and become lazy and heedless of God's anger. Here is the warning: God is slow to anger, but He will not always strive with us. There will be a time when God will not hold back His anger anymore. We may look at nations (even our own nation) and wonder how long will God wait before He brings His righteous indignation against that country, but this is personal; David points to *us*, God's people, and says, 'He will not always strive with us.'

Take time today to look at your life and see if you have let any habits or attitudes slip in. Is there any worldliness you indulge in, does your way of life honour God? He is patient with us, and His mercy and grace are boundless. There will be a time when, although His mercy and grace will not have run out, they may not be immediately available to us. We have an opportunity to repent of our sins before God. Take that opportunity today, you do not know how long it will be there.

This is a psalm of praises to God, so bless the Lord that He does strive with us, putting up with our human weaknesses.

19th August
Psalm 103:9b
'Nor will He keep His anger forever.'
God's righteous anger

The fact that God is 'slow to anger' implies that He does eventually get angry. It is not wise to continually test God, pushing Him to His limits. There will be a day when God runs out of patience with us and He will no longer be able to keep back His righteous anger from us.

There is hope; you are reading this today and God is merciful and gracious. Bow before Him in repentance, confessing your sins. God's anger should be a reminder to walk in His ways and to repent when you stray. It should not be a trigger to run and hide as Adam did in the garden. Don't run from God, face Him humbly even if He has reached the place of discipline. It takes a lot for God to move with indignation in an individual's life and if there is any remorse God sees it. God's righteous anger is reserved for those who do not care that they offend God; God's discipline is shown to us who seek to follow Him in our human frailty.

Pray that God would fill you with His Holy Spirit to lead and guide you each day; He will direct your paths to holiness and away from God's anger.

Praise God today that He is holy and that He will not stand by while His Name is blasphemed. Bless the Lord also, that He has made a way of escape for those who trust in Him.

20th August
Psalm 103:10a
'He has not dealt with us according to our sins,'
The wages of sin
The wages of sin is death (Romans 6:23a), but God has not given out our just reward for our actions, no He has given us life (Romans 6:23b). What more is there to say?

The truth is we all die eventually. It is the inevitable end of everyone. From the richest king to the poorest slave, all die. Since Adam sinned in the garden, all his descendants have died, but today we are alive; God has not dealt with us according to our sins. The Lord has every right to wipe us all out, as He did in Noah's time, but He doesn't. Death is the inevitable end, but God has given you life right now! Take a breath and praise God for His gift of life to you.

If the wages of sin is death, then the free gift from God is Eternal Life is Jesus. He has not dealt with us according to our sins but made a way for us to live forever with Him. He has given you Eternal Life; that life starts the day you refuse your wages and accept God's gift. Christians are living Eternal Life right now. Our bodies wear out, but our life goes on forever with Jesus.

Bless the Lord that He has given you Eternal Life as a free gift, and that starts today.

21st August

Psalm 103:10b

'Nor punished us according to our iniquities.'

Amazing forgiveness

This is amazing! The righteous Judge of the whole world has chosen to forgive us and let us go free! We have all sinned, we have committed iniquities that deserve God's punishment. Fear is the first punishment that comes from sin. When Adam sinned, even before God punished him, he feared what God would do. God did not punish Adam according to his iniquities, yes, he would die, yes, he was cast out of the Garden, but the Lord clothed him and made a way of salvation for Adam and his descendants. Put fear aside; we who are covered by the Blood of the Lamb are forgiven and can be forgiven for all our iniquities. We can walk boldly, yet humbly, into God's holy presence and repent before Him and He will forgive.

We are human, and all humans sin, this is not an excuse and God does not let us off because we are human. God will punish people according to their iniquities, but he will not punish us who are saved by Jesus' sacrifice on the Cross and covered by His righteousness. David didn't know the joy of the assurance of Jesus living in him, and yet he understood that God didn't treat him as he deserved. If God could forgive David, before the Cross, he can forgive you today. Don't live in the fear of God's punishment, live in the joy of His forgiveness.

Bless the Lord that he has not punished us according to our iniquities.

22nd August
Psalm 103:11a
'For as the heavens are high above the earth,'
How high are the heavens?

This verse compares God's mercy toward us with the height of the heavens above the earth. By heavens David was referring to space, where the stars are. So, how high are the heavens? How far does space reach? These are questions that science tries to answer, and it can be breath-taking when we see the numbers; but for David and for us the actual distance that the heavens reach is not relevant; all we need to know is it is huge.

David was not trying to quantify mercy, on the contrary he was implying that God's mercy is immeasurable. As David looked up into the night sky he could see no end of the stars, and yet he was only seeing a tiny fraction of the universe. Today, as people look further and further out, they find there is always a bit more to see. No matter how far you peer through a telescope you will never reach the end of the universe. Whether or not it is infinite is not in the scope of this devotion, but the universe is vast, beyond all human understanding. Keep these things in mind as we go on to the second part of the verse and consider God's mercy which just may well be infinite.

Bless the Lord who has created the whole of the universe and holds it together in His hands.

23rd August

Psalm 103:11b

'So great is His mercy toward those who fear Him;'

How vast is His mercy?

David compared God's mercy to the height of the heavens. How high does space go? No-one knows for sure, but it is big! God's mercy is like that, we can't measure it in any quantifiable way. It can't be weighed on a scale or measured in distance. As we experience God's mercy for ourselves, we find each time we think we must have reached the end there is in fact much more left for Him to give. God is truly mercy-full.

This begs the question, "If God's mercy is so vast that it has no end, can we just go on sinning because God's mercy is always enough?" In the words of Paul, 'Certainly not!' Paul asked this question when discussing God's grace and concludes by saying, 'How can we who died to sin live any longer in it?' Romans 6:2.

Although God's mercy and grace abound toward us and He is always ready to forgive, we shouldn't use this as an excuse to sin. On the contrary, we should look to God's grace and mercy and use it as a catalyst to live a more holy life. God's mercy, as far as we can tell, is limitless, so live in the wonder of that every day. God has mercy enough for you and anything you may have done.

Bless the Lord for the vastness of His mercy and His endless grace towards us.

24th August

Psalm 103:12a

'As far as the east is from the west,'

How far is the east from the west?

How far is the east from the west? This is an important question because it is how far God has removed our transgressions from us. So, how far is it?

It is not about the so-called East and West; these have a definite geological place where they meet. No, the better answer is more profound. Imagine leaving your house and walking due north, if you were to keep on walking in that direction you would eventually find yourself walking south; and if you carried on walking, you'd be going north again. Now, imagine leaving your house, but this time walking due east. It wouldn't matter how far you walked, as long as you always faced in the same direction, you would never be walking west. There is an infinity between east and west, as long as you don't turn around you will never go from one to the other.

So, the answer to that question, how far is the east from the west? It is an infinite distance. Just to be clear, when God removes your transgressions from you, they are not just behind you waiting for you to turn around, they are mindbogglingly far away from you. You do not have to beat yourself up about your mistakes and wrongdoings, God has forgiven you and thrown them an infinite distance from you. Smile, you are forgiven.

Bless the Lord, who is the God of the infinite.

25th August
Psalm 103:12b
'So far has He removed our transgressions from us.'
How far has He removed our transgressions from us?

This question was answered yesterday; our transgressions have been removed an infinite distance away from us. They are no longer a shadow over us; we are free. As soon as God forgave you your sins and welcomed you into His family, He took your sins and transgressions and removed them from His sight. God is the judge of the whole world and He sees and knows everything we have ever done, everything we are doing and everything we will do. They are always before His eyes. When God removes our transgressions from us, He must put them somewhere away from His gaze. God sees everything everywhere. There is nowhere His gaze does not rest, so to put our transgressions out of His eyeline is an impossibility only God can accomplish. If God has taken your sins and placed them outside His gaze they must be in a place beyond infinity!

This is poetic language because of course there can be nothing *beyond* infinity. What David is saying is that God chooses to take your sins and put them out of His sight. He chooses not to see them; instead He sees the righteousness of Christ in you. Why do you always look back at the wrongs you have done? If God has put it out of His mind, isn't it time you did the same?

Bless God, because He has removed your transgressions from you and placed them an unimaginably far distance away.

26th August
Psalm 103:13a
'As a father pities his children,'
What does pity mean?

When I think of pity, I imagine a proud rich man looking down at the poor and pitying their lot, but not doing anything. Is pity a prideful emotion? If not, what is it?

I looked up pity before writing anything, so that I would have a better understanding of what it is. Pity is not proud, it is humble and loving, looking upon the needy and acting on it. It is very much like a godly father caring for his children. He looks at their needs and struggles and cares for them right where they are. He comes down to their level and lifts them up. When I look at my children and what they go through and think of what is up ahead, I don't pity them like the rich man looking down on the poor. I pity them, with all the true definition of that word, love, compassion, care, help. These are action words. Pity should never be passive, it is always ready to come to the aid of others.

This verse compares God's pity with a father's pity. So, to understand God we must understand pity. Never compare God to the lowest form of fatherhood; all us fathers make mistakes, some more than others. Compare God to the best attributes of fathers and father figures you know and then times that by the biggest number you can think of. God cares for you more than any earthly father ever could.

Bless the Lord for godly fathers who have shown us love and compassion when we needed it the most, and have become our own role-models in life.

27th August
Psalm 103:13b
'So the Lord pities those who fear Him.'
What sort of Father is God?

The Lord pities us just like a father pities his children. God looks at us and His heart is moved. Never think of the Lord as heartless and cruel. He is compassionate and kind, He loves and cares for us, always looking for anyway He can help and lift us up.

As a father I try to help my children as they go through life. Although the world is different now to when I was their age, I can still see the same basic needs. I do my best to help and reassure them, but I can never truly understand what they are going through. God has that advantage over me, He knows us inside-out. He knows what you are going through right now: the uncertainties, the dilemmas, the mistakes and sins, the fear. God see and knows all these things and more. The Lord is not a passive observer, He is an active participant and He is working out His plan for you right now. Hold on, the Lord knows.

As I write this the whole world is facing uncertain times, everything has changed overnight; everything except God. He is the same, He was not taken by surprise and His Father heart goes out to all who fear Him. He has a plan when governments are in disarray.

Trust Him.

Bless the Lord for His Father heart, He loves and cares for you.

28th August
Psalm 103:14a
'For He knows our frame;'
He knows you

Are you fearful? Do you worry day and night what will happen? Does death loom large in your thoughts? The truth is you do not need to be afraid because God knows you; He knows you inside and out. In Luke 12 Jesus said He knows the number of hairs on your head. He also said, you have value in His eyes (verse 7). Jesus went on to say you do not need to worry about food, drink or clothing, God knows you need these things; trust Him.

God knows you. He knows your ailments and weaknesses. He knows your underlying health problem, that no-one else knows. He knows that I have Neurofibromatosis 1 and the issues that causes me. He knows. You do not need to be afraid. The God who made you knows how your body works and He also knows how your mind works. He will never put upon you anything that you cannot handle with Him by your side. Take a moment to consider if you really trust Jesus with your current situation. Now let go of that fear and anxiety and rest in the knowledge that God knows you. The road ahead may be hard, beyond my imaginings, and tougher than you can bear, but God is with you in it all and you will not bear it alone.

Bless the Lord today because He knows your frame.

29th August
Psalm 103:14b
'He remembers that we are dust.'
He remembers what we are

What does it mean that 'He remembers that we are dust.'? There certainly is the idea that God remembers our frame, that we are fragile and in need of His care. He remembers we are small.

There is a greater thought here also; a high, lofty grandeur in these words. God remembers we are dust because that is the substance He used to create us. We were made by God's hands and for His purposes. We, however, are not just 'walking dust', if we read Genesis 2:7, we will see just how much more than dust we are, 'And the Lord God formed man of the dust of the ground, and breathed into his nostrils the breath of life; and man became a living being.' We are special because God has breathed life into us; He has given us life and purpose and that life and purpose finds it's fulfilment in Christ.

Yes, the Lord remembers you are dust, but in doing so He also remembers that He gave you life and your life is wrapped up in Him. He knows you, because He made you, He fused every atom of your body together. Always remember you are precious in His sight.

Bless the Lord your Creator, for He remembers you are dust and that He personally breathed life into you. Your life is safe with Him.

30th August
Psalm 103:15a
'As for man, his days are like grass;'
Days like grass

God remembers that we are dust, made alive by His life-giving breath. The question is do we remember how fragile we are?

Our days are like the grass, spread out before us. As we gaze across the meadow of our life it can seem endless, but it is not. At any moment the grass can be destroyed. It may be blighted by famine; or washed away in a flood; or trodden down under foot. Our lives are much like that, an unexpected event can end our lives at any time. This can make us fearful, petrified, unable to move or do anything in case we die. We do not need to be afraid; God is with us and He knows our frame. He knows our lives are like tender grass, that can break at any time, this is why He has made a way of Salvation. We may not be promised tomorrow, but we are promised Eternal Life with Jesus.

Do not fret over what happens in this life but set your mind on things above. God is with you and He will lead and guide you every day of your life, and at the end He will be there to welcome you Home.

Bless the Lord, because He is gentle with us and walks with us every step of the way.

31st August
Psalm 103:15b
'As a flower of the field, so he flourishes.'
Flourishing like a flower

This section of the psalm is about the frailty and mortality of man, however, there is something else to notice. David said we flourish like a flower of the field. The word he uses means to blossom, to shine, to gleam; all these words point to the glory of humanity. We may not live forever here on earth, but there is a dignity in mankind that is like a wildflower. If, like me, you are not the most green-fingered person around, you will have noticed that weeds are much easier to grow that cultivated plants; they will grow almost anywhere. The flowers of the field are hardy and strong. Being compared to a flower is not a bad thing it is a compliment. We are strong, we shine out the glory of God every day of our lives.

Being called a 'weed' is usually thought of as a derogatory term, but no, it is a great compliment of your strength and beauty - you are a beautiful flower in the field of God, and nothing will stop the spreading of the seed of God in you. Plants can buckle and crack concrete allowing them to grow through and God will give you the strength to push through any difficulty in order to display His glory through you to all those around.

Bless the Lord today by simply being a flower in His garden.

1st September
Psalm 103:16
'For the wind passes over it, and it is gone, And its place remembers it no more.'
Fades like a flower
Yesterday, we saw how we flourish like a flower when the glory of God shines out of us. Today, we see that our life is so short, it is over in the blink of an eye. The flourishing of the flower is destroyed by the wind blowing over it, and our youthful flourish fades as the years pass by. Over and against the thousands of years the earth has been here our lives are miniscule, we do not have a lot of time. This is all the more reason to get our lives right before God today.

We may be the centre of attention today and forgotten about tomorrow. Time moves ever onwards. Take this opportunity to pray and confess your sins before God. Don't be obsessed with being remembered by the World, but always desire to be remembered by God. Be like the thief on the cross next to Jesus and cry out, 'Lord, remember me!' The Lord will reply, 'Assuredly, I say to you, ...you will be with Me in Paradise.'

Remember the Lord every day of your life, put Him first in all you do, and He will remember you when the World forgets.

Bless the Lord, He is the One who will remember you for all Eternity.

2nd September
Psalm 103:17a
'But the mercy of the Lord is from everlasting to everlasting on those who fear Him,'
Everlasting mercy

God knows you are dust, He understands that you are mortal, but He also knows you have an eternal spirit that will live on forever. You need to know the God whose mercy is not constrained to this life, but rather is from everlasting to everlasting. Remember who God is and live your life in the light of that knowledge. Do not fear what the World might do; do not fear death; fear the Lord who is forever merciful to those who fear Him.

There is a fear and respect we should have for the Lord. He is the King of kings and we should approach Him in reverence. He has opened His gates to us and invites us to come in to His Throne Room and dwell with Him; this is a great privilege we have been given, but do not take it for granted. Always remember He is the Lord. There is a great balancing act between remembering His holiness and remembering His mercy, but we must hold both of these in our hearts and minds. He is forever merciful but on those who fear Him.

There is a danger we can become over familiar with God. He is, after all, our Friend and Saviour. Always approach Him with reverence and fear in the clear knowledge that He is merciful not just now, but forever.

Bless the Lord for His mercy is from everlasting to everlasting.

3rd September
Psalm 103:17b
'And His righteousness to children's children,'
God's righteousness from one generation to the next

There are caveats to this statement, and we will look at them over the next couple of days, but for today we will look at God's righteousness being passed from one generation to the next.

It can appear that God's righteousness is not getting passed down as it should. There is a feeling that as one generation passes to the next so God's righteousness is not so much passed down, but rather watered down. Do you feel like this? There have been times more barren than now, and yet God's righteousness was still passed on.

It can be hard to communicate God's love in today's society, when Christian values are not held as highly as they once were and many other voices drown out the 'still, small voice' of God. Do you honestly think God is thwarted by these things? He is able to pass His righteousness on, so that our children's children will worship Him in Spirit and in truth and their children's children will worship Him too. We need not fear, the future of Christianity is in safe Hands; not our feeble hands, but God's Almighty Hands.

Bless the Lord today because He will pass on His righteousness from one generation to the next, and He will use us to help Him do it.

4th September

Psalm 103:18a

'To such as keep His covenant,'

Keep the covenant

The eternal righteousness of God is reserved for those who keep the covenant. A covenant is a legal contract or treaty between two people; in this case it is between God and you. All biblical covenants were ratified or signed off by blood; a sacrifice had to be made, then the two parties were legally bound, often with an exchange of names. Father God sent Jesus to this world to die on the Cross as the sign of the covenant. His blood made the covenant binding. There was then a change of names. Jesus became the Son of Man, and you became the son or daughter of God.

Jesus promised to forgive all your sins and make you righteous and ready for Heaven. The Lord said He would never leave you or forsake you and would fill you with the Holy Spirit of Power. There are many more promises God has made, and He has kept every one; have you kept your side of the covenant? There are many promise you have made to God, whether you realise it or not; by saying 'yes' to Jesus you have signed the covenant and ought to be keeping it. This means putting Christ first in your life, reading the Bible and praying. We are to live holy lives. Choose today to keep the covenant.

Bless the Lord that He always keeps His side of the covenant and always will.

5th September

Psalm 103:18b

'And to those who remember His commandments to do them.'

Not just about remembering

Many Christians today do not like the idea of 'commandments'. We are free, they say, and therefore not under compulsion. It is no wonder many Christians do not know the Ten Commandments as found in Exodus 20. You may not be able to remember them, but can you remember the two succinct commandments Jesus gave us? Jesus said, "'you shall love the Lord your God with all your heart, with all your soul, with all your mind, and with all your strength.' This is the first commandment. And the second, like it, is this: 'You shall love your neighbour as yourself.' There is no other commandment greater than these." Mark 12:30-31. I'm not going to ask you to remember the Ten Commandments, but do remember these two commandments; commit these verses to memory.

According to David, remembering commandments is not enough, you have to *do* them. Each morning remind yourself to love the Lord with all your heart, soul, mind and strength and your neighbour as yourself and then live like it. There will always be people who *know* the scriptures better than you, but emulate those who *live* by them. It's not just about remembering facts, it's about living humbly before God and the people you meet.

Bless the Lord, that He has not given you rules to remember but a glorious life to lead.

6th September

Psalm 103:19a

'The Lord has established His throne in heaven,'

The Lord's throne is established in Heaven

Today let us take a step back from looking at our lives and the world around us in despair and meditate on the truth that God's throne is established forever. God Himself has established it. He is God Almighty and when He establishes something it remains established. We do not need to be afraid or alarmed at the news of the day, God is in control, He is over all. Turn to Him and smile in confidence. God has not gone away. He is ever near and always watchful; He knows.

I do not know what you are going through as you read this, but I do know the God who sits on His Eternal throne and judges. He sees you, turn to Him in your distress and He will establish you. His throne is built on an unmovable Rock, and there is room enough for you on that Rock too. Take this opportunity to rest in the Lord; pour out your heart to Him and leave your troubles at His feet. God is over all and He has won the victory over sin and death. There will never be a day when God is ousted from His throne. He is totally established and you can rely on Him always being there.

Bless the Lord for He has established His throne forever.

7th September
Psalm 103:19b
'And His kingdom rules over all.'
His Kingdom is over all

Following on from yesterday, we do not need to be afraid. God's Kingdom rules over all other kingdoms; He is the King of kings. This may cause us to say, 'If God is in control, why does He allow all this suffering to happen?' There is no easy answer to this, however, God has given us all freewill and we can choose to do what is right or what is wrong. God, the King, has set out His rules and anyone who disobeys will be judged, if not in this life then in the one to come.

The kingdom of Satan rules over the World and we can see that in the sinful decisions governments make. God's Kingdom rules over Satan's, and time and again God intervenes to bring His purposes to pass. We can read about some of these in the pages of scripture: Judges, Job, Esther, David, Acts to name but a few. Esther is a great example of how God rules over all; Haman hated the Jews and plotted to have them all killed, he tricked the king into signing a law that could not be broken. There was no hope for the Jews, even the king could not countermand this law. The Lord had already put His master plan in place by making Esther Queen and when the time was right, He moved and the Jews were saved. Not even the law of the Medes and Persians could stop God.

Bless the Lord because His Kingdom reigns over all.

8th September
Psalm 103:20a
'Bless the Lord, you His angels,'
Tell the angels to bless the Lord

Angels are the messengers of God; they go out and tell us what God has said. The angels stand round the throne of God constantly praising and ever ready to do His Will. Who then is David to tell them to 'bless the Lord'?!

This is David's exuberance bubbling over. He has been giving reason after reason why we should bless the Lord and now at the end of the psalm he is encouraging everyone and everything to bless the Lord. Yes, this is over the top, exuberant and yes, he doesn't need to encourage the holy angels to bless the Lord, but his joy is so overwhelming that his desire is that all of God's creation would feel the same.

The angles bless the Lord in word and deed; they love to praise Him and love to serve Him. Nothing can stand in the way of their mission. Just think of the angel dispatched to comfort and answer Daniel. He was held up by the forces of evil, but he would not back down and with Michael's help the message got through. We can learn much from the angels. Choose today to do the Lord's will no matter what obstacle may be in your path.

Bless the Lord with the exuberance of David.

9th September
Psalm 103:20b
'Who excel in strength, who do His word, Heeding the voice of His word.'
Bless God like the angels

The angels David encourages to bless the Lord excel in strength, do God's word and heed the voice of His word. These angels are able to bless the Lord because of their attitude. The excellent strength of the angels is rooted in God, they derive their power from Him, just as we do. Notice how they do not merely obey commands like robots, they heed God's voice and live by the word. The angels bless God because through their God given strength, they are not only hearers of the word but also doers and they are not only doers of the word but hearers. They listen to the voice of God and allow it to penetrate to the centre of their beings and only then do they do it.

If we are to bless the Lord with our lives, we should act like the angels. When you hear a word of the Lord that is personal to you, a word of direction or command, take a moment to let it enter your heart and change you; heed the voice. It is only when the word of God has changed you on the inside that you will be ready to carry out that word in the strength of God. May that process be swift.

Bless the Lord, who has given us holy examples in the angels.

10th September
Psalm 103:21a
'Bless the Lord, all you His hosts,'
Bless the Lord with the Angels

If David in his exuberance crossed the line by telling the angles to bless the Lord, he totally left the line miles behind by saying to the hosts of heaven, 'bless the Lord'! The hosts are the army angels of God, they are the warriors that go out and fight for God's Kingdom. They are the top rung of the angels and David shouts to them, 'Bless the Lord, all you His hosts!'

Of course, they bless the Lord all day and all night and David knew that. It wasn't that they were not blessing the Lord, but rather he wanted to join in with them in their joyous shout. Is that your heart's desire, to bless the Lord along with the hosts of Heaven? The door is open, and they are waiting for you to join with them. I sometimes wonder if they look at each other and shrug asking, 'Why are God's people not joining in? Why are they so quiet?' David was not quiet as he exuded joy and praise even when he was in the darkest place. Come on, throw off the shackles of restraint and stand shoulder to shoulder with the hosts of heaven and encourage them to bless the Lord.

Bless the Lord that we can encourage the armies of Heaven to bless too.

11th September
Psalm 103:21b
'You ministers of His, who do His pleasure.'
Ministers who do His pleasure

When calling on the hosts of Heaven to bless the Lord he called them 'ministers', but what does that mean? We hear a lot about minsters, both in the church and in politics, but it is not always clear what is meant by that. The word minister in the Bible is the same as servant - a minister is a servant. If a minister is not a servant, they are not a minister. If the hosts of Heaven serve why don't we? The hosts of Heaven are the armies of God, the most powerful angels and yet they bow the knee daily to God and do nothing on their own volition but only do His pleasure.

This is a shout out to any who call themselves Ministers of God that are reading this, are you a servant or are you a master? Do you have a servant's heart, or do you crave power over others? Take a moment to consider these things. Now, regardless of where you think you stand in God's Kingdom, bow the knee and seek to do His pleasure, as the heavenly hosts do. We are all servants of God and therefore all ministers. Live like a servant waiting on God's every word and then fulfil it for His pleasure and blessing.

Bless the Lord, you His ministers.

12th September
Psalm 103:22a
'Bless the Lord, all His works, In all places of His dominion.'
Everything everywhere

David has called on the angels to bless the Lord and he then turned to the armies of God to give their praise. He now turns to everything else, 'Bless the Lord, all His works, in all places of His dominion.' or, to put it another way, 'Let everything that has breath praise the Lord.' Psalm 150:6.

Read Psalm 103 again and remind yourself of why you should bless the Lord. You can bless the Lord as the great king David has encouraged you to. You are part of the 'all His works', you are included. Others may exclude you, but God has included you and made you His servant. Listen to Him, humble yourself and do as He commands, even if that is contrary to what you want. If the hosts of Heaven bow, then so should you and I. Is there any area in which you are stubbornly proud, where you will not yield to God? That area, however small, will prevent you from blessing the Lord as He deserves. He has done everything for you, surely you can do the same for Him?

Okay, now get off your knees, stand up with your hands raised high and bless the Lord with all your might. You are not praising God alone but joining in with the heavenly choirs and every believer on the planet; not to mention the animals, the birds, the sea creatures and all the heavenly bodies that fill the gulf of space.

Bless the Lord, you are not alone in doing so.

13th September
Psalm 103:22b
'Bless the Lord, O my soul!'
Back to the beginning?

This has been a long journey through this psalm. David began by trying to convince himself to bless the Lord and now at the end he says the exact same thing, 'Bless the Lord, O my soul!' Has he gone back to the beginning? Has he learned nothing?

The truth is David has come a long way since the opening verse of this psalm. At the beginning it was a statement of intent. He desperately wanted to bless the Lord but his circumstances were standing in the way. Now he has risen above whatever was happening to him at that time and is able to tell himself to bless the Lord with the same exuberance as he called on the angels, the hosts of heaven and everything else so to do. David has made the breakthrough and is able to bless the Lord from the depth of his soul.

What about you, are you back at the beginning or are you now in a new place, where you can bless the Lord with exuberant joy. As we have travelled through this psalm, we have ended each devotion with a reason to bless the Lord taken from the part of the psalm we were looking at. Today I leave that open to you: start with David's words, 'Bless the Lord, O my soul!' and then fill the air with your personal praises to God.

14th September
Psalm 51:1a
'Have mercy upon me, O God, according to Your lovingkindness'
Have mercy on me!

This psalm David sang to the Lord after his sins were revealed to him by the prophet Nathan. Not that he wasn't well aware of them before, but now he was faced with them. This psalm is a prayer of repentance by a man who is absolutely sorry for the terrible things he has done.

David was the king of Israel. God raised him up and gave him the throne of Saul because David's heart was inclined to the Lord. David did many great things but failed totally in one. In the incident with Bathsheba David broke most, if not all, of the Ten Commandments in one go. He thought, as king, he could do as he pleased and so made himself above God; God should be first. He coveted another man's wife, he committed adultery with her, he lied about it, and he murdered her husband. I dare say, all this dishonoured his father and mother. He couldn't get much lower.

You may not have sinned as David did, but do you feel crushed by your actions? When David said, 'Have mercy on me', he was placing himself as a worm, a nothing; helpless and hopeless. If that is how you feel about your sins cry out to God, as David did, according to His lovingkindness; His goodness. God's goodness is contrasted with David's sin, and he relied on God's greater goodness to eclipse his sin. God forgave David, and He will forgive you if you will humble yourself before Him.

15th September
Psalm 51:1b
'According to the multitude of Your tender mercies, blot out my transgressions.'
Erase my sins from Your book

You don't need to bring your sins to mind; if you are truly repentant, they will be front and centre. They are also front and centre in God's mind too. Your transgression is written on the pages of your life that is ever before the Judge of the Universe. David begged God to 'blot out' his transgressions, to erase them from his copybook so that they would not be held against Him. David didn't say, 'Blot out my transgressions because of all the other good things I have done!' It is quite clear from this psalm that is not how David saw himself. No, David prayed, 'According to the multitude of Your tender mercies, blot out my transgressions.' The word translated 'mercies' means compassion, in the sense a mother has compassion on her children, even before they are born.

God's mercies are tender, loving and without end. They are not unconditional, in the sense that we have to be in the right place to receive them, but they have no end and can save even the most wayward soul.

There is nothing you can do, or have done to deserve your sins being erased, but God will do it according the multitude of His tender mercies.

16th September
Psalm 51:2a
'Wash me thoroughly from my iniquity'
A thorough wash

Sin of any kind makes us unclean; dirty, smelly, unhygienic. You may feel like that today, unclean, and however hard you try you just can't get it off. Everything you do reminds you of the stench and everywhere you go people look at you as if they know - whether they do or not makes no difference. You can go to the doctor and she may prescribe a drug to lessen the feelings of disgust. You may go to a therapist and he may help you think differently about yourself. There are many options out there, but they are all useless at getting to the root cause; they cannot cleanse you and remove the stain of sin.

Turn to the Lord, your Heavenly Father, and ask Him to bathe you in the waters of cleansing. He will wash you thoroughly, inside and out, washing away your iniquity. Your sins will be flushed down the drain forever, never again will they cling to you and make you feel dirty.

It is easy to turn to human answers, everyone is talking about them and lauding them, but they cannot wash your sin away. Be careful you do not place well-meaning help before God's help.

If you are repentant you need a thorough wash.

17th September
Psalm 51:2b
'And cleanse me from my sin.'
A spiritual cleanser

Last time the thought was of washing, this time it is about cleansing. A cleanser is used to clean deeply into the skin, often right into the pores where grease and grime can accumulate. The Lord uses His cleanser in much the same way; He cleanses our spirits right into the pores. Spiritual pores are the places we often forget about, but overtime they get the grit of self-righteousness and the grease of pride lodged in them. It is here sins are conceived and it is not long before full grown sins are born and will need washing away. Before that can happen the Lord desires to cleanse you from sin.

Don't be content with the Lord's thorough wash, even though it is better than anything else you can get. Allow God to cleanse your soul deeply, it may hurt, cleansers can be rough, but the result will be worth it. It is our responsibility to keep our spiritual pores clean by coming daily to God.

There is one more amazing truth that comes from the word translated 'cleansing', and that is the Lord pronounces us clean. Your conscience will no longer accuse you. If God say's you are clean you are clean indeed.

18th September
Psalm 51:3a
'For I acknowledge my transgressions'
Don't live in denial

David said, 'I acknowledge my transgression'. He tried to cover up his sins, but this just made things worse. He lived in denial, until Nathan challenged him over his actions, and then he bowed the knee to God and fully acknowledged his sin. It was only at this point David opened his heart and sang the words of this psalm. This is one of the key elements in this psalm of repentance.

What about your sin? Are you living in denial, thinking it's not that bad, or others do worse things, or as long as nobody gets hurt, or it's okay if no-one knows? These lies hide the awful truth from yourself but never from God. You can deceive yourself, living a life of denial, but you can't deceive the God who sees everything. You know the sin that you try to cover up, but do you acknowledge it? Kneel before your Father in Heaven and open your heart to Him, be honest with yourself and Him. There may need to be confession and restitution made, but the first step is to acknowledge your transgression before the Holy God. Everything we have covered so far, and everything left in this Psalm hangs on this. If you are truly repentant and desire forgiveness you must prayerfully acknowledge the wrongs you have done. Be honest with yourself, uncover the sin and lay it bare before yourself. Be honest with God, tell Him everything; He already knows anyway. Once you have done this you are ready for cleansing.

19th September
Psalm 51:3b
'And my sin is always before me.'
Nowhere to run

Try as he might David could not get away from the terrible things he had done. He tried to cover them up, but they just kept breaking out. Yesterday we saw how important acknowledging your sins is and this time we shall consider the damage of not dealing with them.

David said, 'my sin is always before me.' He remembered his actions day and night; his life was tormented by what he had done. He knew there was nothing he could do to undo his transgression and so the memory of them haunted him. There are things we have done that cannot be rectified and these can haunt us day and night, causing anxiety and depression. Thoughts of the past on constant repeat, even in your dreams. The sins are too great, nothing can be done. No, wait, there is an answer: Jesus' blood can make the worst offender clean. The Lord forgave David his trespass and restored his soul and He wants to do the same for you. Cry out to God in your distress, tell Him your affliction and be honest with the root cause. Prayerfully allow God to restore your soul as He did for David.

You are not alone; everyone is a sinner needing the restoring work of grace. It doesn't matter how big or small your sin is, God is able to deal with it and renew your mind (Romans 12:2) so your constant thoughts will be on the goodness of God.

20th September

Psalm 51:4a

'Against You, You only, have I sinned, And done this evil in Your sight'

Remember who you have offended

David had committed adultery with another man's wife, got her pregnant, lied and schemed to cover it up and then arranged to have that man killed in battle. His trespass was against Uriah and Bathsheba in the sense he had wronged them, but ultimately he had sinned against God. David's offence was before God, the God who sees all saw and knew what David had done. The king's high-handed behaviour was an offence to the Lord who had raised him up to the place of honour.

There are people you have hurt and upset by your actions and words. There is no getting out of it, and some restitution may be needed, but you have offended God. The Lord, your Heavenly Father has raised you up to be royalty, a prince or princess in the family of Jesus. Your trespasses and sins were seen by God and you have dishonoured his name. Your sin is against Him and Him alone because He is the King of the whole world and His Law has been broken.

Don't be cast down, there is hope. If you are truly repentant and sorry for your actions, kneel before God, lift up your head and say, 'Against You, You only, have I sinned, and done this evil in Your sight. I come before you in humble repentance and turn from my sinful ways. Forgive me, my Father.'

21st September
Psalm 51:4b
'That You may be found just when You speak, And blameless when You judge.'
The Just Judge

We now get the setting of the psalm: David is in the dock and God is the Judge. David is pleading with the Judge for forgiveness. It is not, '*will* God forgive' but, '*can* God forgive.' If God is the Just Judge He must judge justly and proclaim the same judgements every time, otherwise we will never know what He might say or do. God is the Just Judge and He does judge justly every time.

Many people brashly state, 'only God can judge me!' and so they continue in their transgressions and God will judge them for their arrogant disregard of His Laws. David understood how to approach the Judge. He knew the Lord, he knew that a broken and contrite heart He would not despise (Psalm 51:17). It is only by being open and honest with the Lord and coming in repentance before Him that the Just Judge can justly judge favourably towards you.

Not even God is above His Moral Law. He cannot turn a blind eye to your sins because He must judge them justly, or else there is no justice. Salvation in Jesus is written into the Law and by coming humbly before Him and acknowledging that God is your Judge and you are deserving of death, you can seek forgiveness and restoration. Repent before Him and the Just Judge, who sees your heart, will proclaim you innocent and let you go free.

22nd September
Psalm 51:5a
'Behold, I was brought forth in iniquity'
Born that way

You don't need to be around young children for long to see that they instinctively misbehave. No-one needs to teach a child to do wrong, it comes very naturally to them. David knew this and looking back over his life he could see from his earliest memories he had sinned. He was born in iniquity. Sinfulness was his default setting. He was born that way. That did not excuse him or mean he could get away with his wrongful behaviour. The fact of Original Sin does not get us off the hook, God still holds us responsible for our actions.

We are all born sinners, and we all need a Saviour. Saying, 'this is just the way I am', will not impress God the Judge. He expects 100% holiness and His court demands perfection. The Lord knows you are a sinner from birth, so don't pretend your actions are okay, admit your sin, acknowledge it before the Judge.

God the Judge want's to forgive and set you free, but you must be willing to meet His standards, and that begins with kneeling humbly before His Throne and yielding your life of sin to Jesus. Only then can God proclaim you free. "God resists the proud, but gives grace to the humble." James 4:6b.

23rd September

Psalm 51:5b

'And in sin my mother conceived me. '

Sin is a family trait

Today's verse is 'And in sin my mother conceived me.' This does not imply that the sex act is sinful. Within the safe and secure boundaries of a loving marriage a man and woman can enjoy each other in the deep bonds of sexual love. Nor, does it imply that David's mother was a prostitute or 'loose woman'. No, David is saying that sin runs in his family; it runs in each of our families too.

There are sins that seem to follow families around, and pass from one generation to the next, you may call it a family trait. The truth is sin is a family trait and has been passed to us from our first parents Adam and Eve. Again, David is not trying to make excuses for his foolish actions, he is stating a fact. What about your family? Is there a thing that easily entangles you, that you see in your brothers and sisters, mum and dad, etc.? Come to God to break the hold that sinful trait has over you. If there isn't an obvious trait, acknowledge the sin that you inherited and is now yours. Ask God to free you from the bonds of Original Sin. 'For sin shall not have dominion over you, for you are not under law but under grace.' Romans 6:14.

24th September

Psalm 51:6a

'Behold, You desire truth in the inward parts,'

True to the core

It was through this experience that David realized that God desires us to be true to the core. This doesn't mean we never make a mistake nor even lie; it does mean we are honest about our actions. Don't ignore the sin in your life but bring it to mind and acknowledge your weaknesses and faults. Be truthful to God and yourself over all the wrong things you have done. God is waiting to forgive you, whatever it is you have done, but He can't unless you are true to the core of your life about it.

Repentance is born out of truth. You can't repent while you are living in denial. Repentance comes from the very centre of your being and works its way out. If the ladder of truth doesn't reach to your inward parts then repentance will never emerge, and you will be left in a state of filthy sin forever.

You know the area God is pricking at the moment; the part of your life He is convicting you of. Get down on your knees and talk to Him about it. Let truth penetrate to your core, and so allow repentance to bubble up into forgiveness from God. Be truthful and repent about it.

25th September
Psalm 51:6b
'And in the hidden part You will make me to know wisdom.'
Truth becomes wisdom

Sin is an act of foolishness. We foolishly believe we know better than God and we act in a high-handed way because of a lack of wisdom in our hearts. We don't acquire wisdom by actions, or a long life, we acquire wisdom by being truthful and honest about ourselves before God. True wisdom comes from the Lord; He alone gives it out. As we have seen, having truth reach to our core allows repentance to bubble up before God. That truth in our inward parts prepares the ground for God to plant His seeds of wisdom there.

There is no wisdom without truth. We will run from one folly to the next until we stop, get on our knees and confess our sin before the Judge. When He sees the garden of our heart is clear of the weeds of lies and the rich soil of truth is prepared, He will plant wisdom in that place, wisdom that will guard our hearts from future sinning. This will mean not just preventing the repeat this current sin, but it will begin to move us away from all sin. James understood the necessity of wisdom and the only way to receive it, 'If any of you lacks wisdom, let him ask of God, who gives to all liberally and without reproach, and it will be given to him. But let him ask in faith, with no doubting, for he who doubts is like a wave of the sea driven and tossed by the wind.' James 1:5-6. You cannot ask for wisdom in faith while you are living a lie; get your heart right and receive this unparalleled gift from God.

26th September
Psalm 51:7a
'Purge me with hyssop, and I shall be clean;'
Purification

Hyssop was used in many purification rituals that the Priests performed. It was used to sprinkle the blood of sacrifices, and water of cleansing. It was also used as a part of a burnt offering. One of the most important times hyssop was used was to daub the lambs' blood on the door posts and lintels during the first Passover. Hyssop is not special in itself, but the inference it brings is one of sacrificial purification.

David prayed, 'Purge me with hyssop, and I shall be clean', this is a direct reference to sacrifice. David knew and understood that, 'without shedding of blood there is no remission.' Hebrews 9:22b. The writer to the Hebrews again referenced the sprinkling of blood as the only way to purify someone or something. We do not purify with the blood of cattle and sheep, but blood must be shed and sprinkled in order for you to be clean. Jesus' blood is enough. When He shed His blood on the cross He made it possible for you to be truly and absolutely clean, but you have got to want to be purged with the blood and now there is no hyssop, it's a cross of wood. Purification is costly; it cost God everything. It is also painful, to come to the Cross of Jesus will break your heart; but fear not, Jesus will give you a new clean heart.

27th September

Psalm 51:7b

'Wash me, and I shall be whiter than snow.'

Absolute cleansing

David visits the idea of washing again. He entreats the Lord to wash him, and why does he desire that? Because the Lord will wash him whiter than snow. There is nothing purer than newly laid snow, it covers everything in a beautiful blanket of white. It can be so white that it can blind. Skiers wear protective eyewear to stop the brilliant glare of the snow hurting their eyes. God will make your heart like that!

Ask the Lord to wash you clean and He will make your heart so white and dazzling that you will not be able to hide what He has done. Some may find it hard to look at you because of the purity of your heart, their sinfulness being blinded by the Lord's glory in your life. Pray for them that they may find what you have found, but leave them to the Lord. Don't let their dirtiness mar your purity.

Dive deeply into the Lord's bath and allow every area of your life to be washed by Him. Don't be afraid, it may be painful, but God is gentle and kind and He knows what He is doing. You might not remember what it is like to be pure, but it is worth getting used to. Get a wash from the Lord and be whiter than snow.

28th September
Psalm 51:8a
'Make me hear joy and gladness,'
Happy thoughts

When the Lord is convicting you of sin it can be a distressing time; a time when your thoughts are brought low. At these times it can be nearly impossible to hear joy and gladness, even if it is right in front of you. David was desperate to hear those wonderful things, and so he asks God to change his mind so that he could hear.

To truly hear and appreciate joy and gladness, you need joy and gladness in your heart. These are gifts from God to those who are close to Him and under the protection of His wing. Sinners are far from Him and so do not have His inner joy and gladness. Repentance means a change in direction; a turning around and heading the other way. Turn back to God, and more, go back to Him so that you can enter the place of joy and gladness and receive them as gifts from God. Sorrow always goes hand in hand with repentance, but afterwards comes everlasting joy.

Do you long to hear joy and gladness? Get right with God and He will make you hear joy and gladness on the inside, in your heart and mind, and then all the wonders of Creation will be audible to you.

29th September
Psalm 51:8b
'That the bones You have broken may rejoice.'
Rejoicing in brokenness

King David was broken; the pain of his broken relationship with God was like his bones had all been shattered. The Lord had to break the relationship; David needed to feel the consequences of his foolish behaviour. The Lord would not allow David to get away with his sin and He will not turn a blind eye to yours either. By sinning you have broken the relationship you had with God. The Lord will not hold you guiltless until you repent and come back to Him. This is why the pain of breaking the relationship with God is so raw; if you feel nothing you will never turn back, but the utter pain brings you to your knees in humble prayer, even if it takes a very long time.

Joy and gladness are the signs the relationship is repaired (Psalm 51:8a). When you regain that joy, rejoice in the pain you felt; the pain that brought you back to God. This may be a devastating time for you, a time when all seems lost and God is far from you, but rejoice because this devastating pain will be the catalyst for repentance and restoration.

Not all suffering is punishment for sin. Sometimes suffering is the wake-up call we all need to repair the damage done in the relationship between God and ourselves. In all your sufferings turn to God for help and salvation; He is ready to receive you home.

30th September
Psalm 51:9a
'Hide Your face from my sins'
Should God ignore our sins?

Is David asking God to ignore his sins; to look the other way? We have all sinned, and may hope that God will look the other way, or cover His Holy eyes from our deeds, but should we ask Him to? and would He do it anyway. If the Lord were to ignore our transgressions and sins, He could no longer be the Just Judge. He may wish He'd looked the other way and not see the horrid things we do all day, but He cannot. He watches everything and knows all we do and our hidden motives behind them.

If David isn't asking God to overlook his sins, what is he saying? David is falling on God's grace and mercy. The Lord promises to bury our sins in the depths of the sea (Micah 7:19), and place them as far as the east is from the west (Psalm 103:12). This is what God will do for the repentant sinner, He will put your sins out of His mind. The Lord has a perfect memory and cannot forget anything, but He chooses not to remember sins He has forgiven.

David was not asking God to ignore his sins, but rather to forgive them as only He can. If you come to God in repentance He will do the same for you.

1st October

Psalm 51:9b

'And blot out all my iniquities.'

The Lord will erase your sins from His copybook

Do you realise everything you do and everything you say and every thought you have had is written out before God? Just think of all those hurtful words you have spoken, those spiteful deeds you have committed and those thoughts you hoped no-one knew about all written large before God and He will read them out in the Court House of God. How ashamed will you be?

David knew this and it bothered him enough to ask the Lord to blot out his iniquities. What grounds did David have to expect a positive response to this request? David had come in repentance before the Lord, he was more than sorry for his actions, it wasn't just embarrassment for being found out. He had broken his love relationship with God and all those actions were written in God's book and were open before Him. How can God forgive and put the deeds out of His mind if they are written in front of Him? He can't, they must be erased first.

If you want your sin erased from God's copybook the only legitimate way for that to be able to happen is for you to do as David did and get down on your knees and repent before God. Do it today.

2nd October
Psalm 51:10a
'Create in me a clean heart, O God'
New hearts for old

David's heart had been tarnished by sin; there was nothing he could do to clean in. God's deep clean had purified it, but it was still tainted by his sins. What David needed was a new, clean heart, one that had never been affected by the filth of sin. The very essence of David's life had to be replaced, and the same is true for you.

You may say, 'I'm a Christian, I've already had my heart renewed!' Well, I say, 'Hallelujah, for that, but, you have sinned and tarnished that heart, and it needs replacing.' A part of getting right with God is accepting that you have taken God's gift of renewal and then turned to your own way and acted as you desired, which has brought you to this point. Ask God for a new heart. This isn't about whether or not you can lose your Salvation, this is about losing your communion with God. Allow God to take your tarnished heart, throw it away and replace it with a new, clean, pure heart. The Lord will do it for you in a moment, and in that moment you must choose never to go down the path of sin again. You have a fresh start, make it count to the glory of God.

3rd October
Psalm 51:10b
'And renew a steadfast spirit within me.'
A renewed spirit

The word 'spirit' is often linked with life, energy, vigour, those kinds of thoughts. When we are at a low point, people say, 'he has lost spirit' or, 'she has lost the spark she used to have.' The spirit is the life within us. David had lost his spirit, he was down, weak and sick. God is able to renew your spirit within you, to give you life where before you had lifelessness, hope where there was hopelessness.

There is more to this than normal human life or spirit. David was asking for the renewing of the Holy Spirit within him. David knew the Holy Spirit had departed from him. The Holy Spirit, as His name suggests, is holy, He cannot live in an unholy place. God is omnipresent, meaning He is everywhere, even in the darkest sin pit you may dare to imagine, but God doesn't dwell there. God makes His home where holiness is. If our hearts are made holy by God, He dwells in us by the Holy Spirit. David longed for the renewal of the Holy Spirit in Him. The Holy Spirit is steadfast, immovable, strong, and He gives life to those He dwells with. Holy Spirit Life is more precious than all the gold in the universe. If you want the renewing of the Holy Spirit within you, God must first renew your human spirit, then quite naturally the Holy Spirit will move into your life to dwell. Keep your life clean and He will never leave.

4th October
Psalm 51:11a
'Do not cast me away from Your presence,'
Don't cast me out

I said previously that God is omnipresent; He is in all places at all times, but there are places where He doesn't dwell. David didn't want to be sent to one of those places. In Genesis 4 the Lord cast out Cain when he killed his brother Abel, verse 16 reads, 'So Cain went out from the LORD's presence and lived in the land of Nod, east of Eden.' The land of Nod was a place of lonely, aimless wandering, a place where sinners live lonely, aimless, wandering lives. David did not want to go to a place like that.

How desperate are you for God's presence? What will you do to remain in His Land? The Great King David begged the Lord on bended knee not to cast him away from His presence. Have you got to the point where you are willing to beg God as David did, or are you still too proud? For Cain, the land of Nod was a real physical place, for you and me it is a spiritual and psychological place where we wander round and around in self-pity. There was no way back for Cain, but for us we can turn around and return home, better still not to have ever left. Beg God not to cast you away even for one hour. May your desire be to always dwell in God's presence.

5th October
Psalm 51:11b
'And do not take Your Holy Spirit from me.'
Do not take Your Holy Spirit from me

The Holy Spirit is God's possession, and more than that He is God. We never own the Holy Spirit, He is never ours; it is more true to say we are His! The Holy Spirit is the Lord's to give to whomever He chooses, and He chooses to give Him to those people who belong to Him. However, the Holy Spirit remains God's possession alone. The Lord can choose to take Him back, if He so desires. He cannot dwell in an unholy heart no matter how 'saved' you are. You may remain saved, but you would have no joy, assurance, or Godly guidance until you repent and return to the Lord.

The removal of the Holy Spirit was of genuine concern to David. He detested the thought of God removing the blessed anointing from Him. David had seen first-hand what happens to a man whom God has removed the Holy Spirit from. King Saul was amazingly blessed by God. He prophesied with the prophets and the Lord gave him many victories over enemies, but Saul forgot God and acted high-handedly, so the Lord removed the anointing of the Holy Spirit from him and gave it to David. Saul was not left empty; a troubling unholy spirit moved in and destroyed his life and family.

Whether or not God would take His Holy Spirit from you is not for me to say; but are you desperate enough to fall on your knees before Almighty God just in case?

6th October

Psalm 51:12a

'Restore to me the joy of Your salvation,'

Is there joy in your salvation?

God may not have cast you out or removed His Holy Spirit from you, but is there joy in your salvation? The Joy of the Lord is the hallmark of salvation. Christian joy is like no other, it wells up within us no matter what is going on around us or even what goes on within us. The joy of the Lord isn't an anti-depressant. Even the most depressed person can experience the joy of salvation even if no-one else knows. You know if you have lost the joy; salvation itself becomes distant and meaningless to you. What happens when you lose the joy? Do you fall into depression? No, as I have already said, depression has no bearing on spiritual joy. What happens when you lose the joy of your salvation is you start looking for joy elsewhere.

There is no worldly joy, no matter how noble, that can take the place of the joy of your salvation in Christ; stop looking for it, give it up as a bad job. Come back to God and ask Him to restore the joy of salvation, and do not be satisfied until the cup of joy He pours out on you exceeds the previous level you once knew.

If you do not know what I am talking about, ask God to fill you with His joy today and you will never want any other joy to take its place.

7th October
Psalm 51:12b
'And uphold me by Your generous Spirit.'
God's generosity

To be upheld is to be kept in place, safe and secure. The Lord longs to lift us up in His arms but we are too grown up for that; we are independent and strong; we don't need to be upheld by anyone. Stop thinking like that and start thinking like a little child with his arms raised up to his daddy.

There is a generosity in God's love. It is all encompassing, it will enfold you and uphold you when all other loves are falling away. Like all of God's attributes, God's love cannot be near anything impure, He cannot love anything unholy. This does not imply He hates you or anyone else for that matter, but it does mean the true nature of God's generous Spirit cannot come near while you are separated from Him by deliberate sin. David could ask this only because he was in a state of repentance.

Until there is a longing in your heart to be upheld by God's Spirit you will never come to Him with repentance. Like the prodigal son, you must make the move to return home; the Lord is already waiting to lift you in His loving arms. Let go of your worldly props, and lift your arms to your Heavenly Father who is the only one who can totally uphold you and will never let you down. Allow God to be generous towards you today, and you will become generous towards Him and others.

8th October
Psalm 51:13a
'Then I will teach transgressors Your ways,'
Tell of the goodness of God

When God moves in your life and He has forgiven you your sin, restored your joy of salvation and has welcomed you back home like the father of the prodigal, what will be your response? I trust it will be one of unbridled thankfulness and praise towards your generous God. You may sing songs, laugh, dance and show all the wonderful signs of a sinner forgiven; but what about telling others about God's ways?

David longed to tell others about His loving God who forgave his sin, although it was big. David wanted others to know that God would do for them what He had done for him. 'Look, the Lord has taken away my shame and welcomed me back into His fold. This is the God I serve. He is waiting to forgive you, no matter what you have done, it's not just for me it's for everyone.' That is part of God's ways that David wanted to teach. This psalm would not make sense if that was all of God's ways. God's ways do encompass forgiveness, love, mercy and grace, but they also cover, holiness, judgement, punishment and rejection. Without the hard side of God's ways, the soft side is just that "soft"; we do not serve a "soft" God but an Almighty God. When you paint your word picture of God, don't only paint half of Him paint the complete picture, telling what He was like before repentance and also what the Lord did afterwards. You know because you went through it.

9th October
Psalm 51:13b
'And sinners shall be converted to You.'
Repentance multiplied

What is the response of teaching transgressors God's ways? David believed the answer was that they would be converted to Him. The word 'converted', may be better translated 'return to', meaning to repent.

When sinners hear your testimony of grace and see how God has restored you to His place of blessing, their hearts will yearn for the same to happen to them, and they will return to the Lord. There will be those who mock and refuse to be converted, but I am not interested in them. Your repentance will be multiplied. Your simple, if tough, act of turning away from sin and back to God will be the catalyst for others who have similarly sinned to also turn back to God and this will trigger others to do the same and so on.

Repentance multiplied like a chain reaction spreading out from the church first and then out into the world, but it takes someone to start it. Will you be the one who not only repents of your sins but tells others of the initial judgement of God and His subsequent grace and mercy? Your honesty will cause others, who may be wavering, to also make that step, and their testimony will be the nudge others need and so repentance is multiplied exponentially.

(If you don't believe me, just consider all the people who have repented on the basis of David's testimony in this psalm.)

10th October
Psalm 51:14a
'Deliver me from the guilt of bloodshed, O God, The God of my salvation,'
Delivered from guilt

At this point it is safe to say David had been forgiven by God, and yet he still felt the weight of guilt on his shoulders. Is this how it should be? After all David did have a man killed to cover up his adultery! David didn't think so, and neither do I. There are consequences to sin, just read the account of the end of David's life and you will see how tough it got for him, but that does not mean a child of God need's to live with guilt. The Lord has forgiven you for your sin, isn't it time you forgave yourself!

You can see by David's word's that he found this difficult, Great king David, who was close to God's heart could not forgive himself, even after the Lord had forgiven him. He knew he needed to be free from guilt. David prayed to be delivered from the guilt; to be saved from that unbreakable prison. Although it is true that we must forgive ourselves for the sins we have done, we cannot break the chains on our own, we need the Saviour's help. Jesus died on the cross for our salvation, that is complete salvation from sin and the guilt it leaves behind. Don't hold on to that guilt as if it were a 'battle scar' reminding you of past failures, ask for deliverance from that guilt and replace it with godly wisdom, which is a much better protection from sin. Be free from guilt.

11th October
Psalm 51:14b
'And my tongue shall sing aloud of Your righteousness.'
Sing loudly

When our hearts are racked with guilt the last thing we want to do is sing. Guilt is crippling, it tears up our insides and brings us low, but when we are delivered from that guilt joy rises up within us and we overflow with singing. David was a singer who loved to sing, but his heart was heavy, and no words would come out of his mouth. David longed to sing songs of praise to his God, but he could not because of the guilt of sin he carried. This longing was the catalyst for deliverance and salvation. If David didn't care he would have died with a guilty conscience, but He did care, he cared enough to do something.

Do you want to sing praises to God? Perhaps you once did but now your tongue cleaves to the top of your mouth and your heavy heart will not release praise to God. The solution is not to open your mouth and wait for it to be filled with beautiful words; the solution is to fall on your knees before the Judge of the whole world and ask Him to deliver you from the guilt of sin in your heart. If you are truly repentant the Lord will free you from the bonds of guilt and singing will flow quite naturally from you. Now don't hold back, open your mouth and sing aloud of God's righteousness.

12th October
Psalm 51:15a
'O Lord, open my lips,'
Let God open your mouth

Was David holding back? No, he held his peace until the Lord opened his lips. David was so conscience of his sinful nature that he daren't even praise God in case His words did not make the grade. Yes, king David, who sang and wrote many of the psalms we have, knew his words were not good enough for God. He kept His mouth closed until God opened it again.

Don't be too quick to open your mouth to speak, wait until the Lord gives you the words to say. It can be hard to know where to start and how to put things so that you are understood. The Lord knows everything, and He knows who you are talking to and He will fill your lips with words that will resonate with them. Let God open your mouth, trust Him to give you the right words at the right time and then leave the rest to Him. Do you trust God enough to not share your deliverance until He prompts you to? Wait for God to open your lips and when He does let your heart flow out to all who will listen; they will be His words and His testimony in your life.

13th October
Psalm 51:15b
'And my mouth shall show forth Your praise.'
Flowing with praise

Following on from the past few verses we now have an outflow of praise. It starts with the creation of a clean heart and the renewing of your spirit. The removal of that guilt that was in your heart is like the removal of a stopper of fizzy drinks bottle, the bubbles just come up. Be wise and allow God control of your mouth, but flow freely with praises to Him. You are liberated, set free, no longer bound by sin and the guilt it leaves behind. If God is not stopping you, what is? Shout and sing, let your praises show in not only your words but your whole face. How did David's mouth show his praise? Surely it was in his beaming smile! Show your praise in your smile, let the joy of the Lord be seen on your face, radiating through your eyes and clearly seen on your mouth. It's like a testimony without words, everyone will see and know that the Lord has done a wonder work in you.

There are people who will never hear you speak, but they will see your face, let that show forth God's praise all the time. Has God done something in your life? Show it, let your eyes, mouth, gait, words, everything show forth praise to God.

14th October

Psalm 51:16a

'For You do not desire sacrifice, or else I would give it;'

God does not desire sacrifice

You may be surprised by this statement that 'God does not desire sacrifice', but it is true. Israel were commanded to sacrifice animals on the alter in Jerusalem for the remission of sin. If a person sinned, they could go up to the Temple and take an unblemished lamb with them and the priests would kill it and burn it on the alter before God. Did God really want animals killed for peoples' sins? Someone had to pay for the trespass, if not the person who did it then who? The lamb was killed in the place of the sinner, life for life. The lamb's blood was spilt so the man or woman could go free. Makes you think, 'what about that person, he sinned and got away with it, surely he will go away and sin again.' Yes, that is a real possibility and definitely happened. Sacrifice is not repentance.

This should make you think of the ultimate sacrifice. Jesus the Lamb of God gave His life for you and me; His life for yours, His blood for yours. Jesus was punished for your sin, His death means you can walk free from God's Courtroom. Does this mean we can go on sinning? No, unless you change from the inside and allow the Holy Spirit to reign in your life, Jesus' sacrifice will not benefit you.

God doesn't want sacrifices, He desires true repentance; will you give that to God today?

15th October

Psalm 51:16b

'You do not delight in burnt offering.'

Is God blood thirsty?

Blood sacrifices are a part of many religions: worshipers will sacrifice animals and sometimes children to please their god. They believe by spilling blood their god will grant them a good harvest or forgive some misdeed. Is our God like that, is He blood thirsty? David didn't think so, he declared that, 'You do not delight in burnt offerings.' David knew God, and knew He loved all of Creation. God did not desire anything to die, and certainly not to be killed for His pleasure. However, sacrifices and burn offerings are necessary in our sin soaked, fallen world. Sacrifices were needed, and the pleasant aroma went up to Heaven to cover the stench of our sins. It was only because of sin that God required them and never human sacrifices.

We do not need to give burnt offerings and sacrifice animals; Jesus' blood is more than enough. Jesus death was not a delight to the Father, it was heart-breaking but necessary to bring Salvation to all. Never trivialize Jesus death on the Cross and make out God wanted to do it. Yes, the sacrifice brought forgiveness to us all and opened the doorway to heaven, but He would rather us never to have sinned in the first place.

16th October
Psalm 51:17a
'The sacrifices of God are a broken spirit, a broken and a contrite heart'
The sacrifices of God

God does not delight in burnt offerings and animal sacrifices; the kind of sacrifice God delights in is the sacrifice of a broken, contrite heart. Feeling remorse is not enough; saying sorry every 5 seconds is not enough; trying to do better next time is not enough - God does not want those things. God desires you give Him your broken heart to heal and in true contrition come to Him in humble repentance. It takes great effort to make this kind of sacrifice. It is all too easy to try to go it alone, or to think now we have sinned we deserve to suffer. We want to heal ourselves or try the latest remedy for the feelings of shame and guilt. We are told to, 'leave your mistakes in the past and move on to better things.' It's far too humiliating to go to God for help.

That last line is the exact point, it is humiliating to bow before Almighty God in repentance and ask for forgiveness, but it is that sacrifice God is waiting for. If you feel the need to do something to pay for your sins, then stop running everywhere else and go to the Father. Be humiliated before Him, broken and contrite in heart. That is all you can do; that is all you need to do, leave the rest with God.

17th October
Psalm 51:17b
'These, O God, You will not despise.'
God will not despise you

The first part of this verse is, 'The sacrifices of God are a broken spirit, a broken and a contrite heart' the second part is, 'these, O God, You will not despise.' Why is this important to mention? Because the World does despise these things. Society may make out it loves the humble, the broken and the contrite, but really it despises them. What the World loves is strong people, powerful individuals who make an impact all by themselves or despite setbacks. How many times do you hear of 'strong women' or 'powerful men'? They are honoured and sometimes rightly so, but what about the truly repentant, the men and women who know they are sinners and bow before their stronger, more powerful God, when do we hear about them?

God's view is very different. He is not impressed by power or strength, what pleases Him is humility. God will not despise you, whoever you are. It may sound as if I am saying God despises strong women and powerful men, but no, God sees the heart and He knows we are all weak no matter what front we put on. Be honest before God and bow humbly before Him, He will not turn you away. He will lift you up and fill you with His power and strength which will never end.

18th October
Psalm 51:18a
'Do good in Your good pleasure to Zion;'
Restoring damage done

David was the king of Israel and what he did affected the whole kingdom. His final thoughts on the matter of his atrocious sin were not of himself but of Zion. Zion is another name for Jerusalem often associated with promises and prophecies, but here it symbolized the nation of Israel. David was asking God not to punish Israel for his sin but instead to richly bless it. Our sins, whatever they are, always have an impact on others. The biggest impact they have is tarnishing the Name of God in the eyes of others. Family and friends watch to see what we will do as Christians; is your life of faith genuine? When we fail, they only see the failure and they are put off from following Jesus. What is the answer to this tragedy? Pray for them. Ask God to do them good in His good pleasure. God loves them more than you do, and His desire is to draw them in. He uses us as witnesses but we are bad at it, especially when it comes to family, so pray that God would do for them what only He can do.

It is time to stop looking inward and start looking out. Pray that the Lord would prevent your misdeeds from affecting others around you. Pray that they would see the wonder-work God has done in your life, that your repentance has brought deliverance from the guilt and shame of sin and you have been restored to the joy of salvation. May that fact leave a lasting impression.

19th October
Psalm 51:18b
'Build the walls of Jerusalem.'
Strengthen the weak

David had taken the city of Jerusalem and made it strong. The previous occupants, the Jebusites, believed the walls were impregnable, but David's men broke through. David fortified the city, built the walls and made it stronger than before. However, David's faith was not in bricks and mortar, he believed it was God who protected Jerusalem. When David prayed, 'Build the walls of Jerusalem', he was not meaning the physical walls, but the spiritual protection the Lord set up. David's sin had meant God had withdrawn from Israel and the wall of protection had been weakened. David asked God to rebuild those spiritual walls around Jerusalem. David's eyes were ever on the Lord, and his heart was for his people.

As you come out of this time of repentance, turn to God and ask Him to 'build the walls' in your life, to keep you safe from stumbling. Remember too those around you who have been rocked by your trespass. Ask God to strengthen them and cause them to hide behind God's walls of protection. Although sinning is never good, let the end of this difficult journey bring glory to God by seeing your friends and family brought into His Kingdom. This has been a tough road to walk but the end is in sight; may the blessing of the Lord's protection be on you and those around you today.

20th October

Psalm 51:19a

'Then You shall be pleased with the sacrifices of righteousness, With burnt offering and whole burnt offering;'

Adding back In

David had previously said that the Lord does not desire or delight in burnt offerings and sacrifices (verse 16) but now David is saying that once he had repented of his foolish, sinful ways and his heart is made anew then the Lord will be pleased with them. What has changed? David has. God is the same as before, but David has been restored to righteousness, he has changed his ways and God has changed his heart. It is only now that David could add back in the prescribed worship of God.

It is not right to enter God's holy presence with high-handed sin in your heart. Whatever that sin is, however big or small, it disqualifies you from worship, you are unclean, blemished. This may sound like you have to stay outside the camp, but no, come in and get yourself right with God, go through this psalm of repentance and be made clean. Once your heart has been replaced and made clean and your spirit renewed, you can begin to add worship back in. Only the sacrifices of the righteous are pleasing to God and we are made righteous through the redeeming blood of the Lamb. Come to Jesus for cleansing then lift up your hands to God and worship him in righteousness and truth, He will be pleased to accept your offerings of praise.

21st October
Psalm 51:19b
'Then they shall offer bulls on Your altar.'
Worship is restored

The final step in repentance is that worship is restored. This psalm started with David crying out for mercy, there was no worship only utter desperation. At the start of the journey of repentance there can be no worship because your heart is not right before God; anything you bring to God is sullied by your sin. Once the process is complete and God's seal of forgiveness and restoration is stamped on you, worship can begin again.

Open your mouth and worship God, get on your knees before Him. Before you got on your knees to beg for forgiveness, now you are there to declare the mercies of God. As you turn your face to God, He will lift you up into the heavenly places and you will know the blessings of God once more.

At the start of the journey you were alone but now you are surrounded by others also worshipping God. They are your brothers and sisters in Christ standing with you in your restored condition. Some have been Christians for years, but some are the ones who have watched you go through the pain of repentance and have seen the work of God in your life. There is a sense of growth in this last portion; a seed was planted and now a tree is sprouting up with new leaves on every branch. God is glorified by your humble repentance. So smile, lift up your hands and give glory to God, but endeavour to never have to travel this way again.

22nd October
Psalm 24:1a
'The earth is the Lord's, and all its fullness'
The King of all the world

David was the King of Israel and because of his many victories other nations paid tribute to him as their kings were under David's authority. Nobody likes being ruled over by someone else and even less by another state or institution, but these things are a fact of life. We are not free, we are all under the authority of someone or other. David knew he too was under authority, the Land of Israel was God's possession. God owned and ruled it, David was merely the human figurehead. Just as David's rule went beyond Israel so did God's, He ruled even where David did not.

The Lord is the King of the whole world. This planet we call home, belongs to God because He made it. Everything we see is His. There is nothing at all that does not originate with Him. Every single wonderful invention man has dreamt into being was created using chemistry and physics God spoke into existence. Even the intelligence to make things is a God given gift. Everything around us belongs to God; He is the King and we are His humble servants.

What kind of servant are you? One that serves your Heavenly Master, or one that serves himself? How dare you think it is okay to do as you please, 'the earth is the Lord's and all its fullness' and that includes you.

23rd October
Psalm 24:1b
'The world and those who dwell therein.'
And that includes you

The earth is the Lord's, He created it and He is the King, therefore, He gets to decide what is right and wrong and also what punishments or rewards are given out. This makes God an easy target for haters who ask questions like, 'If God is good, why do bad things happen?' The truth is, bad things happen because of bad people, not because of God (Isaiah 59:1-2).

You are the Lord’s, you belong to Him. You may feel this entitles you to a cushy lifestyle, provided entirely by God. Well, God's plan for you is eternal, not just here on earth, so you may go through discomforts now, but His will is for you to live eternally in Heaven with Him. This is not God's waiting room, but God's mission field. We are His workers ever waiting and anxious to do His will. Or that how it should be. God has no time and Heaven no space for useless, lazy slaves who are only out for their own pleasure. If your good works are not done for God, they are a waste of time. Dedicate your whole life to God, your King, Creator and Owner, and He will dedicate eternity to you.

24th October
Psalm 24:2a
'For He has founded it upon the seas'
Built on water?

What does it mean 'For He has founded it upon the seas'? it doesn't make any sense. How can the earth be founded or built on water?

Psalms are poems and this is poetic language. It alludes to the creation of the earth in Genesis 1. Do you believe God created the world in six literal days as described in Genesis? David did and this whole psalm depends on this being true. If God did not create the world in the way He said, it is not His. I will stand with David on the foundations of the world and unravel this mystery.

Genesis 1:1 starts with God creating the heavens and the earth; the earth is described as formless and void, but it has substance, there is 'the deep'. God began His creation with water. Then in verse 9 He gathered the waters together to reveal the land. The inference is everything came out of water. The seas are the foundations of God's creation in that they were step one.

I do not pretend to understand these things. Men and women cleverer than I debate them but I will take God at His Word and will declare this to be true. What about you? Do believe what God, your King, says about Creation or do you only listen to men?

25th October
Psalm 24:2b
'And established it upon the waters.'
Water sustains the Creation

The waters are the foundation point, or beginning of the creation of the world, but the waters didn't end there. The earth, as we know it, is established on water; nothing can live without it! The idea is one of ongoing development.

The waters of the deep (Genesis 1:2) are a marvellous mystery and we may never fully understand them. What is certain is that those waters are of no use to us whilst existing only in the past; we need water today. God has established His world with water. He keeps it working and all His creatures alive by this wonderful provision. It is thought that Mars once had seas on its cold red surface. They, however, are long gone now, but God has protected our waters against evaporation into space. It is God who sends the rain in its season and it is He who withholds them should He so wish.

God's desire is that all people should be established with fresh water. Beyond that, His overarching desire is that we should be established and sustained by the Waters of the Holy Spirit welling up within us. Ask God to make the foundation of your life the Waters of the Spirit and that His Spirit would establish you in all you do for Him.

26th October
Psalm 24:3a
'Who may ascend into the hill of the Lord?'
Who can go up to meet the King?

People often talk about going 'up' to London, no matter what direction or elevation they are coming from. This is taken from the Jewish idea of going 'up' to Jerusalem, God's holy city and in particular the Temple. The Temple was the highest place in Jewish worship, maybe not physically but certainly spiritually, it represented where God was. This is the picture David is beginning to paint. He has said that the earth in the Lord's, He is King, so who is worthy to walk up the mountain to God? We shall look at that in a later devotion, but today we shall consider that God is above all, He is holy and righteous, faultless in all His ways.

Who would dare approach Almighty God? If you do not qualify you will never get close. His brilliant glory surrounds Him and the unworthy is slain and thrown to the foothills. Can the angels' approach? The mighty seraphim cover their faces in His presence (Isaiah 6:2); they dare not look directly at Him. Jesus, the Son of God, has access because He is God, He is worthy to sit at the right hand of Father God. We are small, fragile creatures in comparison to angels and Jesus. Our smartest clothes are dirty rags not worthy of the King.

The door of Heaven is open and God beckons you up, but only those qualified will make it. Pray, call out to Jesus for cleansing and then begin your assent up God's mountain.

27th October

Psalm 24:3b

'Or who may stand in His holy place?'

Who is worthy to stand before God?

So, you have taken the step to climb God's mountain, but now you must enter into His awesome presence. Are you worthy of an audience with the King of kings?

'As it is written: "There is none righteous, no, not one."' Romans 3:10. Paul declares that no one is worthy to stand before God because none of us are righteous. It doesn't matter how many good things you do it will never be enough to outweigh your sins; God will not allow a sinner into His sinless throne room. Who then may stand in His holy place? Jesus is the righteous one, He stands before Father God and intercedes for us, and more than that He shares His righteousness with us! We may enter the holy place, not by our righteousness, but by Jesus' righteousness. As sons and daughters of God we share in the righteousness of the Son; we are family. Throw away your old worthless righteousness and put on the righteousness of Christ with prayer. It is not an easy transaction, as we shall see because we may need to repent.

28th October
Psalm 24:4a
'He who has clean hands and a pure heart'
How do you measure up?

We have been asking the question, 'Who can ascend into the hill of the Lord? Or who can stand in His holy place?' (Psalm 24:3). We have seen that only Jesus is worthy of an audience with God, but He shares His righteousness with His brothers and sisters. It is not enough to sit back and enjoy God's company under Jesus' protection, we must make a transaction.

You must examine yourself, by asking if you have clean hands and a clean heart? Think critically about all you have done. Have you sinned, corrupting your hands in some way? Have you stolen something, a pen from work or school. Maybe you have acted aggressively against someone who provoked you. We have *all* sinned, we all need to bow before Jesus and wash our dirty hands clean in His powerful cleansing blood.

On the other hand, you may have kept your hands clean by not yielding to the impulses of your eyes, but what about on the inside, how is your heart. Have you ever had impure thoughts you have allowed to settle and take root in your heart? Jesus, in Matthew 5:21, 22, 27, 28, said that sins that only exists in your heart, are no different to if you were to carry them out. Kneel before Him and accept God's offer of a new pure heart in the place of your dirty one, then ask the Holy Spirit to give you the strength to keep it pure.

29th October
Psalm 24:4b
'Who has not lifted up his soul to an idol'
Who is first in your life?

Who is first in your life? Where does God come in your list of priorities? Before you shout, 'He's number one!', take a moment to see if that is true. Take Sundays for instance, what stops you going to Church? There are many legitimate reasons why people can't get to Church, health, job, transport. These may or may not be as legitimate for you as for others, so take stock, and ask if God is really number one in your life or is there something else keeping you away?

Do you desire to spend time with God? What gets in your way, and does that thing prevent you from doing other things you want to do? Idols are not just things, they can also be excuses. Put God first, not just in word but also in deed.

You will find great freedom in structuring your life around God, rather than structuring God around your life. Repent of all your idols, bury them, as it were, in the deepest sea. If necessary, throw things away literally; do whatever is needed to get your priorities right.

Who is first in your life?

30th October
Psalm 24:4c
'Nor sworn deceitfully.'
Do not lie

We have seen that it is not a light thing to ascend the Hill of the Lord and stand in the Throne Room of God. This last part hits us all; have you ever lied, broken a promise, wilfully deceived someone to their hurt? The ninth Commandment is: 'You shall not bear false witness against your neighbour.' Exodus 20:16, this goes beyond lying or even the list I just made. We must be wary of our speech as what comes out of our mouth is important. God hates deceit and will not fail to judge accordingly. The people of God are meant to be known for their honesty, that if they are asked something, they will give a truthful answer, but do we? Do people trust your words, or do they assume you are lying?

Do not be deceitful but be wise in all you say. There are those who will try to use your honesty against you, affectively swearing deceitfully, they will ask pointed questions that if you answer will put you in a place of opposition to the World View; so be wise. Don't be afraid to speak the truth, even to your hurt, but keep your ears open to what God is saying; perhaps it is sometimes better to say nothing.

In all your ways keep a clear conscience and so walk boldly before God. This may seem tough, but if God is first in your life then all these other things will naturally fall into place.

31st October
Psalm 24:5a
'He shall receive blessing from the Lord'
A just reward

It is not an easy thing to enter God's Holy presence; it is all or nothing. You may think that it is all for God and nothing for you, but this is not the case. The one who has clean hands, a pure heart, who has not lifted up his soul to idols or sworn deceitfully will be blessed by God. The King of kings, the ruler of the whole earth will pour out His blessings on you. He will give you the gift of the Holy Spirit, the assurance of Heaven and Jesus as your closest friend. The blessing of the Lord comes with something else, something only the King can grant and that is an offer of peace between Him and you. Before, you were the enemy of God but now He has made you His ally. All charges are dropped, past sins forgiven and forgotten. This is the just reward for living a life worthy of the King.

God knows all your weaknesses, but His blessed gifts will give you the strength to withstand all temptation, so that your standing before Him will never falter. If, however, you do fall into sin, there is always hope in the blessed blood of Jesus. Being forgiven by God is a wonderful blessing and one that we can share with others. If someone has wronged you choose to bless them with forgiveness.

Come to God and receive your just reward of abundant blessings today.

1st November
Psalm 24:5b
'And righteousness from the God of his salvation.'
Righteousness from the Lord

We have seen that our righteousness is not good enough to enter God's Holy Throne Room; we can't even begin to climb the mountain it is on. How then can you enter? You must choose to be different, to seek God to cleanse your hand's and heart of all the wrong contained there, to put away idols and things that take God's place in your heart and speak the truth in love. The Lord, who sees the sincerity of your heart, will then do what only He can do: He will fill your life with blessing and your heart with His righteousness. This is the transaction of Salvation; you make your offering to God by the actions you take, and He accepts them and fills you with His Spirit of Righteousness.

Make that choice to come to God today, put your life in order and reach out to Him. The Lord is just and will always come to you and do all His work of Salvation in you. Open your heart to Him and then place your foot boldly on the hill of the Lord. His righteousness in your heart gives you access to Him meaning that you are no longer an outcast but rather, you are welcome to stand in the holy place.

2nd November
Psalm 24:6a
'This is Jacob.'
The people of the King
If God is a King and He has a Kingdom, surely He must have a People! When David wrote this psalm, he was referring to Israel, the Jewish nation. They were, and are, God's special chosen people. Israel are the descendants of Abraham, although they were named after his grandson Jacob. Jacob was not a nice person, he manipulated family situations to suit his needs; most notably tricking his older (if only just) brother, Esau out of both his birthright and blessing before running away to be taught a lesson from his uncle Laban.

Jacob may have tricked his way to gain the blessing, but that does not diminish his rightful place as the son of promise; God chose Jacob and rejected Esau. While at Laban's house the tables were turned on the master manipulator and he received a taste of his own medicine. By the time Jacob returned home he was a broken, more humble man. God met with him in that state and changed his name to Israel, and his descendants took on that name, but the name Jacob, the son of promise, went along with it.

Israel is the nation of God's promise. If you have received God's blessing and righteousness as previously discussed, you too will be a part of 'Jacob', the son of promise. You may not be Jewish, that's a separate thing, but you will be one of the 'People of the King'.

3rd November
Psalm 24:6b
'the generation of those who seek Him'
The character of the people of the King

The historical character Jacob was not a good role-model. He was crafty, manipulative, selfish and unkind, but Jacob, the son of promise, is very different. To be like the son of promise is to be one who seeks the Lord; that is the character of the People of the King. Those in God's Kingdom seek Him out and bear their hearts before Him.

A generation can be described as those on the same level of a family tree, siblings and cousins, for example. All believers, no matter their age, gender or the number of years since being saved are all on the same level of the family tree of the King. We are *one* generation. There is wisdom in years and dynamism in youth, both are vital for the ongoing growth of the Kingdom, but more important than wisdom and drive is the discipline of seeking God.

Seek God every day, get your life on His track, pray, read the Word and talk to other believers about the Lord. Ensure you are always believing the right things. We are one generation so mix with all of your brothers and sisters and help each other to seek God more.

4th November
Psalm 24:6c
'Who seek Your face. Selah'
The character of the person of the King

We are one generation, one people worshipping one King, but we are also individuals and we must seek God's face as a *Person* of the King. Life is busy and can all too easily feel like a roller-coaster that just won't stop. The word 'selah' is usually understood to mean a musical pause, i.e. a rest. Pausing, resting, stopping before God is so important. We must actively seek God's face, but we do this by pausing. This is an oxymoron, actively pausing! Unless we pause from our busy lives and spend time seeking the face of the King we will drift further and further away from Him. If your life is going out of control, stop and call on God. Take time to rest in His love.

Sometimes 'selah' is said to mean a crescendo; a building up of the music. This too is found in seeking God. The noise of life can be deafening, drowning out all others, but the crescendo of God's blessing is an ever-growing melody of beautiful music that, if you let it, will itself drown out the noise of life. God's music will lift your heart up and up as you sit quietly before Him. Take time to be swept away by His love before entering the hectic world outside.

The character of the Person of the King is one that actively pauses before His face and waits for the crescendos of God's blessing to lift him up each day.

5th November
Psalm 24:7a
'Lift up your heads, O you gates!'
Open the gates!

There is here the idea that the King is coming and so we should open the gates with great joy. The King is God and the gates are the gates of His Temple. The King is coming home to dwell.

The gates are the outer entranceway into the house, the first line of defence. The gates are kept shut against enemies but can be safely opened when the King comes. Have you been badly hurt by people and so keep the gates of your heart firmly shut against everyone? A lot of people are like that, hiding behind the gates in case they get hurt again. Such people find it hard to open up even to God. It is a big thing to open your gates and bear your wounded heart to God but do it and do it with great joy. The King is gentle and caring and will heal your heart and patch up your wounds, so don't be afraid to let Him in.

Fling wide the gates, lift your head and sing praises due to the King of kings as He makes His way towards you. Lay palm leaves before Him and bow the knee and be glad because the King is coming.

6th November
Psalm 24:7b
'And be lifted up, you everlasting doors!'
Open the doors of the Holy Place

If the gates are the first line of defence, then the everlasting doors are the entrance to the innermost part of the Temple, the Holy of holies; God's Holy Place. This gives a different slant on verses 3 and 4, take a moment to read them again. Surely the King of kings can enter the Holy Place? Of course He can, it is His Throne Room. There is a place in your heart that God wants to dwell in; the innermost part of your life.

It is not enough to 'open the gate' and let God into the outer courts of your life, you must swing open the doors of the Throne Room in your heart. Only God has the right to be there, so clear it out, throw out the usurpers and interlopers and make it ready for the King. Solomon gave that space to his many wives and turned away from God, how foolish of the wisest of all men. If Solomon can make that mistake so can we. As God, the King, enters your heart and life, open the everlasting doors to Him only. Allow God to dwell in your Throne Room; no longer you, or anything else in charge, let the King of kings rule over your life.

It is a solemn act, the crowning of the King of your life, but an essential one. Only God has the right to go through the everlasting doors to the innermost part of your life; only He is worthy and able to keep you in all things. Don't leave the King in the outer courts, open the doors to the Holy Place.

7th November
Psalm 24:7c
'And the King of glory shall come in.'
The King will come in

'Lift up your heads, O you gates! And be lifted up, you everlasting doors! And the King of glory shall come in.' If you open up your heart to God, He will come in and dwell with you. This isn't just Old Testament poetry, this is New Testament truth. In Revelation 3:20 Jesus said, 'Behold, I stand at the door and knock. If anyone hears My voice and opens the door, I will come into him and dine with him, and he with Me.'

Open the door and Jesus will come in. Jesus will not reject you nor hurt and abuse you; your heart is safe with Him. There is no doubt Jesus is waiting to enter the very centre of your life and if you open up to Him, He will come in.

If you have never opened the outer court gates of your heart to Him, open them now. If you have done that, but never opened the inner sanctuary of your heart to Him, do that now.

Don't leave Jesus on the outside of your life, let Him in. He is the King of glory and He will bring His blessed glory into your life. If you are hesitating and wondering, 'Who is this King of glory?' then we will answer that in the next couple of days. In the meantime, don't hesitate, take a step of faith, open the gates of your heart, 'Taste and see that the Lord is good.' Psalm 34:8.

8th November
Psalm 24:8a
'Who is this King of glory?'
The big question

We have been considering the 'King of glory', but you still may not be sure who He is. 'Who is this King of glory?', 'Who is God?', 'Who is this Jesus?'. Questions like this don't have to be negative but can be the queries of an enquiring heart. The answers are too big for this psalm, and certainly too big for me, but the Bible is God's Word and it contains all the answers you will ever need.

Read God's description of Himself in the pages of the Bible. His goodness is contrasted with the evil of men and women. From cover to cover God revels Himself to sinners, so that a person can choose to either follow or reject Him. You and I can never find God on our own, He must come to us, however, it is our choice whether to go with God or go on alone. As a first step to discovering who God is, we will, with the psalmist, begin to answer this tough question. You are not alone so kneel quietly and ask God to reveal Himself to you, then open the Bible and read what He says. Be willing to ask questions of the Pastors and Elders at your Church. If you really want to know who the King of glory is, you will find out.

9th November
Psalm 24:8b
'The Lord strong and mighty'
The big answer

Yesterday we asked the question, 'Who is this King of glory?', today we get the first answer.

What do you imagine God to be like? He is the God of love, gentle and kind, but He is also the Lord, strong and mighty. We do not serve a weak God, He is the Almighty One who stands strong in the heavens and judges the ways of Man. He is a Holy, Righteous Judge and is able to carry out all His plans.

Our King is able to withstand any onslaught from the Enemy. He is the protector and defender, who stands between you and the wiles of this World. We are safe if we are on His side. But those who stand against Him will come to nothing and more they will perish, vanishing away. The King will not budge from His statutes or change His stance on sin, no matter what the World may say. If you say He is your King, do you stand with Him on all things? Or, do you side with the worldly society around you?

The King of glory is strong and mighty, take care that you are on His side in all matters.

10th November
Psalm 24:8c
'The Lord mighty in battle.'
The warrior King

Do you picture God as a 'Warrior King' striding out to battle? Isaiah 59:17-18 describes God as putting on His armour and going out to war, and more than that, He wages war against His enemies. God does not change; He will still go out to battle for righteousness.

We may look out and see all the bad things that are happening in the world and ask where God is in all this. Isaiah 59 answers this by saying God is still there, but He will not fight for the wicked, nor will He go out to battle for the unrighteous, or lift a finger for the sinner and He will disregard the one who disregards Him. He will, however, battle against those people.

Are you small, weak, disenfranchised, marginalized and hated? Then turn to the Lord, mighty in battle and He will fight for you. Are you willing to give up your rights to do as you please and let the Lord be your King? If so, God will see to it that you are safe and protected and free and loved. Stand with Him and He will stand with you through your trials and enable you to conquer all.

11th November
Psalm 24:9a
'Lift up your heads, O you gates!'
Open the gates!

The psalmist has repeated himself, and you must take note. The King of Glory is coming, the King strong and mighty in battle is coming. What will you do? Bar the doors and lock Him out, or open them wide and allow Him entrance into your life? If you do not open the gates of your heart He will not batter them down or force His way in, no, He will honour your decision and walk away, but you will find, however, that it is not God that is shut out but you!

Take a breath, open the door and let Him into your life because you have nothing to lose and everything to gain. He is the Mighty King and He wants you to dwell with Him - wait, shouldn't that be the other way around!? You are opening the doors of your heart to Him so surely He is dwelling with you. No! Remember you are the Lords, 'The earth is the Lord's, and all its fullness, the world and those who dwell therein.' Psalm 24:1. Your life is His already anyway, you had merely usurped the throne. Give it up for the King and dwell with His riches in your heart. This is one decision you will never regret.

12th November

Psalm 24:9b

'Lift up, you everlasting doors!'

Open the doors!

This isn't just a repeat of a previous thought; this is clipped and to the point. Open the Doors to the inner part of your life. Allow God access to the centre of you where your thoughts and feelings originate. Let the Holy Spirit reign over all your deepest thoughts and give Jesus the keys to the treasure chest of your emotional life. It is not enough to open the gates of your life to Him. Making a start is good and proper but the King must be welcomed into the Throne Room of your life.

To be a servant of the King of kings, is to give Him everything and every part of you. He is able to govern your wellbeing so much better than you. You may think you are doing alright but God can do it better. You may think that your life is a mess and that there is no hope but God can sort out all your inner difficulties and give you hope and peace in ways you never thought possible.

What will you do? Be content at being a half-way Christian or go all out for the King?

Fall on your knees in reverence before the King of glory, give Him the Throne of your life and see what He will do.

13th November
Psalm 24:9c
'And the King of glory shall come in.'
What are you still waiting for?

The King of glory, the King of the Universe, the King mighty in battle is waiting to dwell and commune with you and you with Him. What are you waiting for? Open the gates, open the doors, and welcome Him in. He will come in and change your life around from the inside out. He will be strength in your weakness, light in your darkness, truth where you have been lied to. The deeper you allow God to penetrate into your soul the more He will unravel the knots you have in your life. Things may not change on the outside, but you will change on the inside.

Stop blaming everyone and everything else and start to allow God to change *you*. He is waiting today to enter your heart of hearts and change you all around. God spoke through Isaiah these words, 'To console those who mourn in Zion, to give them beauty for ashes, the oil of joy for mourning, the garment of praise for the spirit of heaviness; that they may be called trees of righteousness, the planting of the Lord, that He may be glorified.' Isaiah 61:3. When Jesus referenced Isaiah 61:1-2, He was saying that was what He had come to do. Verse 3 is the natural continuation and working out of that statement. Jesus wants to do something in you so stop looking to the left and to the right for your help and look up. Open the gates of your heart, open the doors of your inner life and the King of glory will come in, and you will never be the same again.

14th November
Psalm 24:10a
'Who is this King of glory?'
So who Is He?

Who is this King of glory? The King of glory is the Creator of the world, the rightful ruler of everything around you. Look around yourself, everything you see is ultimately God's. It doesn't matter if a person designed and made it and you paid for it, the materials, the skill and your money all belong to God. Now look in a mirror. The person you see also belongs to God so whatever you think of yourself, you were created by God. The King of glory made you and He has owners' rights over your life. You can't do as you please, you are not your own, your Creator knows what is best for you to live a happy life.

It is time to put your house in order, the King is coming. Put away your idols, think pure thoughts and act in a right way before God. Choose to live as God desires and not as the World dictates. Open up the gates of your heart to the King, open the doors of your innermost life so that He may even enter there.

If you are willing to turn your eyes away from yourself and take an honest look at God, you will see that the King of glory is your King and to disrespect and ignore Him is treason. Kneel before Him in reverent praise. He loves you and only wants the best for you. Give Him the opportunity to prove Himself to you and your life will be full of blessings.

15th November
Psalm 24:10b
'The Lord of hosts'
The Lord's army

The term 'the Lord of hosts', brings up more questions than answers. What does it mean? Who are the hosts? and how does this impact us?

The Lord is the King and this is the underlying theme of the psalm. A king needs an army. This phrase 'the Lord of hosts' implies the King is over a mighty army, and indeed He is. The armies of God are the angels, they are mighty in battle and obey their Captain's commands down to the letter. What does this mean for us?

Armies protect the Kingdom and ensure the citizens are safe. We are the citizens of the Kingdom of God so the Lord dispatches the angels to protect us from powers too mighty for us. They guard us and fight for us, keeping the Kingdom of God safe. We are not to be passive citizens enjoying the peace ensured by the angels, we are to put on the full armour of God (Ephesians 6:10-18) and join the fight. We are to stand up for righteousness in an unrighteous world. We are to hold to biblical principles and morals in a society that declares everything, but these things, to be okay. We are to actively do our part for King and His Kingdom.

The King of glory is the Lord of hosts. Will you join His ranks today and fight for a better future?

16th November
Psalm 24:10c
'He is the King of glory. Selah'
Now you have been introduced, what will you do?

Psalm 24 is about The King of glory and how we can relate to Him. Like all parts of the Bible this psalm demands a response so what will you do? The Lord, King of kings is waiting to be your king and to fight and defend you in your life's battles.

The King of glory is the Creator of the whole universe, including you. You are His possession because He designed and made you, you are no accident or freak of nature you are God's handiwork. What will you do? Will you ignore this and carry on pretending you are the ruler of your destiny, going the World's godless way, or will you kneel before the King your Maker and give yourself back to Him.

There is a choice to be made, what will you do? Open the gates of your heart and let Him enter into the outer courts of your life. He will come in and dwell there with you, but there is more; open the door to the centre of your life, the 'Holy of holies', where the king of your life sits. Give that throne to God and allow Him to rule in your life. He will lead and guide you and will protect your innermost life. He will protect your thoughts and emotions and will make you strong.

Now you have been introduced to the King of glory, what will you do?

17th November
Psalm 100:1
'Make a joyful shout to the Lord, all you lands!'
Shout to the Lord in joy

When reading through the psalms we often come across a psalmist calling out to God in some distress. He might be asking for help or guidance, or perhaps it is a cry of complaint. Today we see something different, the psalmist encourages a shout of joy.

Shout for joy today, don't hold back in 'Christian reserve'. Take a deep breath and tell the Lord all the happiness in your heart. It doesn't have to be long, there is a feeling here that it is a spontaneous shout of joy for all He has done. Think of all He has done for you and let that feeling of gratitude well up in your heart, then let it out to Him in a shout of praise.

You say to me, yes, but this was addressed to 'the lands' not to individuals. It is true that all the countries of the world have much to praise God for, and by and large they do not. The psalmist *was* imploring the lands to shout out as one to the Lord, but don't let that be an excuse for you not to do it. Be the first, be the loudest and shout joyfully to the Lord.

18th November
Psalm 100:2a
'Serve the Lord with gladness;'
Serve with gladness

Servants are low down in the pecking order. They are told what to do and are expected to get on and do it. Servants do not expect thanks for their work, they are only doing what they are paid for. Most of us work because we have to, not be because we want to. We may enjoy what we do but does it make us glad?

The psalmist says we should serve the Lord with gladness; that is to be overjoyed at working for the Lord, even if you get no recognition for it. It is the highest honour to serve the Lord. He is the King of kings and Lord of lords and He has asked you to be His servant! Choose to serve Him with a joyful heart.

This glad attitude is not limited to workers in the Church. Whatever you do, do as unto the Lord. Be glad in your work as servants of God, not looking at the worst things, but always the best. Don't strive for recognition, or some kind of reward, work gladly in your lowly place knowing your great reward is in Heaven.

19th November
Psalm 100:2b
'Come before His presence with singing.'
Sing in God's presence

Do you feel like singing today? Some will shout 'Yes!', others will whimper, 'No, not really.'

This psalm is a psalm of joy; joy in who God is and what He has done for us. We don't always feel that joy. Even that person who is always bouncing around with a smile on their face, has some time in the valley. We should never try to work up joy in our hearts, or worse fake it. Sing to the Lord a song of praise, for His goodness. Job is a song and in much of that Job is in deep depression, and yet his words are full of hope in his Lord.

Sing a song from your heart to God's. Lift up your heart, whatever state it is in today, and open your mouth to sing. Listen to the words you utter, and ask they reflect who God is, or who you want Him to be. In other words, is He the God of the Bible or the god of your imaginings? Bend your heart's song to point to the true God and His never-failing faithfulness and your time alone in His presence will become refreshment to your soul.

Sing to the Lord a new song, your song, and commune together friend with Friend.

20th November
Psalm 100:3a
'Know that the Lord, He is God;'
Know that the Lord is God

Do you know that the Lord and Master of your life is God? Tomorrow we will see why God has the right to be your Lord, but today be content to know that your Lord is God.

Once you have made that step of faith towards God, He will run to you and welcome you into His family. We are children of God. We are also servants of God; He is our Lord and Master. Before Salvation Satan was master. He led us into all the lusts of our flesh, ultimately leading to destruction. God is our Master now and He only leads us into righteousness with Eternal Life as our destination. The road may be hard and God's plan for us may take us places we would not choose to go, but remember He is our Lord and we, as servants, simply obey, knowing that our God is a good God who only want's the best for us and leads us down the paths that will make us into the men and women He longs for us to be.

Your Lord is God, obey only Him. His ways are righteous and will always reflect the words of the Bible. It is not a fearful thing to be a servant of God, no, it is the highest honour bestowed on humanity.

21st November
Psalm 100:3b
'It is He who has made us, and not we ourselves;'
We are God's workmanship

In today's world we are told that if you work really hard and keep focused on your dream, you can be anything you want to be. This is a lie; it is God who made us, and it is He who directs our paths. The Lord your Creator has a plan for you, a plan that might not fit into your ideals for yourself, but it will be significant in the Kingdom of God.

Hopes and dreams are not a bad thing, and working hard for your goals is admirable, but remember you are not your own and God's ultimate plan for your life may be different. He made you and He knows where you are best suited in His Kingdom on earth. You have gifts and talents and they too are God given so use them for His purposes. God's plan might involve your gifts, but then it might not; I never expected to be used to write as it is not my natural gifting, but God wanted me to do it anyway. Keep your eyes on God and follow where He is leading you. Remember He made you, He knows you and He will never lead you down a path that is wrong for you.

Trust God with your life for it is God who is making you; yield to Him.

22nd November

Psalm 100:3c

'We are His people and the sheep of His pasture.'

We are God's people

The psalm has been building to this point, this is why we should make a joyful shout, serve the Lord with gladness and come before Him with singing: The God of the universe, the God who made you has brought us into His fold! We are God's people and He is our God, there is a relationship between us and He will care for and protect us as a shepherd cares for and protects his sheep.

As we are God's people, let us start acting like it. We don't have to be ashamed of who we are, we stand in the highest place of honour there is. We should live as people of God: holy, righteous, humble, bold, joyful. We are His people and He is our God.

If God is our God, then we can expect to see His hand in our life. He will lead us down the best paths and guide us to the most verdant pastures. There will be blessing in our lives. Sometimes life will be tough, but no matter how bad it gets God will always be with us. We can face the day, not because of our own strength, but because we are people of God, someone He intimately cares for. God is with us.

23rd November
Psalm 100:4a
'Enter into His gates with thanksgiving,'
How to enter God's presence #1

There is a right way to enter God's presence. He is your God, He made you, He is holy and righteous, and you must enter in an appropriate way. The psalmist says to 'enter His gates with thanksgiving', but what does that mean?

To enter God's gates is to cross the threshold of God's House; Israel would have understood that to be the Temple in Jerusalem, but it has a wider meaning in that it covers worship wherever you are. As you begin to worship God, give Him thanks for all He has done. This is not about exuberance and over-the-top displays of 'joy and happiness', no, this is about telling God how grateful you are for His work as your Shepherd. God cares and protects you, He gives you what you need, so take time to thank Him for all these things.

How often do we come to Church, or even our Quiet Times expecting God to do or say something? We think we come into His gates to get something from Him, but no, we come to give something. We who have nothing, give to Him who has everything; we give God thanks for His goodness to us and then God responds by answering us in our current need.

Remember to say thank you next time you enter God's presence.

24th November
Psalm 100:4b
'And into His courts with praise.'
How to enter God's presence #2

Yesterday we looked at entering into the Lord's gates, the initial stepping through into His holy presence. Today we take it further. Don't linger in the gatehouse, carry on into God's inner court, right into the Throne Room of God. This is a place of awe and wonder, and the psalmist encourages us to praise the Lord there. No longer thanking Him for what He has done, but now praising Him for who He is. It is right and proper to tell Him how much He means to you and to extol the wonders of the unsearchable God.

If you have trouble thinking of anything to say, start by jumping ahead to verse 5 of this psalm, as this will give you plenty to begin praising God with. What a way to start your praise journey! The goodness of God, the mercy of God and the truthfulness of God; there is the foundation for endless praise that will lead inevitably to God's grace, love, peace, faithfulness, power, trustworthiness, etc.

Always come into God presence ready to give Him praise; let His wonderful attributes fill you with awe filled words. He is worthy of our praise and adoration, and it is wrong to remain silent before His throne. Prepare in your heart today something to bring next time you are at a service.

25th November

Psalm 100:4c

'Be thankful to Him, and bless His name.'

How to enter God's presence #3

Over the last two days we have learned the necessity to thank the Lord for all He has done and to praise Him for all He is. This final phrase sums this up for us. As we enter into God's presence we should remember to be thankful and to bless His name. We do not come to God to get but to give; He has already given more than we could ever deserve or repay.

It is so easy to come to God with a question on your heart, expecting Him to answer. Standing before God in silence, ignoring the opportunities to praise whether in prayer or song. If you treat the worship at church like that, when the word comes you will hear nothing and go away disappointed. The more desperate you are to hear from God the more fervent should be your praise. Not that praise and thanksgiving gives you extra points in God's book, no, they draw you into the right place before Him to receive the blessing He has already prepared for you.

Don't go away disappointed. Enter into His gates with thanksgiving and His courts with praise, open your heart to Him and He will open His heart to you.

26th November
Psalm 100:5a
'For the Lord is good;'
Reason to praise #1

While thinking about praising God in His courts I said to skip on to read verse 5 for some inspiration. Now we will look at those things more closely.

The first thing the psalmist brings to mind is the wonderful truth that God is good. When the Bible calls God 'good' it means just that. Think for a minute what that word means to you. All the underlying meaning of goodness is found in God.

God is good for you; He does you good. His ways are good; the things He does are always good. His intentions towards you are good; you can trust in Him. Where He leads you is good; even if it doesn't feel that way at the moment. His judgement is good; you can rely on Him to come to the right decision. It is not possible for God to do something that is bad; because of His righteousness He will always do good. There are countless other expressions of God's overwhelming goodness.

Spend time today praising God for some aspect of His goodness you have seen in your life. If you can't think of anything recently look back at your life and see His hand of guidance and how He brought you to Himself.

God is good.

27th November
Psalm 100:5b
'His mercy is everlasting,'
Reason to praise #2

If you are still finding it tough to praise God, think about His mercy. God's mercy is everlasting; it doesn't run out. He is the Judge that has mercy on us; He looks upon us and our sinful ways and chooses to forgive! The same undeserved mercy the psalmist knew, is available to you today!

Look back over your life and ask yourself if you can see the mark of God's everlasting mercy? Can you call to mind the times you deserved God's indignation and you received His love? There is nothing you have done, or will do, that is bigger that God's mercy. To the Christian it is the assurance of home; you know that God is there waiting for you to come back to Him. God does not punish us with a big stick as we deserve, but rather He welcomes us in like the father in the parable of the Prodigal Son.

Although there are inevitable consequences to our high-handed actions that we must face, our Lord and God, our Maker will show mercy and forgive us, sparing us from the consequences of offending Almighty God.

We have all sinned and have fallen short of God's glorious standards (Romans 3:23), but He shows His everlasting mercy to all who call on Him.

Praise Him for His everlasting mercy.

28th November
Psalm 100:5c
'And His truth endures to all generations.'
Reason to praise #3
This verse starts by saying God is good, it then states that His mercy is everlasting, but that was written a long time ago; has God changed His mind? We can be assured of God's goodness and His never-ending mercy because His truth endures for all generations.

Something that was counted as true to people in generations past is considered with disdain by today's generation. Truth changes from one generation to the next as we set out to make our mark on history. No matter what your generation or mine may say, God's truth does not change. We can know what God's view is by reading the Bible; if it was sin when God spoke it, it is sin now. Life can be troubling in a world without a fixed understanding of truth, that is why it is so wonderful that God's truth endures to all generations; we can rest in God's unchanging Word.

Take time today to praise God for His enduring truth. While other truths come and go, God's truth remains. Praise Him that He sent Jesus, His representative of Truth, into the world to demonstrate that truth to us. Don't get lost in the World's ever-changing 'truth', come to God's perfect, enduring Truth.

'Jesus the same yesterday, and today, and forever.' Hebrews 13:8.

29th November

Psalm 8:1a

'O Lord, our Lord,'

A very personal beginning

This psalm opens in a beautifully personal way. By singing this we are saying that the Lord is our Lord, our Master. He is the one who guides and directs us, not we ourselves. How can we declare these word's and then not listen to His voice? He is our Lord.

This is very personal, I can't do this for you, and you can't do it for me, but we must do it, we must put the Lord first in our lives. There can be negative connotations to placing oneself under the authority of another and God can be seen as a hard task master. However, this is not the theme of this psalm. This psalm is an awe inspired love song to God, so take a moment to read it, as the words are amazing. I do not ask you to submit to a hard, distant god that is uncaring. No, I urge you to make the Lord who, in spite of holding the entire universe together, is mindful of you (verses 3-4).

He is ours and we are His, there is a relationship here, yes, He is the Lord, the Master, but He is also the Covenant God who has revealed His name to us. We can call Him by that name and cry out, 'O Yahweh, our lord!'.

30th November
Psalm 8:1b
'How excellent is Your name in all the earth,'
An excellent name

What comes to mind when you read about an 'excellent name'? Do you see your name as good, or perhaps you don't like it. Would you say that yours or someone else's name was excellent? As hinted at already, names are rather subjective, two people may have the same name and one loves it and the other hates it. All my children like their names and get offended when they are contracted. This isn't about our names but the Lord's. God's Name is Yahweh and that is an excellent Name, but we're talking about more that the status of God's wonderful Name compared to ours, it speaks of God's renown over the whole earth.

There is no name that is higher and more worthy of praise than God's. His Name is exalted in every corner of the world. In this sense it doesn't matter at all whether men and women lift His Name up or use it as a curse word; His Name is excellent right in their midst, because He is the King of every inch of this planet. Therefore, don't use His Name lightly or as an expression of shock of revulsion (you know what I am saying), instead glorify His Name and praise Him for His excellent Name. Get into a habit of praise. Psalm 8 is a psalm of praise and wonder therefore use it to put God's Name back in its rightful, excellent place.

1st December

Psalm 8:1c

'Who have set Your glory above the heavens!'

Beyond the earth

We have seen that the Lord's Name is the most excellent name anywhere in the world, but have you considered God's renown goes beyond the earth. God's glory extends above the heavens; the heavens is the sky, and beyond that to the end of the universe. To see where God has set His glory, go out on a cloudless night and look up (even better if you are away from light pollution), those countless stars, that are many millions of miles away, are just the edges of the universe. God's glory and His excellent Name goes far beyond all we can see even with the most powerful telescope. As you gaze at the immensity of space and the beauty of the stars, it should bring you to a place of awesome wonder of how powerful God is to create all that with just one Word.

'The earth is the Lord's, and all its fullness...' (Psalm 24:1a), but God's glory is not contained by this planet. In fact, the entire universe is not big enough to contain God; His glory is above the heavens. Never let your vision of God be limited to what you can see or understand because He is so much bigger than anything we can dream up. He has set His glory above the heavens and we should praise and worship Him in a way that reflects that awesome truth.

2nd December

Psalm 8:2a

'Out of the mouth of babes and nursing infants You have ordained strength,'

Out of the mouths of children

This verse is often misused by people when the weak, young or those deemed of lesser intellect say something that reflects their views; let us not fall into that trap. So, what is this verse saying?

David wrote, 'Out of the mouth of babes and nursing infants You have ordained strength' or as Jesus quoted it in Matthew 21:16 after cleansing the Temple, 'Out of the mouth of babes and nursing infants You have perfected praise'. Young children have no problem seeing God all around them. The beauty of Creation cries out for a Creator and children know that. The simple faith and praise of a child is worth more than a thousand theological doctorates. It strengthens God before His enemies; no wonder the World is so quick to teach them folly and doubt!

I am often amazed at the deep understanding children have of God and His ways. I will never forget the Sunday my daughter spontaneously sang to the Lord a new song of praise as God filled her mouth, a totally natural moment, a moment between her and God to which I was only a spectator.

Let the children praise; teach them the truths of God, tell them of His excellent Name and show them the wonders of His glory. Build on their natural foundation of praise and guard them from fools who wish to knock it down.

3rd December

Psalm 8:2b

'Because of Your enemies, that You may silence the enemy and the avenger.'

Silencing the enemies

The first half of this verse speaks about small children bringing strength or praise. The godly strength of a child is more powerful than the rantings of a worldly warrior. When we speak a simple word of peace we silence the hateful ravings of the enemy. It is easy to see the difference between the godly battle cry and that of the World: a godly person always speaks in love and forgiveness covered with righteousness from on high; whereas the worldly person may speak of love and sometimes even forgiveness but it comes from self-righteousness.

When children try to speak like adults it causes strife and anger because that is how they perceive adults to conduct themselves. But, when we humble ourselves and speak as little children, our faltering words will silence the enemy.

We are God's children and He alone brings the victory. Immerse yourself in God's Word so that you will know how to answer the avenger. It doesn't matter if you're not a 'mature Christian' yet, as long as you are regularly taking the milk of the Word so that He can speak strength and peace through you. Remember it is not your word but His, and He can use you, yes even you, to silence the enemy.

4th December
Psalm 8:3a
'When I consider Your heavens,'
Do you consider the heavens?

Do you ever look up at the sky on a clear night and marvel and wonder at the beauty of the heavens? Next time there is a clear night look and consider where those countless stars came from. Were they the result of cosmic chance; even cosmic chance influenced by God? Or, did God speak them into being on Day Four of Creation Week? 'Then God made two great lights: the greater light to rule the day, and the lesser light to rule the night. He made the stars also.' Genesis 1:16. How Big does God have to be to make all the stars of heaven (visible and invisible) in one moment, just by speaking their creation! The God revealed in the Bible is bigger and more powerful than the gods of our imagining. A god who fits in to our limited knowledge and understanding is no god at all; and that goes for anyone reading this with umpteen degrees!

There is a natural beauty in the heavens, that fills us with awe and wonder; how hard must be the heart that is not touched by the glory of the heavens. Now, consider this; how hard must a heart be not to bow down and worship the God who created them! Open your eyes and see God's awesome creative power displayed for all to see, right before you in the stars above. Sing praises to Him who made all the stars with just one word.

5th December
Psalm 8:3b
'the work of Your fingers,'
God's handiwork

Have you considered the wondrous truth that every single star and every planet and moon that orbits them were handmade by God? He designed and made them for His pleasure. It is true that we also garner pleasure from the heavenly bodies. It fills us with joy looking up at the night sky, but there are stars that even the most powerful telescopes will never see; God sees them and knows them all by name.

Consider the awesome power of God's creative acts; if the Bible's account of Creation is true, we have a God for which nothing is impossible. He is able to do amazing things in your life. He can turn your life around in an instant, from going down and down to going up and up. He is able to open any closed door before you and lead you through. In your darkest hour He is the Light. Consider this too, even if He doesn't change things in your life, He is with you through all of it and He is able to sustain you through it. He is an awesome powerful God that made by hand every single star in the heavens, and He is able to meet you at your need today. That insurmountable problem is no problem to Him.

Pray to the God of Creation and ask Him for help in your need. He made the stars, He can help you.

6th December
Psalm 8:3c
'The moon and the stars,'
The moon and the stars

Notice that David draws our attention to the night sky, he doesn't mention the sun at all. This is not because God didn't make the sun, of course He did, but rather that when David couldn't sleep and he looked up during those long dark nights, what he saw brought to his mind the awesome glory of God. When we are in the light, we don't need to consider God greatness in the same way; it is easy to praise God in the good times. During the night-time of life, when all is dark and you can't see what is up ahead, when praising God seems hypocritical, these are the times to look up and consider the wonders of Creation.

Paul wrote in 1 Corinthians 15:41, 'There is one glory of the sun, another glory of the moon, and another glory of the stars; for one star differs from another star in glory.' Have you thought of that, the fact that no two stars are exactly the same? There are red, blue and yellow stars, but each individual star differs from the rest. What about the moon? Not only does it light up the night, it also regulates times and the tides are guided by it. It would be difficult for us to survive on earth without the moon. God has made these heavenly bodies for our joy, but also to bring glory to Himself. The God who made the sun, moon and stars is the God who is holding your hand in the dark night of your life; look up and bask in His glory.

7th December
Psalm 8:3d
'which You have ordained,'
Everything in its place

What comes to mind with the word 'ordained'? Is it a Vicar or Pastor that has been ordained for ministry? When a man or woman is ordained as a Minister, we are saying that God has placed them in a position of pastoral leadership over His Church and that He has established them for that vocation. When God ordains a person they are ordained forever and this is also true for everything God has ordained. King David wrote that God has ordained the moon and stars; He has set them in place and established them forever. There is order in the heavens, the stars do not fly off out of their constellations and the moon is not going to leave our orbit above us. Yes, they move through time, but they are constant in their vocation. They are so amazingly constant in their movements that we know where each star was thousands of years ago and know where they'll be in thousands of years time, should Jesus tarry that long. There are charts that tell us when each phase of the Moon will be, and every lunar eclipse is dated. You can find out when the next Blue Moon will be!

What God has ordained is established, everything in its place, so that nothing can shake or alter anything God has set in order. This is why Ordination is such a serious matter. Pray for your church leaders, that they may be established in the Lord.

8th December

Psalm 8:4a

'What is man that You are mindful of him,'

What is man?

We have been looking at the grandeur and majesty of the universe. God created everything we see around us. Every single star in heaven was fashioned by Him, the Moon with all that it does for us was designed by God. Not only did He make the universe, but He also upholds it and keeps it in order. So why would Almighty God, the Lord of heaven and earth, think about you or I?

We are so small and insignificant compared to the rest of Creation, or so we are led to believe. There are those who would go as far as to say Creation would be better off without us. This is not God's view. He is mindful of us, think about that, His mind is full of us! He thinks about us all the time. What is man, what is woman? We are the centre of God's Creation, we are the pinnacle of all that He has made. There is no salvation for the rest of Creation, but Father God sent His only Son to die for you, so that you may be saved and restored to Him.

If you are in the forefront of God's mind, surely He should be in the forefront of yours! Kneel before God your maker and receive His gift of salvation today.

9th December
Psalm 8:4b
'And the son of man that You visit him?'
The Lord visits you!

This is an intriguing thought, but what does it mean? Son of man literally means son of Adam, or a descendent of the first humans, Adam and Eve. We are all sons and daughters of Adam, human beings made in the image of God. What is it about us that God chooses to visit us? God created us to have a loving relationship with Him, and He is determined for that to be the case for all the sons of man.

You may have noticed that 'Son of Man' is the title Jesus gave Himself while He walked on earth. He did this not only to associate Himself with us but also for a much more wonderful reason. Jesus is the Son of God, but He changed His name to the Son of Man so that we could change our names to sons and daughters of God.

There has been a change of names for all who come to Jesus in repentance. There was nothing we could do to become sons and daughters of God, so He came down and visited us, becoming the Son of Man so He could lift us up to a new status. Jesus has done it all, the only thing left for us to do is accept His glorious gift. Humble yourself before God, and allow Him to raise you up in Christ; no longer a son or daughter of man, but now a son or daughter of God.

10th December
Psalm 8:5a
'For You have made him a little lower than the angels,'
A little lower

At first glance it seems strange to praise God for making us lower than the angels. Our pride says that we are the pinnacle of God's Creation and should be higher than the angels. Look again, David says we are a little lower than the angels, and by little he means by the tiniest of margins. In the Bible angels are always depicted as mighty and powerful and when they appear it causes fear. The angels stand in God's holy presence waiting to be sent on an assignment, and when they get the call, they move at lightning speed. They can appear and disappear in an instant, they can do many other marvellous things that are beyond our understanding. For all the things that seem to make angels far above us, God has made us only a little lower than them.

There is a dignity for us, God has placed us as second only to angels and then only by a tiny margin. We ought to live up to God's billing. Think about what God did to the rebellious angles; He cast them out without any hope of redemption. We are granted what the angels were not; we can come to Jesus in repentance and find forgiveness and redemption. Live as God intended you to live, in peace with God, obeying His blessed commands. You were made a *little* lower than the holy angels so start living like it!

11th December
Psalm 8:5b
'And You have crowned him with glory and honour.'
Crowned by God!

Take a moment to take that in, for the God who created the universe has crowned you with glory and honour! I'll say it again, God has crowned you. This is like being knighted; the king or queen gives the person a status above everyone else. You may think some deserve it more than others, but all those knighted have the same honour. We do not deserve to be crowned with glory and honour, but God does it anyway. We are not 'knighted' for services to anything, we receive honour because we are sons and daughters of God. Jesus became the Son of Man so that we can become sons and daughters of God, if we trust and believe in Him. When we do take that step, bowing before God, He comes down and crowns us with glory and honour.

After someone is knighted they may not feel or notice any difference in themselves, and that can be the same for Christians. We may not 'feel' the glory and honour bestowed upon us, but take it by faith, if you are a son or daughter of God you have a status that places you above all others. Believe and accept that highly exulted place, but walk humbly before God and man. Let God make your crown visible to all; He will make it shine for all to see. You don't have to point it out, they will see it, and when they ask, tell them that a crown of glory and honour is available to them too if only they will humble themselves before God.

12th December
Psalm 8:6a
'You have made him to have dominion over the works of Your hands;'
Hands are for work

God made the heavens and the earth in six days; He spoke the Word and it happened. There is, however, the idea that God made everything we see with His hands. Remember things are different in Eternity and God has 'time' to make things and also say a single word. This world and everything in it is the work of God's hands (Psalm 24:1) and God has entrusted it to us; we have dominion over it. God has given us rule over His works and we are to govern wisely as representatives of God. How are we doing?

I have entitled this devotion 'Hands are for work', and they are. All we see around us is the work of God's hands and He expects us, as those with dominion, to work with our hands to make this a safe place to live. We have a privilege and responsibility to govern this world in God's Holy Name.

We are not 'mini gods' and there are things we cannot do, but what we can do we must. Are you wondering what God has called you to? Start by looking after the world around you, actively using your hands to make this world beautiful; this is what all people are called to do. The King will take an accounting of all people, Believers or not, on how they represented Him in their God given dominion over the works of His hands.

13th December
Psalm 8:6b
'You have put all things under his feet,'
Under our feet

This is very direct language; God has placed all things under our feet. We are under God, and everything else is under us. This doesn't include angels who are little higher than us, but everything we see around us is under our feet. This may be offensive to some people, that our dominion over this world means we decide the fate of all animals, birds and fish. This doesn't give us the right to treat animals as we please, no we are to govern responsibly as representatives of God. We are to treat all living things with the honour they deserve, but no more than that, we are not to treat them as equals to us; God has not made them that way.

Look to Jesus, He is our Head and we are under His feet. How does He govern the world? He reigns with equity and justice, with wisdom and honour and we should do the same. How we treat our world is a reflection on how we see ourselves. Do not govern with pride as if you have no one to answer to, and do not govern as if it is all down to you and God's arm is short. We're to govern in God's Name as representatives of Him. So read His Word and get to know Him, in order to manage His world as He desires.

14th December
Psalm 8:7
'All sheep and oxen - even the beasts of the field,'
Over the land animals

God has placed us over the land animals, all of them. David puts these into two groups, the sheep and the oxen and the beast of the field. The sheep and oxen represent the domestic animals, whether they are kept for food, clothing or as pets, etc., Whereas the beasts of the field are wild animals. Both wild and domestic animals are under our protection and it matters how we treat them. Even if we are breeding them for food they must be treated properly, but never as equals. Remember it was God who gave them to us as food.

All animals around us are under our dominion and care, and God is watching to see how we use our dominion. Do we mistreat them, abusing our power? Or do we try and lift them up to a status that God has not given them, usurping His power? Prayerfully consider how you view animals, because this will colour not only how you treat them, but also the way you treat other people. Animals are God's Creation and they are His. He has charged you and I with caring for them. May the way we treat animals bring glory to our God.

15th December
Psalm 8:8a
'The birds of the air,'
Over the birds of the air

There is a majesty to the birds, the way they fly so effortlessly and the ever-shifting patters of flocks as they migrate, their beauty and of course their songs. Birds are designed for flight, with feathered wings and light yet strong bones. They may fill us with awe and wonder, but we have dominion over them. Although they inhabit the air, they are under our feet (verse 6).

God has given the birds to us to look after, but how well do we do this? How well do you manage the birds? To be honest, they do just get on with their lives without much input from us, but our responsibility is to ensure they have all they need available, and to make sure they are safe and secure to thrive and fill the skies.

As with the land animal, birds are bred for food, and God has given them to us for this purpose. This should encourage us to look after them more and treat them properly. Let us think about God's abundant provision for us and cut waste down. The birds of the air are for our food and sustenance, but God will judge us on how we have fulfilled our mandate to govern them the way He would, with wisdom and righteousness. How well are you doing?

16th December
Psalm 8:8b
'And the fish of the sea that pass through the paths of the seas.'
Over the fish in the seas

As I write this, the plight of the seas is front and centre in the news. What can we do to keep the seas a safe environment for the creatures who live there? The answer is to turn back to God. God's desire is that all His created things should be safe and provided for, that is why He put us in charge. We haven't fulfilled our mandate to govern the world with wisdom. The Lord has filled the seas with good things to eat, but if we mis-manage them, there will be nothing left.

Like all living creatures, fish will get on with their lives with no help from us, however, God has given us dominion over them and so we should intervene and do all we can to make their lives better.

The great God of the universe has given us a task to perform for Him, so how well are you doing it? The natural world is God's. He made it and ultimately governs it, delegating to us the responsibility for all the living creatures on land, in the air and in the sea. We should look after them and treat them properly. We are a little lower than the angels, and the animal world is a lot lower than us. Ask God for wisdom in how best to fulfil your God given responsibility.

17th December
Psalm 8:9a
'O Lord, our Lord,'
A thoughtful end

The first and last verses in this psalm are the same. Verse one is a statement of fact, the Lord is our Lord. Verse nine says, in the light of this psalm, He is our Lord. After journeying through this psalm is the Lord your Lord?

The Lord has made everything we see around us. His glory fills the highest parts of heaven and even children can know and understand Him so that their praise lifts Him up. The God who made the stars, made you and knows you! He has made you a little lower than the angels and given you His world to manage. All this is true of the Lord, but is He your Lord? Do you do as He commands, or do you go your own way? In the light of His delegated role He has given you, do you neglect the creatures He has entrusted to you? Or, do you assume He has no power and it's all up to you to stop the world falling apart? Take a moment to think about your life as a whole and ask yourself is the Lord, your Lord?

We all fall short of God's glory (Romans 3:23), and there are often areas that we hold back from Him. Take time today to give one of those areas to God so that He will be a little bit more your Lord and Master.

18th December

Psalm 8:9b

'How excellent is Your name in all the earth!'

A truly excellent name

After reading through this psalm, it is clear to me that God is far above all; His Name *is* excellent. We judge people by their names, 'He's got a bad name', 'she's got a good name'; it is not by what they are called but what they do. When you hear a name, your heart may either rise or sink, or alternatively their name may mean nothing to you. Bring to mind someone you know with a 'bad name', and ask yourself why they make you feel like that. Now, bring to mind someone with a 'good name' and ask what they have done to deserve such an honour? God's Name is not dependent on our opinions, it is excellent far above all.

Now concerning the one you know with a 'bad name', pray for them. You may need to pray for yourself first, and then pour out the blessings of God on them. As for the one with a 'good name' pray for them too, that they may know God and inherit a truly good name.

What about your name? How do others perceive you? You have been given a position a little lower than the angels and have been entrusted with dominion over the earth; do not let that fill you with pride, but rather be humble before God and men, showing God's excellent Name in favour of your own. God has a truly excellent Name, let others see that through all you do.

19th December
Psalm 150:1a
'Praise the Lord!'
Commanded to praise

This psalm is a call to praise, and more than that it is a command to praise. How should we obey this command? What does the psalmist mean when he says, 'Praise the Lord'? You may think you need to be a Bible scholar or look up the word in a concordance, this isn't the case here. The psalmist himself unravels the depths of praise we are expected to give.

Our praise should be joyous, unfettered, loud, unbounded and boastful. We are to praise the Lord with all we have, all we are and with all our talents. Hold nothing back from Him, be yourself but be uninhibited.

Remember how King David praised God as the Ark of the Covenant was brought into Jerusalem? He danced, he leapt, he whirled around shouting and blowing trumpets and most of all he did it for the Lord. As he explained to his wife Michal who despised him for his actions, 'I will be even more undignified than this, and will be humble in my own sight.' 2 Samuel 6:22a. David was 'undignified' in his praise. Will you praise God with abandon, not necessarily in a linin ephod, but with no care what others think except God Himself.

The Command is 'Praise the Lord!'

20th December
Psalm 150:1b
'Praise God in His Sanctuary;'
Praise Him in the place He has chosen

The Sanctuary of God is the place He chose for Himself to dwell in here on earth. For the ancient Jews it was the Tabernacle or Temple; but not just any tabernacle or temple, no, it had to be the right one in the right place.

You are the Temple of the Holy Spirit so His Sanctuary is wherever you are; but beware, do not go into a place that is not chosen by God and think you can praise Him there. His Sanctuary is never the home of foreign gods or places of utter wickedness. What would you be doing in such places anyway!

As we are ourselves, God's Sanctuary on earth, we have more freedom to praise and worship than the Jews of old, but that doesn't mean we can praise Him anywhere and in anyway. Listen to the voice of your conscience, amplified by the Holy Spirit, and discern for yourself whether you, as a Christian, should be in that place; and if it is okay to be there, then, Praise the Lord with all your might.

21st December

Psalm 150:1c

'Praise Him in His mighty firmament!'

Let your praises reach to the ends of heaven

What on earth is the 'firmament'? This is the wrong question to ask because the firmament is not on earth, it is above the earth; it is the heavens.

In Genesis 1:6-7 God created this firmament and calls it the heavens. The firmament is a mystery; space is not firm! What does it mean? Some things have no easy answer; God knows what it is and that is enough for me.

We are to fill the heavens with our praise, and by heavens, I mean firstly space, the universe, and right into the heaven of Heavens where God, Himself sits. That is some praise! When I was in Junior School, we were encouraged to sing out so powerfully the roof would fly off. This never happened, but it is a good example of what we should be aiming for in our praising. Don't praise small, praise BIG. Let your thoughts of God expand, let Him be magnified in your eyes (Psalm 34:3). Bring to God abundant praise, let your cup overflow with joy. As you bring to mind all the things God has done for you, add to it all things He means to you and sing out your love songs to Him. Don't hold back, let your praises reach to the ends of heaven, and try to blow it's roof off!

22nd December
Psalm 150:2a
'Praise Him for His mighty acts'
Praise the Lord for all He has done for you

Open your mouth and praise God for all He has done for you. At first it may be hard, as you think, 'what has God done for me?' Then you remember the best thing of all, Jesus went to the Cross for you. Praise Him for that, praise Him for saving you and forgiving you your sins. These are praises that are true for all believers, but there are others too. As you enter that arena of praise, what else comes to mind? What has God done for you personally, that He hasn't done for anyone else. He is your Father and He cares for you in a unique way. The mighty acts has He done for me will differ from the mighty acts He has done for you.

It's wonderful seeing God move in other people's lives and we should praise Him for it, but never let that cloud what He is doing for you. It is so easy to look at others and think God is working for them, but I am not worthy of such blessing. Whether or not you are worthy is irrelevant, God *is* working in your life. Take stock of all the good things He has done, and give Him praise for it, because He is worthy.

23rd December

Psalm 150:2b

'Praise Him according to His excellent greatness!'

God is great, praise Him for it

Praising God for what He has done for us can be tough, but it pales into insignificance when we turn our minds to God's 'excellent greatness'. God is great, He is wonderful and marvellous, I find I quickly run out of superlatives to describe Him. But, let's do our best. Praise Him for all that He is; enter into His presence and expound your love for Him; open your mouth and let your praises fill the air. I like the way the Bible says we should praise Him '*according* to His excellent greatness', because that speaks to me of intent more than content.

Even if you do not have the vocabulary to say everything you desire to say to Him, let you heart sing out in praise. Do not be hindered by the smallness of your words, allow the bigness of your love to speak volumes. Just when, even that runs short, the Holy Spirit will step in with His deep groanings (Romans 8:26), and you will know that you are praising according to His excellent greatness.

This is a wonderful leveller, because it does not matter how wordy you are, the greatest wordsmith stand shoulder to shoulder with the most word blind person when it comes to expressing God in His excellent greatness. No one has enough words to praise, but the more we try the bigger our vision of Him becomes.

24th December

Psalm 150:3a

'Praise Him with the sound of the trumpet'

Praise Him with trumpets (even if you don't play)

But I don't play the trumpet, do you? Whether the answer to that is 'yes' or 'no', we can all obey the heart of this command. The trumpet was used by the Jews as a call to worship, it's loud, resonating sound broke through the clamour of the day and drew the people to worship. We can do the same. With a heart filled with praise our words and actions can attract people around us to worship God.

Examine yourself, and ask if your demeanour encourages others to lift their voice in praise, or does it drain the room of God's presence? Be a trumpet for the Lord, by letting your life resonate praise to all around, so that when they see you their hearts are lifted, and their mouths are filled with praises to God. A trumpet is meant to be heard, and your praises are meant to be seen on your face. Let everyone know that it is time to worship by the smile on your face and the lilt in your step. David was glad when he was able to go into the house of the Lord (Psalm 122:1), and his gladness was infectious. Choose to be glad like David, especially when you go to the house of the Lord.

25th December
Psalm 150:3b
'Praise Him with the lute and harp!'
Praise Him with beautiful tones

The first thing that comes to mind when I think about harp music is the beautiful sounds it creates. The skill involved in playing a harp is second to none and to produce such awe-inspiring melodies takes a lifetime of practice. The same is true for praise.

It does not come naturally to praise God in the beautiful, uninhibited way He deserves; it takes practice, lots of practice. To produce the tones of praise that delights God's heart takes a lifetime of praise to get right. As we spend time trying out new chords and practicing new melodies, our praise repertoire increases, and we get better at creating the beautiful praise tones God loves.

This may make you think that at the moment God doesn't like your praise, that it's not good enough, but this could not be further from the truth. God loves to hear your praise, faltering though it may be. Don't give up because you think someone else does it better, keep practicing, every day as the Lord is your only audience and His opinion is all that counts. So, let those beautiful notes resound from your mouth to please the heart of God.

26th December
Psalm 150:4a
'Praise Him with the timbrel and dance'
Praise Him with your whole body

You can't praise the Lord with your hands in your pockets! Get your hands out and lift them high. Use your hands to show how much the Lord means to you. Don't stop there, move your feet, dance! What Dance?! No Way! Yes Way, we must praise God with our whole body. Going back to 2 Samuel 6, where David danced, leapt, and whirled around in joy, he was unfettered, he danced before the Lord without a care. So what if he looked a fool, he'd be a fool for God.

There may be very good reasons why you can't dance the way David danced, from your church tradition to your health, but have that desire to let go and praise Him with everything. God, who sees the heart will know your intent. What about the rest of us, what is holding us back? I'm not one for dancing because I don't like drawing attention to myself, but I need to let go of my inhibitions and trust God. It is not about what others are doing or what they think, your praise is directed to God and He's the One who sees. So what if others laugh, or give you a look, the question is what does God think? Is He smiling on you? If you are giving Him true, honest praise with your dance He will be full of joy.

27th December

Psalm 150:4b

'Praise Him with stringed instruments and flutes!'

Praise Him in a group

I believe a good worship group is made up of an eclectic mix of instruments, not just electric guitars turned up to the max, or a string quartet playing classical sounds. Both of these have their place, but a mixture of different instruments add colour to the sound and makes a unique blend. If you play an instrument, whatever it is, volunteer to be in the worship group; it doesn't matter if it's a dulcimer or a melodica, get up and add your sound to the mix.

I also believe this is a general truth in corporate worship. Each of us has something to add to the offered praise. It may be a long 'word dance' that mixes scripture with your own expressions of thankfulness, or it may be just one word, 'Jesus!' or anything in between. The overall effect is a unique, one off sound, never to be repeated. There is something in bringing your offering of praise that adds the finishing touches to corporate worship.

You are unique, one of a kind and your praise is essential for rounded, eclectic praise. God doesn't want to hear the same type of praise over and over again; He loves variety and when He hears something unexpected it is a delight. Will you bring the unexpected sound next corporate praise time? You may feel you are a dulcimer or melodica, well there is a place for you to add your sound to the mix.

28th December

Psalm 150:5a

'Praise Him with loud cymbals'

Let your praises be heard

It's not easy to play a cymbal quietly, they are meant to be heard. To praise the Lord on a cymbal, is to praise Him with the intent to be heard. Yes, cymbals can be played quietly but the psalmist is calling for volume and passion. Let your praise resound like a cymbal crash that draws attention to itself, not that the attention goes to you but rather the object of your praise.

A cymbal is meant to be heard, but it is also meant to be harmonious with the other instruments, never drowning out the melody, but always there giving definition to the rhythm. If the cymbals are too loud and unrestrained, they draw attention away from the music and towards themselves. Beware that your unfettered praises should never pulls anyone's eyes from the Lord you are worshipping and turn them on you. On the other hand, don't be so meek and quiet that no one really knows if you are praising or not. Let your praises be heard in the congregation of believers, don't hold back your fervour, but also learn to listen and make your sound harmonious to the music the Holy Spirit is making.

29th December

Psalm 150:5b

'Praise Him with clashing cymbals!'

Let your praises clash with the world

At first glance this appears to be saying exactly the same thing as the first half of the verse. Often in the psalms we find repeated phrases, or one verse expanding on the thought of the previous one. Here we find a similar phrase but with a different thought behind it. Last time we looked at the 'loud cymbals' that we must be like in worship, not whispering our praises but equally not drowning everyone else out, but this time it's is different, this time we are to be 'clashing cymbals'.

We are to make a noise and clash with the sounds around us. Our daily life must be like a cymbal that cries out, 'repent!' to all those around us. Everything the World stands for is against the Lord's great Kingdom and we are to shout the battle cries of God. Does your life clash with modern society, or do you blend in with them? It is not, necessarily, about making a protest against unrighteousness, but it is about making a stand for righteousness. We are to be a warning to our unsaved family and friends that judgement is coming and we can only do this if our lives clash with theirs.

Pray for wisdom on how you can be a 'clashing cymbal' to those around you.

30th December

Psalm 150:6a

'Let everything that has breath praise the Lord.'

Can you breathe? Then praise!

It is often put across that this verse is saying, 'If you can breathe, you can praise.' or 'If you can breathe, you should praise.' but what it is actually saying is, 'If you can breathe, then you *must* praise.'

God has given us the gift of air and He has given it to everyone and everything; no-one can say that God hasn't given them anything! It doesn't even matter how difficult you find breathing, God has given you breath, you have life because of Him, and you must praise Him for it. This isn't just a nice thing to say, it is a command. If you have breath, praise the Lord! There is no getting around it, so how grateful are you to God for giving you air to breathe? There is much disdain for those who are ungrateful, and scroungers, those who take but do not give back, and yet how many people who are breathing God's air today will give Him thanks for it?

For believers, we shouldn't need to be commanded to praise God for all He has done for us; but even we need to remember to not take God's gifts for granted. Go on, take a deep breath and praise God for filling your lungs with His precious air.

31st December
Psalm 150:6b
'Praise the Lord!'
Remember it's a command!

Remember right back at the beginning of this psalm? It is a lot like the end! We are once again commanded to praise the Lord. As we have journeyed through this short psalm, we have seen the kind of praise God expects of us. We are to praise with abandon, praise with our whole self, praise Him in union and unity with others, and let our praises clash with the World outside. There is one area from that first verse we have not touched on, and that is to praise Him with all our talents.

I put that thought in at the beginning because of all the musical instruments that are mentioned throughout the psalm on which we can give praise. I will list them: Trumpet, lute, harp, timbrel, stringed instruments, flutes and cymbals. If you are able to play an instrument, play it for the Lord, praise Him with it every day and if you get the chance join the worship group and praise Him on a Sunday with your gift of music. Or, perhaps you could dance for the Lord, let your whole body move to the music in beautiful motion. If your gift is singing, sing for Him. Whatever your talent is do it as praise to God, whether it be, acting, magic, hosting, puppetry, juggling, writing, speaking, gardening, getting along side, poetry, drawing, painting, graphic design; whatever it is, do it for the Lord.

Praise the Lord. It is a command!

For more devotions visit

https://www.facebook.com/ajourneythrough/

Contact:

journey_through@outlook.com

Printed in Great Britain
by Amazon

64766251R00212